A Handbook
for Alcohol Education

A HANDBOOK FOR ALCOHOL EDUCATION

THE COMMUNITY APPROACH

KENNETH C. MILLS
Center for Alcohol Studies, School of Medicine

EDWARD MAX NEAL
Faculty Development Division, Media and Instructional Support Center

IOLA PEED-NEAL
Instructional Development Division, Media and Instructional Support Center

University of North Carolina at Chapel Hill

BALLINGER PUBLISHING COMPANY • CAMBRIDGE, MASSACHUSETTS

A Subsidiary of Harper & Row, Publishers, Inc.

International Standard Book Number: 0–88410–726–4

Library of Congress Catalog Card Number: 81–22913

Printed in the United States of America

Library of Congress Cataloging in Publication Data

Mills, Kenneth C.
  A handbook for alcohol education.

  Includes index.
      1. Alcoholism—Study and teaching. 2. Youth—Alcohol use. 3. Alcoholism—Research. I. Neal, Edward Max. II. Peed-Neal, Iola.   III. Title.
  HV5125.M54   1982   362.2'9286   81–22913
  ISBN 0–88410–726–4   AACR2

DEDICATION

to
Chapel Hill, North Carolina

Contents

List of Figures

xi

List of Tables

Acknowledgments

We would like to thank a few of the individuals who were active participants in the National Institute on Alcohol Abuse and Alcoholism's college alcohol education projects at Northern Michigan University at Marquette, Southern Illinois University at Carbondale, the University of Nevada at Reno, and the University of North Carolina at Chapel Hill. These projects were pioneered by Dr. David Kraft and his staff at the University of Massachusetts, Amherst. Although we have probably omitted many innovators in alcohol programming, we wish to acknowledge the following people who are highly committed to the uphill task of preventing alcohol problems: Jean Beckham, David Boorkman, Donald Boulton, Ann Bowden, Jean Bryant, Susan Burkholder, Sparky Carpenter, Carol Casper, Cathy Cousins, Ginny Davis, Pat Eckert, Steve Felts, George Harpster, Howard Henry, Heddy Hubbard, Kathy Keating, Kim Keef, Michael Looney, Kathy Macbeth, Susan Maloney, Larry Mason, Dieter Mauch, Jack McKillip, E.T. Mellor, Sherry Morrison, Fran Pernetta, Sheila Peters, Suzanne Pfaffenberger, Michael Poore, Jim Ptaszynski, John Reinhold, Fred Schroeder, Gary Shaffer, Betsy Stephenson, Kathy Von Egmond, John Ward, and Jim Whiteside.

We would also like to offer special recognition to Dr. Dennis McCarty who was the evaluation director of the program at the University of North Carolina. Dr. McCarty's clear and logical approach to data collection and program planning made our job much more manageable and accustomed us to using field data as a basis for program decisions. A special thanks to Lucie Minuto of the Student Health Service at the University of North Carolina at Chapel Hill for her inservice training skills, which brought to life many of the blackboard ideas that previously were conceptual fragments. Finally, a special thanks to Hollie Taylor, graphic designer; Margie Myers, our indexer; and Joy Smith, the swiftest typist and editor east of the Mississippi.

Introduction

Problems with alcohol are widespread in our society, particularly among its younger members. The agencies and institutions that deal with youth, such as the military services, colleges and universities, and juvenile authorities, have been searching for effective methods to deal with these problems. Many strategies have been tried, but specific strategies that seem to work in one locale often fail in other communities. Poster campaigns, meetings, public service announcements on radio and television, alcohol education seminars, workshops, and judicially oriented programs have all had some success, but these projects cannot be counted on to replicate successfully, even in communities that are apparently identical. What seems to be lacking is a comprehensive management system by which members of any community can develop strategies appropriate for local conditions. This handbook provides such a system: the problem-specific approach to alcohol problem management.

Using this book, you will be able to:

1. Design and administer a problem-documentation survey to identify specific problems in your community;
2. State your program goals clearly in terms of the targeted problems;
3. Enlist the support and cooperation of community leaders;
4. Train people to carry out program strategies focused on specific, documented problems; and
5. Evaluate the effectiveness of program strategies in preventing or minimizing the targeted problems.

Most people have a vague idea of the patterns of alcohol use in their own communities, and they may also be aware of some community problems (e.g., property damage, excessive litter, and auto accidents). But the extent to which drinking patterns and community problems are linked is not usually apparent. In the problem-specific approach, the documentation of problems helps to establish that link and raises public awareness of the connections between drinking patterns and problem patterns.

The broad goals of an alcohol education program all relate to peer involvement. Members of the community are brought together, formally or informally, to share information about the nature and extent of drinking and alcohol-related problems in their community. Alcohol educators (members of the community who have been trained in the problem-specific approach) help community members develop solutions to these problems and establish a program to avert future problems.

It is important to state at the outset that this system is not a device for developing prevention programs for alcoholism. Many people associate the phrase "alcohol-related problem" with the image of the alcoholic. Although alcoholism is a serious problem, it affects a relatively small proportion of the population. Drinking, on the other hand, is far more widespread and frequently results in immediate and severe problems short of alcoholism.

Since alcohol is a drug, it would be easy to assume that many of the techniques and approaches used in alcohol education could be applied to drug education. However, drug use and abuse encompasses a wide variety of social, legal, and medical problems not shared by users of alcohol, and therefore are beyond the scope of alcohol education programs. The problem-specific method does have limited application in this area as long as the basic requirements are met, which means identifying and documenting specific problems and using community involvement to develop consensual solutions.

In a similar fashion, the system can be used to supplement methods of health education. By designing and executing projects related to alcohol problems, community members develop organizational skills that can be used to help solve other health problems. Many traditional health education programs achieve their goals by attention to individuals with problems. By contrast, a problem-specific program focuses on groups (and deals with problems shared by the group). In other words, when carefully planned and carried out, a problem-specific program becomes a model that a community can use to generate appropriate solutions to health problems that affect the whole community.

In the field of health education, as in many other specialties, a number of terms may be unfamiliar to the layman. We have tried to keep these words to a minimum, but some of them have no convenient synonyms. The context in which they are found should clarify their meaning. However, several special terms need to be identified immediately, to serve as reference points from the start:

1. "The problem-specific approach" is the organizational framework for developing a community program to solve alcohol-related problems.
2. "Alcohol education program" is a catch-all term used in traditional and nontraditional alcohol programs. On some college campuses it refers to a single course or series of lectures about alcohol use, on others it is used to describe a comprehensive, participatory program similar to the problem-specific model.
3. "Peer" means, of course, "one of equal standing." In this handbook it is used as a convenient label for students who participate in the organization and operation of a problem-specific program. We may refer to "peer educators" and "peer programs" to emphasize the fact that the individuals involved are equals and that the programs are in the hands of people who share similar outlooks and are familiar with the needs and problems of their social counterparts.

This book is written for use in institutions of higher education, so the specific examples and program strategies it contains are oriented toward university students and their community, but the principles of the problem-specific approach can be applied to programs in any community or institution. It is divided into two parts: Part I (Chapters 1 through 12) presents the model in broad outline, and describes how the system works, the function of each component, and how to set up a training curriculum for program personnel. Part II (Chapters 13 through 19) consists of six self-instructional units for peer educators.

Chapter 1 explains the rationale and assumptions behind the problem-specific model and how it differs from previous attempts to deal with alcohol-related problems. Since this handbook is specifically concerned with adolescent and young adult drinking, the chapter identifies some of the major differences between adult drinking and youth drinking patterns and the kinds of problems that each type engenders.

Chapter 2 draws on national research studies of adult and youth drinking patterns to provide a broad, factual analysis of collegiate drinking. Information gathered by researchers over the last thirty years demonstrates both the seriousness of the problem and its widespread implications for education and society. In Chapter 3, several of the most recent studies on youth drinking are examined for specific risk factors that apply to young drinkers. These risk factors are extremely important for program planners in alcohol education, since they provide a starting point for analyzing local problems.

Chapter 4 introduces the problem-specific model as a management system, delineates the major components of the model, and describes how a typical program would be staffed and operated. In addition, this chapter covers the first two stages of the model: creation of a planning committee and a working committee. These committees form the program's nerve center, providing both executive control and official sanction for the entire operation.

Chapter 5 tells how to identify and document alcohol-related problems in the community, gather information about possible solutions, and evaluate the effectiveness of problem-reduction strategies used in the program. The chapter provides guidelines, examples, and practical techniques for carrying out each phase of documentation.

A formal policy statement is crucial to the success of an alcohol program, and Chapter 6 outlines procedures for policy development. Policy development is a consensual, participatory process that results (ideally) in a compromise between the rights of drinkers and other members of the community. Through a policy statement the program planners publicize the goals, methods, and procedures of their program and define the social, legal, and practical parameters of the local drinking environment. Without a policy statement, a program may dissipate its resources on irrelevant or ineffective activities and may never gain widespread community support. Moreover, the existence of a formal, officially sanctioned, publicly supported statement insures the continuance of the program—it becomes part of the institution's avowed aims.

The core of the system, its operational phase, is examined in Chapter 7. This chapter introduces the Alcohol Use Cycle, an indispensable concept for understanding why people drink and the social factors that promote drinking. In order to have an impact on drinking behavior and its negative consequences, program strategies must be targeted at specific points in the use cycle. Chapter 7 describes methods for focusing alcohol projects on those critical points.

Chapter 8 outlines the development of training curricula for those who will manage the program and for those who will implement it. Chapters 14 through 19 are self-instructional units that teach principles of problem-specific alcohol education.

Chapter 9 covers basic assumptions of the problem-specific method regarding how people make decisions about drinking, how they form attitudes and beliefs about alcohol, and how their attitudes can be changed.

Chapters 10 and 11 explain principles of alcohol education through which one can design, structure, and evaluate communication strategies. They are followed, in Chapter 12, by an examination of the workshop format as one kind of communication strategy.

The remainder of the book (Chapters 13 through 19) is comprised of six student work modules, each of which describes an element of the Alcohol Use Cycle in detail—drinking behavior, biological consequences, behavioral consequences, belief and attitude formation, decisions, and situations.

Part I

THE COMMUNITY SYSTEM

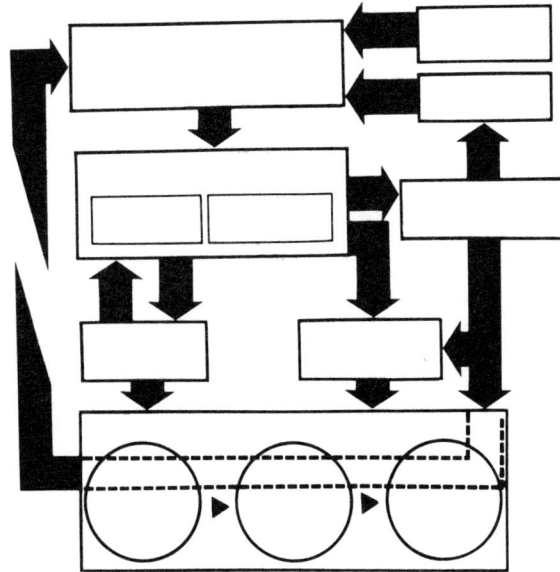

Chapter 1

OVERVIEW

OBJECTIVES

When you have finished this chapter, you should be able to:

1. Describe the problem-specific approach to alcohol education;
2. Identify various types of alcohol-related problems;
3. Describe the ways youth alcohol problems differ from adult problems; and
4. Describe the major differences between traditional alcohol education programs and the problem-specific approach.

The problem-specific approach to alcohol education was developed from principles employed in health education, business management, and organizational development. The system (illustrated in Figure 1–1) provides a framework for organizing a community-based alcohol program—how to choose the community leaders who must lend their support to the program, how to train the personnel (peers) who will manage and carry out the program, how to document specific alcohol-related problems and focus program activities on their solution, and how to develop a policy statement to preserve community changes and insure continuation of the program itself.

The problem-specific system involves organized group problem-solving and is directed toward minimizing or preventing alcohol-related problems in a community. (Although this book focuses on university communities, a community can be a military base, a town, a factory, a school district, or any similar aggregation of people.) This system differs from other forms of health education because it attempts to go beyond simple information passing or skill development and tries to change the way people

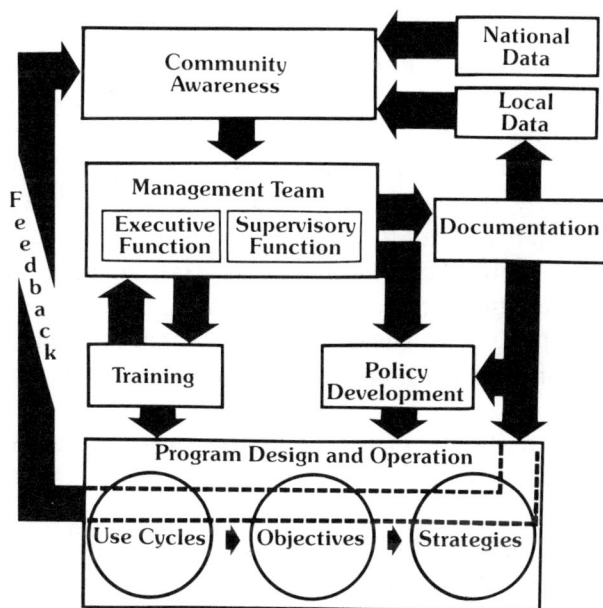

Figure 1–1. The problem-specific system.

5

interact with one another. It is based on the assumption that effective solutions to alcohol-related problems will result only when members of the alcohol-consuming group participate in the derivation of those solutions.

An alcohol program of this nature cannot be used in communities whose members refuse to acknowledge the existence of any problems. On the other hand, one of the objectives of the problem-specific approach is to raise community awareness of alcohol problems. Community leaders are usually aware of alcohol problems if they have begun to affect the quality of life or the goals of the community. For example, the purpose of a college is to educate people for professional careers, and if alcohol problems reduce a college's ability to perform this function its leaders may be receptive to an alcohol education program. Similarly, the mission of a military organization is readiness for defense of the country, the object of a business is to make a profit, and the purpose of a fraternity is to provide friendship and companionship. If drinking problems begin to interfere with the attainment of these goals, the community may be receptive to an alcohol program in order to restore group function.

Since the members of a community will be open to alcohol education only to the extent that they believe alcohol-related problems exist, the first step in creating an alcohol program must be *documentation of problems*. The kinds of problems that may occur in a typical community vary widely, affecting individuals, groups, or whole institutions. They can be divided into eight major categories:

1. *Biological problems.* Overconsumption can lead to hangover, nausea, blackouts, or even death.
2. *Legal and financial problems.* These are primarily restricted to property damage and conviction for Driving while Intoxicated (DWI), but may also include arrest for assault and long-term increases in car insurance rates.
3. *Casualty problems.* Cuts, sprains, broken bones, and other injuries are common when people overindulge.
4. *Problems of litter and noise.* Although these problems are usually associated with parties, they may occur in neighborhoods where businesses sell alcohol.
5. *Problems of crime and aggression.* These include physical assault, fighting, property damage, rape, robbery, and false fire alarms.
6. *Problems involving default of responsibility.* These include missing college classes, job absenteeism, poor study habits, and failure to complete job assignments.
7. *Mental health problems.* These may involve family disputes, depression, deterioration of personal relationships, unwanted pregnancies, and even suicide.
8. *Social problems.* These include isolation, quarrels with roommates, complaints of disruptive behavior, and public drunkenness.

Although some of these problems primarily affect individuals, their effects may have repercussions throughout the community. For example, a person who is frequently late for work because of overindulgence damages his or her career but also reduces the productivity of the entire office. In the same fashion, the student who smashes dormitory furniture or walls while intoxicated may suffer physical injury, but all residents of the hall suffer from higher maintenance costs reflected in higher rent. Chapter 5 describes methods for identifying and documenting specific problems in your own community.

Since this book is intended for use in colleges and universities, it is important at the outset to understand that alcohol-related problems among college-age youth differ substantially from chronic alcohol problems. First of all, young drinkers are unlikely to exhibit the external signs of clinical alcoholism—physical deterioration, family problems, job difficulties, legal problems, or withdrawal symptoms (DTs) when alcohol is taken away. Healthy young drinkers are more likely to suffer the immediate consequences of intoxication—hangovers, injuries from falls, arrests for driving under the influence, fights in bars, and the like. Studies show that people in the eighteen to twenty-four year age bracket share similar drinking practices (and problems), whether they are military personnel, noncollege youth, or university students. The leading cause of death in this age group is the alcohol-related automobile accident.

Young adult problems with alcohol are usually associated with specific drinking situations involving particular group membership. For example, rock concerts and college parties are situations where problems often occur. Fraternities and other college social organizations often encourage heavy drinking (although they may disavow the negative consequences).

Because young adult drinking is related to specific situations and because the norms and values that promote excessive drinking are shared by many people, it is easy for a college student to deny having an alcohol problem. By contrast, chronic drinkers who abuse alcohol are confronted almost daily by their families, employers, doctors, and friends who remind them of the extent of their drinking problems and point out that link between drinking and their other problems. Because young adult problems are usually short-lived and occur within the context of "good times" they are easily overlooked or excused by other members of the drinker's group.

Finally, young adult and chronic adult problems differ in terms of the people who must deal with them. College counselors, health educators, teachers, parents, and occasionally law enforcement officers are drawn into young adult problems. On the other hand, family members of chronic problem drinkers usually get involved first, followed by employers, doctors, any social groups to which they belong, and finally (possibly) religious organizations.

The next two chapters draw on national studies of youth and adult drinking patterns to provide a picture of the scope and seriousness of collegiate problems and to illustrate some specific risk factors that affect young adult drinkers.

The fact that there are differences between chronic drinking problems and those of college-age persons has often been ignored by program planners in the past. The essential difference between traditional approaches and the problem-specific approach is the ability to take such variation into account when developing an alcohol program (see Figure 1–2). Traditional programs begin with the assumption that if young people were simply informed about the terrible consequences of excessive drinking, especially alcoholism, they would avoid the problem. Seldom are the program participants questioned about their drinking habits or the kinds of problem they experience. The designers of these programs decide which problems should be emphasized. They present a vast amount of information about alcohol use, the disease of alcoholism, life

Traditional Methods

- Case studies on alcohol use and alcoholism; medical consequences.

- Emphasis on legal and financial consequences of alcohol use and alcoholism.

Problem Specific Methods

- Analysis of drinking situations and drinking groups.

- Documentation of alcohol-related problems that members of the community find intolerable.

- Itemization of social consequences of community action or inaction.

INPUTS

PROGRAM COMPONENTS

Socialization and Education of Youth

Info. about Alcoholism

Treatment and Rehabilitation Services

Info. about Use

Info. about Laws

Laws and Regulations

Documentation and Planning

Training

Services and Strategies

Participation

Evaluation

Development of Community Guidelines and Policies

PROGRAM GOALS

PROGRAM CONTENT

- Reduce the individual's risk of catching the disease of alcoholism.

- Facts about alcohol and drinking.

- Minimize alcohol-related problems in the community through peer-conducted services.

- Strategies and activities based on the alcohol use cycle of individuals and communities.

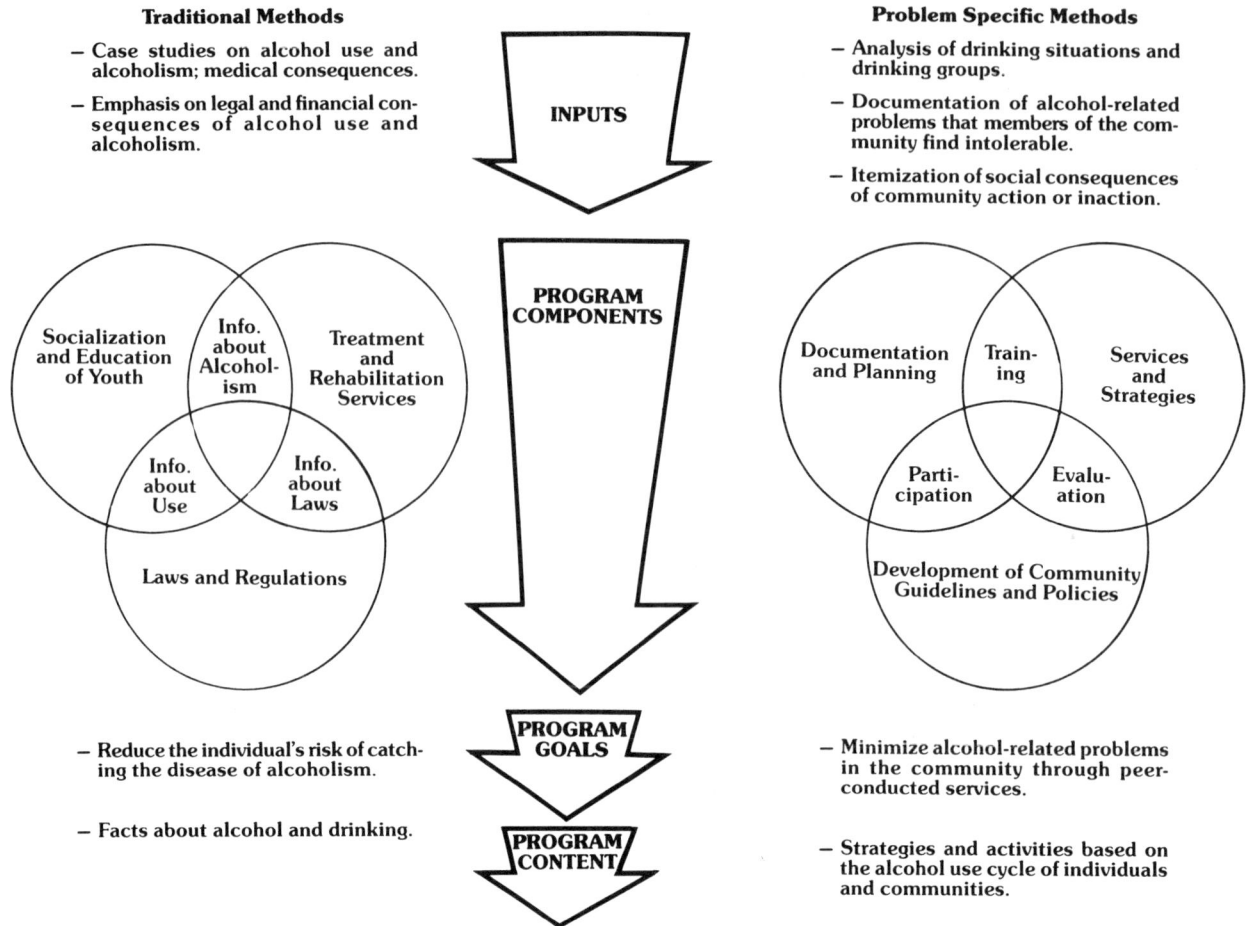

Figure 1–2. Comparison of alcohol education models.

in the family of an alcoholic, and the laws and regulations that affect the drinker. Overall, the goal of the traditional program is to reduce the risk that young people will catch the disease of alcoholism.

By contrast, the problem-specific approach begins with an assessment of the type and extent of alcohol-related problems in the community. Data from a survey provide the basis for the program's content and direction. Instead of presenting indiscriminately all kinds of information about alcohol and its consequences, the problem-specific program focuses on the documented problems and presents only the information necessary to solve them. Although this approach may seem less comprehensive than traditional efforts, it avoids the pitfall of overwhelming the community with information that may not be appropriate for local conditions. The problem-specific approach *requires* peer participation and community involvement. Its goal is to help groups solve their own problems.

To summarize, the problem-specific approach to alcohol education is unique because:

- Specific, documented problems are identified and confirmed by community members as significant and worthy of program attention.
- Problems chosen for solution affect the entire group, not just a few individuals.
- Organized group effort is used to solve the identified problems.
- The strategies used to solve problems are evaluated for their effectiveness in reducing problem levels.

Traditional programs are easy to identify because they involve a lot of one-way communication. The program organizers lecture, present films, produce pamphlets, and sponsor guest speakers. On the other hand, a problem-specific program is rather like an iceberg—its organizational base and support system are not readily visible. Projects and activities in a problem-specific program involve a great deal of two-way communication between the people directing the program and the people participating in it. It is difficult to characterize a typical program, since projects may range from sponsoring group workshops for residence advisers to throwing parties that emphasize nonalcoholic beverages. This book contains examples of a variety of program activities, but they are offered as illustrations, not suggestions. The examples presented below represent only two of the many formats that could be used in a problem-specific program. These projects were parts of much larger, community wide programs.

The production of a play was chosen by a college residence hall government to try and solve problems revolving around dorm parties. Thirty-six student volunteers were led by a residence hall director in carrying out the project. A health education student helped coordinate activities. Problem documentation consisted of a short questionnaire distributed to the 700 residents of the dormitories in their "community." The survey indicated that the most frequent and troubling complaints were drunkenness and excessive noise resulting from dorm parties. The volunteers built a tavern set in which they could portray different drinking situations, illustrate various party themes, and show how good planning can prevent problems.

To manage the project, the group broke into five teams: direction, budget, media/promotion, supplies, and scripts. They had their first opening night eight weeks after the project began. In all, the group made fifteen presentations to key groups on campus (residence hall advisers, student government representatives, Interfraternity Council, etc.). Each member of each team had an assigned role in the project and the script for each presentation was negotiated with the sponsoring group beforehand. These plays effectively (and amusingly) instructed the audience in ways to plan parties so that noise, overconsumption, and crowding could be reduced. This project—the scripts, the tavern, the decorations, and the lively entertainment—changed the nature of residence hall parties at the university and reduced the specific problems uncovered by the survey.

In a totally different setting, an industrial training model was applied in a program to instruct a group of military officers enrolled in leadership training. This model was necessary because only a limited number of hours could be devoted to participation. A survey administered on the military base provided data on local concerns and problems involving alcohol. Experienced alcohol instructors taught class once a week for six weeks to train the officers in discussion and small group techniques that could be used with their men in work settings. Each of the forty officers developed unique designs for their discussion groups and workshops, and each of the designs focused on a specific problem identified in the survey. The curriculum for the six-session program was divided into three parts: goal setting, mobilization, and strategies for communication. Although the industrial training model does not expose the whole community to the experience that can be provided with a community development model (such as the student tavern described above), it does provide an intensive experience for some individuals, who thereby become trainers on their own.

For a college group, the classroom may be the best starting place for the development of alcohol education projects, but any student group can start a program as long as they follow the management plan in this book and adhere to the principles of the problem-specific approach. Chapter 7 describes specific methods and techniques for translating documented problems into community-based solutions once the organizational foundation for these projects has been constructed. The cornerstone of that foundation is the factual data on national drinking trends contained in the next two chapters.

Thought Questions

1. Can you recall incidents of alcohol-related problems that occurred on your campus within the last month?
2. Can you think of any nontraditional approaches that could be used to reduce or prevent these problems?

References

Bacon, S.D. 1978. "On the Prevention of Alcohol Problems and Alcoholism." *Journal of Studies on Alcohol* 39: 1125–47.

Blane, H.T. 1976. "Issues in Preventing Alcohol Problems." *Preventive Medicine* 5: 176–186.

Cafferata, G. 1980. "Taking Responsibility for Health." *College Health* 28: 196–200.

Mills, K.C.; B. Paffenberger; and D. McCarty. 1981. "Guidelines for Alcohol Abuse Prevention on the College Campus—Overcoming the Barriers to Program Success." *Journal of Higher Education* 52: 399–414.

Room, R. 1979. "The Case for a Problem Prevention Approach to Alcohol, Drug and Mental Problems." Paper presented at the first annual Alcohol, Drug Abuse, and Mental Health Administration Conference on Prevention, Silver Springs, Maryland.

Rorbaugh, W.J. 1979. *The Alcohol Republic: An American Tradition.* Oxford: Oxford University Press.

Smart, R.G. 1979. "Priorities in Minimizing Alcohol Problems in Young People." In *Youth, Alcohol and Social Policy.* H.T. Blane and M.E. Chafetz, eds., New York: Plenum Press.

Trice, H.M., and P.M. Roman. 1978. *Spirits and Demons at Work: Alcohol and Other Drugs on the Job.* Ithaca, N.Y.: Cornell University Press.

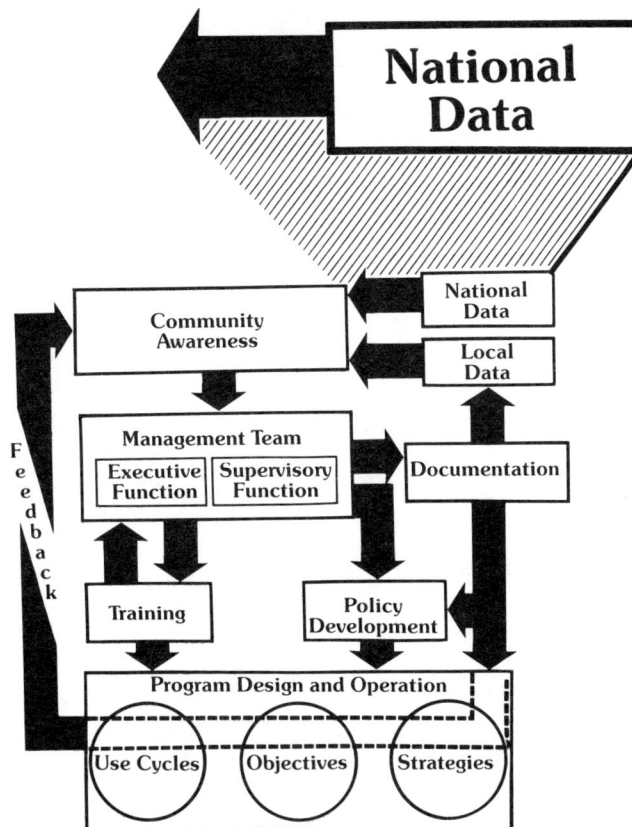

Chapter 2

NATIONAL DATA SOURCES
The Scope of the Problem

OBJECTIVES

When you have finished this chapter, you should be able to:

1. Recognize which groups in the U.S. population are most likely to experience alcohol-related problems;
2. Trace the trends in national drinking patterns over the last thirty years;
3. Discuss the implications of collegiate drinking patterns as revealed by college surveys; and
4. List the types of problems usually present on college campuses.

Additionally, you should begin to think of ways to measure alcohol-related problems in your own community.

Unfortunately, many members of college communities do not believe that problems related to drinking exist on their campuses. That these problems have existed for some time, and are apparently getting worse, has been statistically demonstrated in scores of studies nationwide. This chapter condenses a great deal of research data about drinking trends collected over the last three decades. These data are important because they provide factual support for the existence of drinking problems, and also because the information will help alcohol program planners focus their projects on known risk areas. Although each campus is unique, the problems common to college youth nationwide can serve as a starting point for estimating the type and extent of local problems. Drinking surveys indicate that no other population in the United States has a larger proportion of drinkers than the college student population. Both men and women drink more as they progress through college, and those who drink more also have more problems.

In 1979 the National Institute on Alcohol Abuse and Alcoholism (NIAAA) commissioned Walter Clark and Lorraine Midanik of the Social Research Group at the University of California at Berkeley to conduct a national survey of alcohol use and alcohol-related problems (Clark and Midanik 1980). The survey was designed to study the drinking practices of all age groups (eighteen and older) in the continental United States. Instead of mailed questionnaires, hour-long interviews were conducted in the homes of the 1,772 respondents. The interviewers read questions to the participants and recorded their answers on standard forms. The sample included a wide cross section of drinkers and nondrinkers and about equal proportions of men and women.

One of the purposes of the study was to compare its findings with the results of previous survey research, especially those from a similar project conducted by the Berkeley group in 1976, in order to examine long-range drinking patterns. The researchers also wanted to find out if there had been any marked changes in alcohol use or alcohol problems over the previous ten or twelve years.

The survey data provided a clear picture of drinking patterns across different age groups, but did not reveal any clear changes in alcohol consumption or in problem rates. Early survey work in 1939 addressed the question of how many drinkers and nondrinkers lived in the United States. Although the percentage of drinkers increased from 58 percent in 1939 to 71 percent in 1978, their numbers have remained relatively stable over the last five years. There has also been no change in the average amount of alcohol consumed in this five-year span.

Table 2–1 summarizes some of the data from the Berkeley study. It shows that *regular* use of alcohol is characteristic of about half of our population. Among drinkers, there are fairly well-defined subgroups in which heavy drinking is commonplace. Rates of alcohol-related problems are highest among those subgroups that consist primarily of young people and men. Encouragingly, although heavy drinking among youth is widespread, by the time they reach their thirties heavy drinking and its

Table 2–1. Drinking Patterns and Drinking Problems in the U.S. Adult Population by Age (in percentages)

Age	Abstainers	Light to Moderate Drinkers	Heavy Drinkers	Rates of Social Consequences	Total[a]	Percent Based on Drinkers Only
Males						
18–20 years	5	79	17	15	1,137	37
21–25 years	10	54	36	13	82	28
26–30 years	20	50	29	10	87	32
31–40 years	25	55	19	8	154	21
41–50 years	27	52	21	2	107	11
51–60 years	32	51	17	3	130	8
61–70 years	38	53	8	5	91	11
71+ years	41	45	13	4	72	4
Females						
18–20 years	31	64	5	5	52	24
21–25 years	15	78	6	6	130	16
26–30 years	30	65	5	3	125	10
31–40 years	27	65	9	5	208	12
41–50 years	43	46	10	4	137	9
51–60 years	50	46	4	1	143	8
61–70 years	61	38	1	0	102	0
70+ years	61	39	0	0	103	0
Total Sample	33	54	13	5	1,772	15
Males	25	54	21	7	762	20
Females	40	54	5	3	1,010	10

Note: The percentages are weighted figures and may not total to 100 percent due to rounding; totals shown are the actual number of cases. Slight variations in these totals occur because of nonresponse, and so forth.

[a]To the left of the "Total" column are shown rates of drinking problems based on the total population. To the right of the "Total" column are shown rates based on drinkers only.

Source: W.B. Clark and L. Midanik, *Alcohol Use and Alcohol Problems among U.S. Adults: Results of the 1979 National Survey*, Social Research Group, University of California, Berkeley. Table 8, 1980.

related problems seem to diminish. However, this conclusion was drawn from a cross-sectional analysis of these groups (measurement taken across all age groups at the same time)—a longitudinal analysis (which follows the same group as it ages) might not support the same conclusion.

The survey data also indicate that not only are drinking problems in the general population more rare than expected, but many drinkers actually change their drinking habits as they grow older. Even among heavy drinkers problem rates seldom exceed 50 percent. Table 2–2 shows problem rates reported by men and women (all ages) for the year prior to the study. The most common problem was psychological dependence on alcohol, the least common were problems with the police or one's spouse. Drinkers whose intake is low or fairly low also have extremely small problem rates; problems increase proportionately as the average amount consumed increases.

The results of this comprehensive study are reinforced by research conducted on college-age youth over the last thirty years. One of the pioneer studies in this field was performed by Robert Straus and Seldon Bacon in the 1950s (Straus and Bacon 1953). They polled a sample of 15,000 men and women attending colleges and universities across the United States. Their purpose was to try and measure how much these students were drinking, the problems they were experiencing with alcohol, and the factors that seemed to influence their drinking patterns.

Straus and Bacon found that 79 percent of the men and 65 percent of the women

Table 2–2. Prevalence of Problems Associated with Drinking in the Past Twelve Months for Males and Females in the 1967 and 1979 National Surveys (in percentages)

	National Survey 1967			National Survey 1979		
Problem Area	*Male*	*Female*	*Total*	*Male*	*Female*	*Total*
Health problems	6	5	5	4	2	3
Belligerence associated with drinking	5	3	4	8	4	6
Problems with friends	2	—[a]	1	3	1	2
Symptomatic drinking	11	5	8	20	9	14
Psychological dependence	49	29	37	26	17	21
Job problems	3	2	2	7	2	4
Problems with the law, police, accidents	1	—[a]	—[a]	2	1	1
Binge drinking	1	—[a]	1	1	—[a]	1
Problems with spouse	1	0	1	2	—[a]	1
(N)	(751)	(608)	(1,359)	(762)	(1,010)	(1,772)

Note: The percentages are weighted figures and may not total to 100 percent due to rounding; totals shown are the actual number of cases. Slight variations in these totals occur because of nonresponse, and so forth.

[a]Less than 0.5 percent.

Source: W.B. Clark and L. Midanik, *Alcohol Use and Alcohol Problems among U.S. Adults; Results of the 1979 National Survey*, Social Research Group, University of California, Berkley. Table 6, 1980.

drank before they entered college. (More recent surveys indicate that 94 percent of the men and 90 percent of the women have already begun to drink before they reach college.) Perhaps the most significant finding in this survey was the fact that students who drank heavily were also more likely to experience serious problems—an obvious relationship, but hitherto unsubstantiated. For example, among drinkers, 18 percent of the men and 15 percent of the women experienced blackouts from overconsumption; 11 percent of the men and 1 percent of the women also reported engaging in violent or destructive behavior while drinking.

In 1979 a survey was conducted in thirty-four colleges and universities in five New England states (Wechsler and McFadden 1979). To ensure a representative sample, the questionnaire was mailed to men and women in four-year state and private institutions (both coed and noncoeducational) in urban and rural settings. The undergraduate populations of these schools ranged from 500 to 15,000 students. Data was compiled from the responses of 3,185 men and 3,898 women.

An interesting and useful aspect of this survey is the combination of quantity and frequency measures to create a *typology* of drinking behavior. The researchers crossed four quantity categories—"light" drinkers (two drinks per occasion), "medium light" (four drinks), "medium heavy" (five drinks), and "heavy" (six drinks)—with four frequency categories (ranging from "less than once a month" to "more than two times per week"). Five distinct drinking types could be discerned in the student population:

1. infrequent light drinkers
2. frequent light drinkers
3. intermediate drinkers
4. infrequent heavy drinkers
5. frequent heavy drinkers

Category 1 (infrequent light) contained 29 percent of the women and 15 percent of the men, but at the opposite end of the scale (frequent heavy) the proportions were reversed: 29 percent of the men and 11 percent of the women are in this category. There were more freshmen in Categories 1 and 3 (infrequent light and intermediate), and more seniors in Category 2 (frequent light). Older students (over twenty-two) were more likely to be frequent heavy drinkers.

This quantity/frequency typology is much more useful for uncovering problem areas than either quantity or frequency measures taken alone. For example, in this survey infrequent heavy drinkers might report a low total consumption in a given month but nonetheless suffer (or cause) problems in their infrequent bouts with intoxication. People who drink less, although they drink more often (frequent light drinkers) are less likely to have difficulties.

Table 2–3 summarizes more details of collegiate drinking patterns discovered by Wechsler and McFadden. Generally, less than 5 percent of the students were abstainers. Men drank more than women, and tended to choose beer for a beverage; relatively few women listed beer as their beverage of choice. For both sexes, drinking became more popular as they progressed from their freshman to senior years.

A different approach to data collection was used in the alcohol education program at the University of Massachusetts (UMASS). This program, initiated by David Kraft, is significant in that it was one of the first to use local survey data for five

Table 2–3. Drinking among College Students
(Frequency of drinking, by sex and year in college, in percent)

	Totals	Freshman	Sophomore	Junior	Senior
Men					
Never, not in 1976	3.4	2.9	4.0	3.6	3.2
Less than weekly	27.2	31.7	28.4	26.5	22.3
1–2 times a week	39.9	41.9	43.4	37.2	37.5
3–4 times a week	20.9	18.1	17.0	23.6	24.6
More than 4 times a week	8.6	5.4	7.2	9.1	12.4
(N)	(N = 3,122)	(781)	(745)	(747)	(849)

Chi square = 63.17, 12 df, $p<.001$

	Totals	Freshman	Sophomore	Junior	Senior
Women					
Never, not in 1976	4.0	4.3	3.8	4.0	3.9
Less than weekly	45.6	43.4	46.4	46.4	46.6
1–2 times a week	38.1	41.5	37.8	38.9	33.7
3–4 times a week	9.9	9.1	9.3	8.7	12.6
More than 4 times a week	2.4	1.7	2.7	2.0	3.2
(N)	(N = 3,830)	(1,043)	(949)	(899)	(939)

Chi square = 24.66, 12 df, $p<.02$

Men versus women: Totals, chi square = 429.47, 4 df, $p<.001$; freshmen, chi square = 64.09, $p<.001$; sophomores, chi square = 75.46, $p<.001$; juniors, chi square = 141.58, $p<.001$; seniors, chi square = 163.50, $p<.001$.

Source: H. Wechsler, and M. McFadden "Drinking among College Students in New England, Extent, Social Correlates and Consequences of Alcohol Use," *Journal of Studies on Alcohol* 40 (1979): 969–996. Table 1, p. 975.

consecutive years to plan its program activities. A consumer alcohol survey was mailed to a sample of the undergraduates each year, and thereby the researchers were able to measure trends in drinking patterns that a single survey could not assess (in other words, it was a *longitudinal* study).

The UMASS data showed that over 90 percent of the students (about equal proportions of men and women) drank at least once a year. Parties were the most common drinking occasions, and 90 percent of the subjects reported attending parties at least once a month—between 10 percent and 17 percent attended six or more parties each month.

Over the course of the study, a significant increase was recorded in the average number of drinks consumed on each occasion (from 3.8 drinks in 1976 to 4.8 in 1979). The average number of occasions upon which students drank also increased (from 1.7 to 2.1) in the same period.

Frequency of intoxication also increased in four years and students with lower grade point averages, male students, and younger students reported the highest rates of intoxication. Table 2–4 summarizes some of the data from the UMASS study in terms of age and number of drinks per week. These measures are remarkably consistent over the span of the survey, for virtually every age category shows an increase in the average number of drinks per week.

Table 2–4. Drinks per Week by Age: 1976 to 1979

| Age | Average Number of Drinks per Week | |
	1976	1979
18 or younger	7.8	7.4
19	5.6	7.2
20	6.0	9.1
21	6.4	6.8
22	7.4	8.1
23 or older	5.6	5.2

Source: E. Duston, ed., *Evaluation Report for the University Model, Demonstration Alcohol Education Project.* Rockville, MD: Division of Prevention, National Institutes on Alcohol Abuse and Alcoholism. p. 56, 1981.

Damage to residence halls is a major problem for colleges and universities. Residence hall advisers and other staff members report that the most frequent alcohol-related problems they must deal with are destructive or aggressive acts resulting in damage to the building or its furnishings. In an attempt to document the cost of such drinking-related damage the UMASS evaluation team conducted four different studies of alcohol use and dormitory damage. They found that most damage occurs to men's dorms, and that up to 48 percent of it is associated with drinking. Most of these damages occurred after dormitory parties and were caused by the residents themselves rather than guests from outside. Their survey showed that the damage costs could run as high as $19.24 per student per year.

Up to this point, the surveys discussed have been rather comprehensive and elaborate, but precise, reliable estimates of drinking patterns can also be ascertained using less complicated techniques. At the University of North Carolina at Chapel Hill, student surveys were conducted for three consecutive years as part of an alcohol education program (McCary et al. 1979). In the UNC study, students were asked to recall their drinking behavior only over a four-week period, thereby yielding a more reliable estimate of consumption than surveys that require respondents to remember a whole year of drinking activities. Table 2–5 summarizes some of the results of this study in terms of *who* drinks (by group percentages of men and women, academic class, and fraternity affiliation) and also *how much* they drink (in ounces of ethanol—absolute alcohol—consumed). Clearly, people in some categories drink much more than others, both by proportion of the group concerned and the average amount consumed, but the figures also show increasing percentages of students choosing to drink over the four-year span of their college experience.

The results of these surveys are interesting and valuable for the light they shed on collegiate drinking patterns, but there is a practical lesson to be gained from them as well. Sometimes the quality of the information one gets from a survey depends less upon *what* is asked and more upon *how* and *where* one asks it.

For example, at the University of Massachusetts, the alcohol education evaluation

Table 2–5. Drinker's Mean Ethanol Consumption during the Month prior to the Survey by Selected Characteristics

Characteristics	N	*Percent of Each Group Who Drink*	*Average Ounces*
Sex			
Female	279	83.0	17.37
Male	217	85.4	28.14
Class			
Freshman	116	77.3	21.60
Sophomore	107	88.4	20.60
Junior	132	85.7	23.08
Senior	141	87.0	22.68
Fraternal Affiliation			
Member	113	95.8	26.00
Nonmember	383	82.2	20.93

Note: Ounces of ethanol consumed per month was calculated on the following basis:
One 12 ounce beer = .48 ounces of ethanol
One 4 ounce glass of wine = .48 ounces of ethanol
1.5 ounces of 80 proof liquor = .60 ounces of ethanol
Drinking 26 ounces of ethanol a month is roughly equivalent (eight glasses in bottle) to drinking *fifty-four* (12 oz.) beers or *seven* bottles of wine or forty-three drinks.
Source: D. McCarty et al., *Campus Alcohol Education Service, First Year Evaluation Report*, Center for Alcohol Studies, University of North Carolina, Chapel Hill, NC, 1979.

team found that routine reporting of medical encounters in the student health service in a three-year period showed that only one-tenth of 1 percent of 90,000 visits a year were associated with alcohol use. However, *routine* reporting procedures were not an accurate source of information in this case. A special survey of medical outpatient contacts revealed that 1.4 percent of all medical contacts were alcohol related. Furthermore, when student contacts after normal operating hours were measured, almost 4 percent of the visits were shown to be associated with alcohol use. When weekends were examined separately, as many as 8 percent of the visits were alcohol related.

The UMASS study also found in the mental health clinic, that about 7 percent of the 1,000 new patients seen each year indicated that alcohol-related problems were part of the reason they sought help. Sixty percent of these students were concerned with their own use of alcohol while the remainder were concerned with someone else's drinking. Analysis of mental health clinic contacts between 1976 and 1980 revealed that 14 percent were connected with drinking problems.

Problems related to student drinking can best be documented by reference to "alcohol-related incidents." Any social disruption, legal infraction, injury, or death associated with acute intoxication is an alcohol-related incident. These incidents are usually recorded by authorities who must deal directly with them: police officers, county coroners, university housing officers, emergency room doctors, and similar officials. Others may also be aware of problems that do not reach the authorities—students sharing living facilities know how many times sleep and study have been interrupted by drunken roommates.

It is the function of an alcohol education program to try and measure the frequency of these incidents (from official and unofficial sources) and bring them to the attention of the community at large. An awareness of cumulative alcohol-related incidents often impels an individual to seek help to manage his or her personal problem. Documentation and publication of aggregate incidents in a community will result in increased awareness and concern about the effects of these problems on the health of the community. In both cases, problem awareness is the key to change.

Measuring the extent of alcohol problems is complicated by the fact that they vary in extent, duration, and seriousness. The previous chapter contained a list of the major categories of alcohol-related problems, but for measurement purposes it is easier to examine the consequences of these problems. There are three types of consequences associated with collegiate drinking problems: situational, personal, and communitywide.

Many problems are the result of the behavior of students attending a gathering in which drinking is the primary activity—a single situation in which the drinker's blood alcohol level exceeds .06 percent (about five drinks in one hour for a 150-pound person). This does not mean that the situation is the cause of the problems, but simply that they can most easily be described with reference to that situation. Examples of situational problems on a college campus are litter, noise, and property damage. These problems are often not seen as serious or persistent because they are linked to transitory events, not repeated patterns of aberrant behavior, and can frequently be attributed to the actions of a few individuals.

Personal consequences are also attributable to the actions of individuals of a drinking group, but usually occur after the drinking situation. For example, drinking/driving arrests occur after people leave a party. Hangovers, injuries sustained while drunk, damaged friendships, and similar personal difficulties are also in this category. Personal consequences also accumulate gradually into more serious problems—missed classes, poor grades, failure to graduate, even long-term mental health problems. These consequences do not usually stir widespread concern because they are seen as the individual drinker's responsibility.

Ironically, most of the adverse personal effects of drinking occur to those who are not dependent upon alcohol. Individuals who are dependent often isolate themselves from the physical, social, and legal environment and thereby avoid many of the adverse consequences of their habit. Drinkers who continue to interact with the world around them expose themselves to problems.

Communitywide consequences of alcohol use are by definition also cumulative, and they are characterized by the fact that they affect more members of the community than the individual drinker. People injured in alcohol-related accidents obviously suffer personally and individually—pain, loss of work or study time, hospital costs—but the community suffers collectively in terms of higher insurance rates, greater court costs, and increased burdens on law enforcement resources. These problems are the ones most likely to receive communitywide attention because they are persistent, damaging, and affect virtually everyone in the community. Alcohol education programs usually focus on solutions to this type of problem.

This chapter has introduced some general concepts of data collection and problem documentation. The next chapter will carry these concepts a step further and examine their implications for alcohol program planning on a college campus.

Thought Questions

1. From your own observation, does your campus seem to share the general patterns described by survey research in this chapter?

2. Is there some significant, persistent problem on your campus that was not mentioned in the text?

3. Can you think of several data sources on your campus from which alcohol-related incidents could be measured?

4. How would you characterize the level of problem awareness on your campus—low, high, nonexistent?

References

Clark, W., and L. Midanik. 1980. "Alcohol Use and Alcohol Problems among U.S. Adults: Results of the 1979 National Survey." Report submitted to the National Institute on Alcohol Abuse and Alcoholism.

McCarty, D.; S. Morrison; K. Mills; and L. Mason. 1979. "The Campus Alcohol Education Service—An Analysis of First Year Evaluation Activities: Assessment Process and Impact." The University of North Carolina at Chapel Hill. Report prepared for the National Institute on Alcohol Abuse and Alcoholism, Division of Prevention.

Mills, K., and D. McCarty. In press. "A Data Based Alcohol Abuse Prevention Program in a University Setting." *Journal of Drug and Alcohol Education.*

Straus, R., and S. Bacon. 1953. *Drinking in College.* New Haven: Yale University Press.

Wechsler, H., and M. McFadden. 1979. "Drinking among College Students in New England, Extent, Social Correlates and Consequences of Alcohol Use." *Journal of Studies on Alcohol* 40: 969–996.

University of Massachusetts. 1980. Evaluation report for the university model, Demonstration Alcohol Education Project, University Health Services, Amherst, Massachusetts. Report submitted to the Division of Prevention, National Institute on Alcohol Abuse and Alcoholism.

Additional Readings

Cahalan, D.; I.H. Cisin; and H.M. Crossley. 1969. *American Drinking Practices.* Monograph No. 6, New Brunswick, N.J.: Rutgers Center of Alcohol Studies.

Engs, R.C. 1977. "Drinking Patterns and Drinking Problems of College Students." *Journal of Studies on Alcohol* 38: 2144–2156.

Kraft, D.P. 1979. "Alcohol Related Problems Seen at the Student Health Services." *Journal of The American College Health Association* 27: 190–194.

Noble, E.P., ed. 1978. *Third Special Report to the U.S. Congress on Alcohol and Health*. U.S. Department of Health, Education and Welfare, DHEW Pub. No. (ADM) 79–832. Washington, D.C.: U.S. Government Printing Office.

Polich, J.M. 1979. "Alcohol Problems among Civilian Youth and Military Personnel." In H.T. Blane and M.E. Chafetz, eds., *Youth, Alcohol, and Social Policy*, pp. 59–86. New York: Plenum Press.

Rosenbluth, J.; P.E. Nathan; and D.M. Lawson. 1978. "Environmental Influences on Drinking by College Students in a College Pub: Behavioral Observations in the Natural Environment." *Addictive Behaviors* 3: 117–121.

Wechsler, H. 1976. "Alcohol Intoxication and Drug Use among Teenagers." *Journal of Studies on Alcohol* 37: 1672–1677.

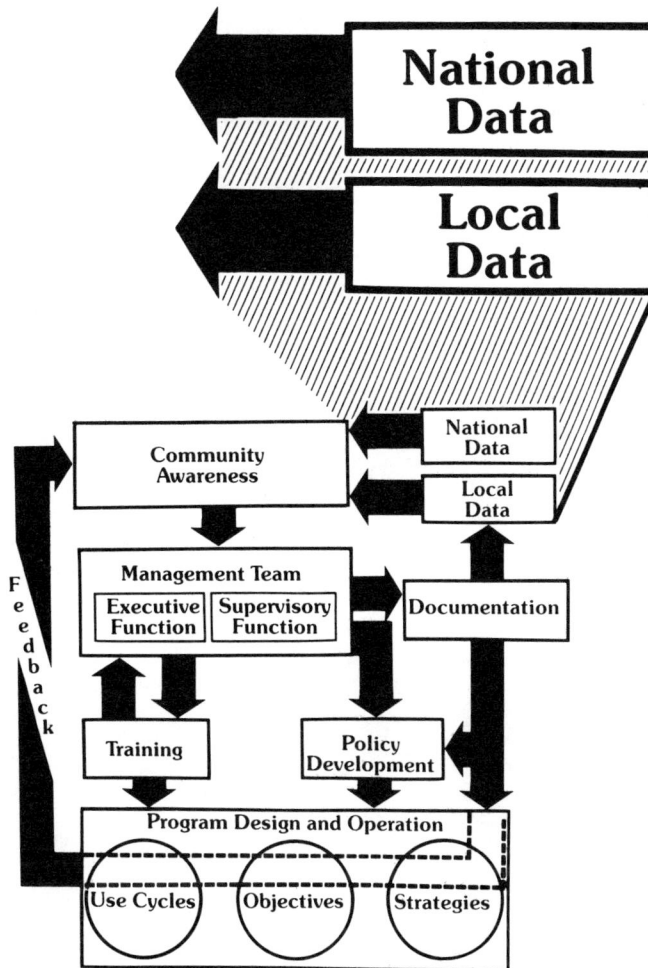

National
Data

Local
Data

Community
Awareness

National
Data

Local
Data

Management Team

Executive
Function

Supervisory
Function

Documentation

Feedback

Training

Policy
Development

Program Design and Operation

Use Cycles

Objectives

Strategies

Chapter 3

NATIONAL DATA SOURCES
Establishing a Risk Profile

> *OBJECTIVES*
>
> When you have finished this chapter, you should be able to:
>
> 1. Summarize the significant trends in youth drinking patterns as reflected in research surveys;
> 2. Discuss the relationship between alcohol use and drug use by adolescents;
> 3. List five risk factors usually associated with youth drinking problems; and
> 4. Begin to compile a list of high-risk groups present on your own campus.

The previous chapter provided factual data about national trends in collegiate drinking and its effects. This chapter uses that data, plus information from additional studies, to establish a "risk profile" of factors that are related to alcohol problems. This risk profile can be used to guide program organizers on a college campus.

A "risk factor" is an event that is associated with a problem. A risk factor may be the proven cause of a problem, verified by logical or statistical means, or it may be related to a problem in some way that is not easily provable. Failure to use a seat belt is a statistically demonstrated risk factor for injuries in automobile accidents. Walking across an open field in an electrical storm is a risk factor for death by lightning. Unfortunately, it is impossible to isolate a single risk factor for complicated problems such as city riots, cancer, heart disease, or street crime. Many risk factors are associated with these problems. For example, cardiovascular disease has been linked with such diverse factors as diet, exercise pattern, family medical history, age, stress level, and even the region of the country where one lives.

Similarly, risk factors for alcohol problems are difficult to isolate, partly because people disagree on the definition of "alcohol problems" and partly because these problems do not just happen and then disappear—they tend to gradually wax and wane, and perhaps emerge again in some other form. Social Scientists have not yet been able to determine whether manyof these alcohol risk factors are causal or simply associated with problems. However, one obvious risk factor is always linked to alcohol problems: alcohol use. The question that researchers have tried to answer is: *What quantity* of alcohol, drunk *how often,* will lead to problems?

In its *Fourth Special Report to the U.S. Congress* the National Institute on Alcohol Abuse and Alcoholism stated that the many variations in alcohol-related problems made a single-concept description impossible:

> Categories such as alcoholism, alcohol abuse, alcohol dependence, problem drinking, and alcohol-related disabilities are of definite although limited value. Each is useful for certain purposes and for certain populations, but none can represent adequately the full range of problems associated with alcohol consumption in American society (Deluca 1981:29).

The report also indicated that the traditional risk profile for adult alcoholics is inadequate and inappropriate for application to youth.

In effect, problem drinking among adolescents cannot be assessed by the same criteria used to assess adult alcoholism or problem drinking. Alcohol-related diseases, classical symptoms of alcohol dependence, and many of the adverse consequences that occur in adult alcoholics are reported infrequently in adolescent populations. Moreover, frequency of adolescent drinking may not be as big a problem as quantity consumed on a given occasion..."(39).

These "classical symptoms" include drinking early in the morning, repeated job absenteeism, treatment for alcoholism, and loss of social status.

Surveys and critical incident data suggest that the frequency of alcohol problems among college students varies considerably. More than 70 percent of student drinkers apparently have no problems related to alcohol, but that leaves a substantial number who do experience difficulties. In the 1979 study by Wechsler and McFadden covered in Chapter 2, nearly one-quarter of the men in college reported that they had been in trouble with authorities after drinking. Twenty percent reported physical fights after drinking. Ten percent said that drinking caused them to have automobile accidents, and another 10 percent recounted that they had been passengers in alcohol-related crashes in which someone was hurt. The most common problem reported by both men and women was that they did or said someting that they would not do or say when sober (men, 42.5 percent; women, 36.1 percent).

Three of the most recent studies of adolescent and adult alcohol use are introduced in this chapter to help construct a risk profile for alcohol problems. These studies were chosen for inclusion because they were intensive national efforts that "fine tuned" many of the research methods used in the past and because they show that drinking patterns are well-established *before* individuals reach college age.

The National Institute on Alcohol Abuse and Alcoholism (NIAAA) commissioned a survey of high school students by the Research Triangle Institute (RTI) of North Carolina (Rachal et al. 1980). The RTI researchers conducted a nationwide survey of adolescents in grades seven through twelve in 1974 and polled a second sample of tenth, eleventh, and twelfth graders in 1978. Some of the students in the 1978 sample had also been included in the earlier survey, so the researchers were able to examine trends of alcohol use over time (a longitudinal study). For cross-sectional data, a separate sample of tenth through twelfth graders (not surveyed in 1974) was taken in 1978. Although the RTI study concentrated on alcohol use, some information about drug use was also solicited.

Prevalence of drug use among high school seniors was specifically addressed in a project sponsored by the National Institute on Drug Abuse (NIDA) and carried out by the University of Michigan's Institute of Social Research (Johnston, Bachman, and O'Malley 1980). The seven classes of drugs examined in the study were marijuana (including hashish), inhalants, hallucinogens, cocaine, heroin, opiates other than heroin, stimulants, sedatives, tranquilizers, cigarettes, and alcohol. The investigators concentrated on high frequency drug use rather than on proportions of people who had ever tried drugs. This was done in an effort to clarify the levels of seriousness and real extent of drug involvement. The subjects of the study were drawn from approximately 130 public and private high schools across the United States. About 16,500 high school seniors were surveyed each year from 1975 to 1980. In this chapter we are primarily interested in the survey data that compare alcohol use to other types of drug use, but the interested reader may obtain a copy of the full report entitled *Student Drug Use in*

America, published by NIDA. (Write to the National Clearinghouse for Drug Abuse Information, NIDA, 5600 Fishers Lane, Rockville, Maryland, 20857.)

Another study, carried out in 1978 by the Rand Corporation, examined the prevalence and extent of alcohol problems in the U.S. Air Force (Polich and Orvis 1979). The results of this study are valuable for the light they shed on the similarity of drinking patterns among youth in both military and collegiate populations. Also, the Rand study was one of the first research efforts in which the investigators made a clear distinction between two types of alcohol problems: 1) dependence upon alcohol indicated by severe and chronic patterns of addictive symptoms; and 2) adverse effects and serious consequences arising from limited, short-term patterns of consumption.

The primary source of data in the Rand study was a questionnaire completed anonymously by a random sample of 3,148 active duty personnel. To validate the data from this survey, Rand researchers also collected information about drunk-driving arrests on air force bases, the number and type of nondriving alcohol-related arrests, and alcohol beverage sales on air force bases.

Similar surveys of military personnel were conducted worldwide by another research company, the Burt Corporation (Burt and Biegel 1980). They found that drinking and drug use were less prevalent in the Air Force than in the other branches of the armed service and are probably representative of the rates in the civilian population.

The results of the Rand study indicate that alcohol problems increase with heavier consumption patterns, and that the problem increase occurred for individuals with addictive patterns as well as for those with short-term patterns. This relationship is illustrated in Figure 3–1, which shows that as soon as consumption rises above an average of two drinks a day the chance of experiencing problems doubles. An individual who consumes eight or more drinks in a day, if only once a month, has a 20 percent chance of experiencing serious, long-term alcohol problems. This rate is five times as high as the rate for those who never drink heavily.

The Rand study also linked serious risk with frequent intoxication and with incidents of warnings from friends or authorities. These conclusions parallel those of the University of Massachusetts study discussed in the previous chapter. The UMASS researchers found that the amount of alcohol consumed per sitting was the most significant risk factor for adverse consequences among college students.

The "serious incident" checklist from the Rand study catalogued the types of problems usually associated with heavy alcohol use (Polich and Orvis 1979:35):

Work Impairment

   Official punishment
   Lower performance rating
   Loss of 3 working days

Physical Damage

   Illness lasting one week
   Hospitalization
   Visits to physician
   Accident with self-injury
   Accident with injury to others or property damage

Social Disruption

Spouse left
Spouse threatened to leave
DWI arrest
Nondriving arrest
Jail
Fights

A similar list of incidents could be compiled for documentation of problems among college students. Most current studies indicate that up to 25 percent of college drinkers experience some type of serious problem in their college career. Only 5 to 10 percent of the air force respondents experienced the problems listed above at any time in their lives.

Since college provides a permissive environment and military service does not, it might be concluded that the degree of permissiveness results in variations of drinking levels. The Rand research took this possibility into account, and, after examining

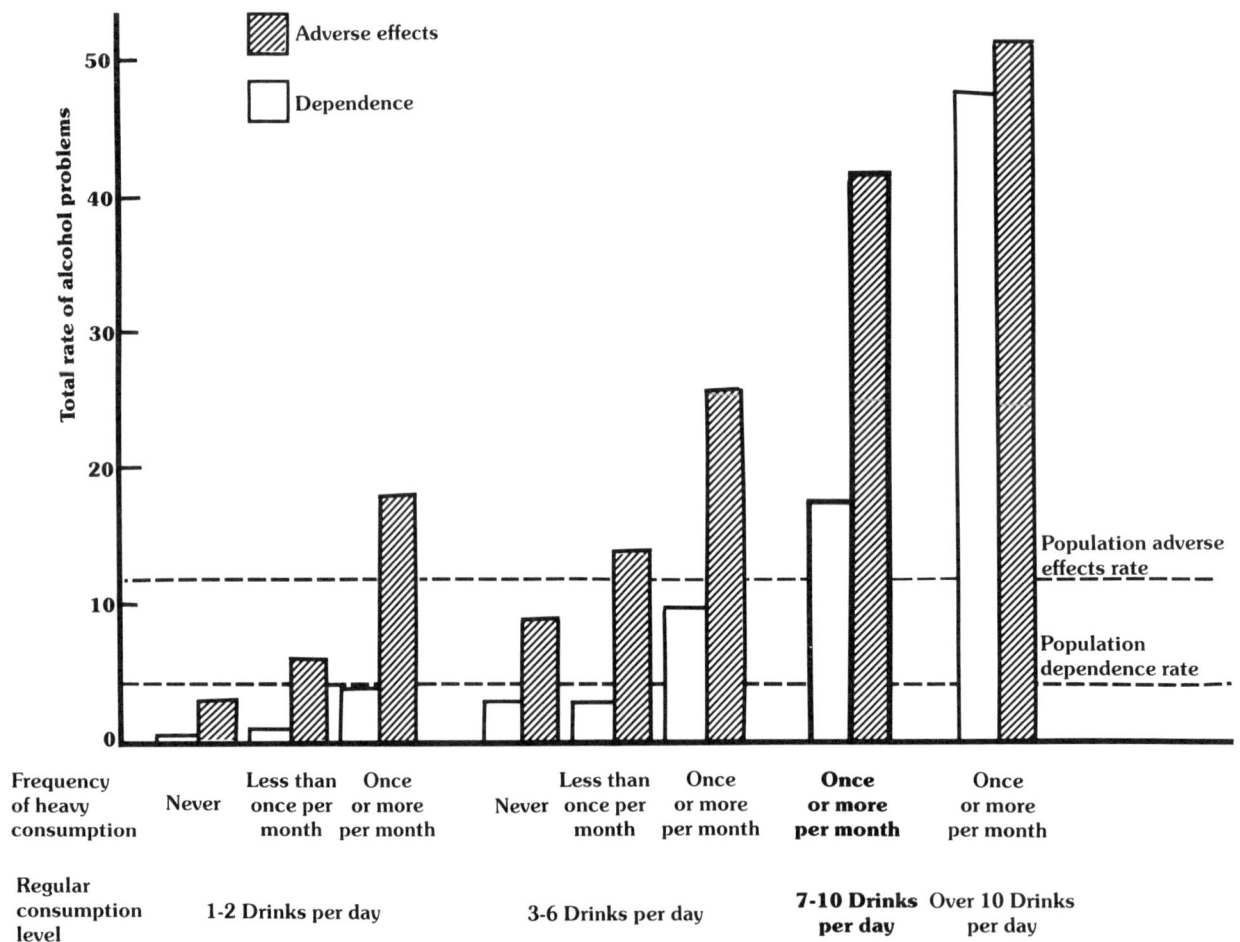

Figure 3-1. Alcohol problem rates by consumption patterns. (Source: Polich and Orvis 1979.)

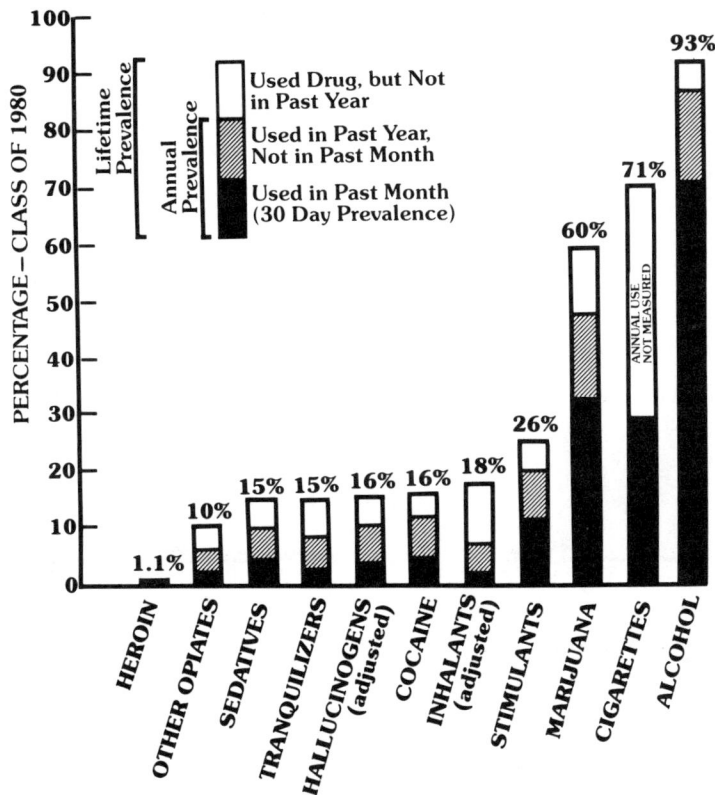

Figure 3–2. Prevalence and recency of use. Eleven types of drugs, class of 1980. (Source: Johnston, Bachman, and O'Malley 1980.)

alcohol consumption across various bases and working conditions worldwide, the investigators concluded that "variation in the permissiveness of environments may account for some of the variance in adverse effects," but "it is clear that the underlying drinking behavior" is more important (Polich and Orvis: 1979, 37).

Other drugs create the same behavioral effects as alcohol, but alcohol poses special problems because (unlike other drugs) it is legal, inexpensive, readily available, and well-promoted through advertising. For these reasons, alcohol is the most popular drug, especially among adolescents. Data from the NIDA survey summarized in Figure 3–2 show just how popular it is. Alcohol leads all other drugs in prevalence, measured over a month, a year, or a lifetime.

Data from both the NIDA and NIAAA studies indicate that alcohol does not replace other drugs. In fact, there is an almost linear relationship between alcohol use and other drug use. A young person who drinks heavily is also more likely to have a wide variety of experiences with other drugs. In the 1978 NIAAA study, only 14 percent of the alcohol abstainers had tried marijuana, but 84.1 percent of the heavy drinkers had tried it. A similar relationship holds for inhalants, hallucinogens, stimulants, barbiturates, tranquilizers, cocaine, and heroin.

More students use drugs, especially alcohol, as they progress through school. This is true for both sexes. Figure 3–3 illustrates this trend with respect to marijuana, stimulants, and alcohol. The use curves on these charts may be assumed to continue beyond graduation; students do not stop using alcohol and other drugs when they

ALCOHOL

MARIJUANA

STIMULANTS

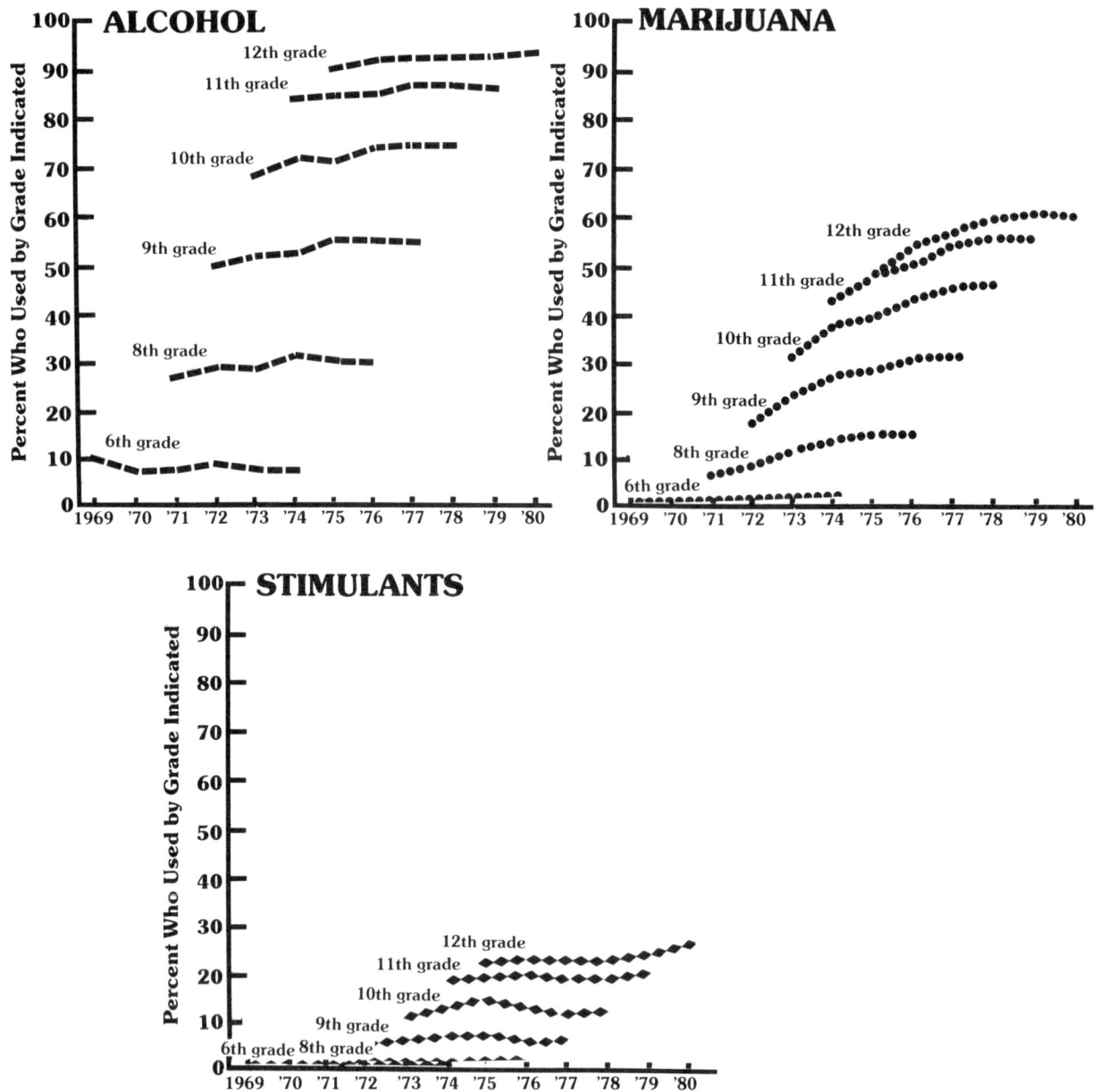

Figure 3–3. Trends in prevalence of alcohol, marijuana, and stimulants for earlier grade levels, based on retrospective reports by seniors. (Source: Adapted from Johnston, Bachman, and O'Malley 1980.)

graduate from high school. Moreover, although men use drugs and alcohol more heavily than women, this difference is disappearing in the case of alcohol use.

Of course, an estimate of problem rates depends not only on prevalence, but on quantity and frequency of use. The NIDA study showed that about 17 percent of high school seniors had consumed five or more drinks on at least three occasions in the two weeks prior to the survey. That means they were getting very drunk an average of once every five days.

The NIAAA research indicated that most teenagers drink frequently, but drink small amounts, and that beer was the beverage of choice. Table 3–1 is a list of the drinking categories used in the NIAAA study. They are similar to the categories used in the Wechsler and McFadden study discussed in Chapter 2. (Either scheme would be useful for problem documentation on a local level, and these considerations will be explored further in Chapter 5.)

Using the categories in Table 3–1, researchers found that 14.8 percent of the students in grades ten through twelve were "heavier" drinkers, 17.3 percent were "moderate/heavier," and only 21.1 percent were abstainers. About 30 percent of tenth through twelfth graders could be classified as moderate to heavy drinkers; roughly the same percentage of entering college freshmen are moderate to heavy drinkers. Generally, the adolescent studies show that teen drinking increases rapidly beginning with age thirteen and that the figures hold for both sexes. In the NIAAA study, 70 percent of the high school girls were drinkers.

There is a clear association between drinking parents and drinking children. Parents' opinions about teenage drinking have little to do with teen drinking behavior. Young people tend to do what their parents *do*, not what they *say*. Approximately 50 percent of the teens with abstaining parents were also abstainers; about 40 percent of the teens whose parents drank regularly were heavy drinkers. A more potent influence

Table 3–1.　NIAAA Drinking Categories

Drinking Level Groups	Definition
Abstainers	Don't drink or drink less than once a year
Infrequent	Drink once a month at most and drink small amounts per typical drinking occasion.
Light	Drink once a month at most and drink medium amounts per typical drinking occasion *or* drink no more than 3–4 times a month and drink small amounts per typical drinking occasion.
Moderate	Drink at least once a week and small amounts per typical drinking occasion *or* 3–4 times a month and medium amounts per typical drinking occasion *or* no more than once a month and large amounts per typical drinking occasion.
Moderate/heavier	Drink at least once a week and medium amounts per typical drinking occasion *or* 3–4 times a month and large amounts per typical drinking occasion.
Heavier	Drink at least once a week and large amounts per typical drinking occasion.

Source: Rachal, J.V.; I.L. Guess; R.L. Hubbard; S.A. Maisto; E.R. Cavanaugh; R. Waddell; and C.H. Benrud. 1980. *Adolescent Drinking Behavior, Volume I: The Extent and Nature of Adolescent Alcohol and Drug Use.* Research Triangle Park, North Carolina: Center for the Study of Social Behavior, Research Triangle Institute. p. 43.

on drinking behavior is that of the peer group. High school and college students drink with friends their own age; parents and older friends are the second most popular companions. This means that they are drinking away from their homes; in cars, at parties, and in bars. Finally, the NIDA study showed that drinking teens tend to drink and associate with one another—more so than teens who use other drugs.

Teens who drink more alcohol often suffer more problems. In the NIAAA study, for example, only 8 percent of the "infrequent/light" drinkers reported problems, but 25 percent of the "moderate/heavier" and 55 percent of the "heavier" drinkers had problems. When the same sample was analyzed with reference to the highest average amount used, the percentages reporting problems were even more dramatic: of those who averaged two to four drinks, 23 percent had problems; of those who averaged five or more drinks, 75 percent reported problems.

It is almost an axiom among alcohol researchers that drinkers progress inevitably upward from lower drinking levels to higher ones as their age increases. This is definitely true for the adolescent drinker, less true for the college drinker, and encouragingly, even less true in older adults. Movement from one drinking level to another appears to happen quite slowly for a given individual, but the change is dramatic when measured over an entire population (as in the NIAAA study of high school youth).

Significant drinking at an early age does seem to lead to moderate or heavy drinking later on, but there is no way to ascertain definitively whether drinking problems in youth lead to problems later in life. Furthermore, experienced heavy drinkers often learn how to adjust their drinking patterns to accommodate new situations and avoid detection. For example, the drinking driver compensates for the effects of alcohol by driving more slowly, hugging the yellow line, taking back roads, and so forth. Some heavy drinkers adjust their living schedules to escape detection, as in the case of the student who never signs up for classes held before eleven o'clock in the morning. The measurable decrease in consumption levels of college seniors may be attributable to the necessity of preparing for graduation and the search for jobs.

Unfortunately, once drinking patterns are established, they are difficult to unlearn, especially for the heavy drinker. A study published in 1976 examined the stability of drinking patterns among problem drinkers over a four-year span. The researchers concluded that "continuity of particular problems over time is low, but continued involvement in some alcohol problems is the rule rather than the exception" (Clark and Cahalan) 1976: 258).

In spite of the measurement difficulties mentioned above and in the previous chapter, at least three risk factors, derived from the research data, can be associated with young adult drinking problems:

1. The amount of alcohol consumed on each drinking occasion. Five drinks (or about three ounces of absolute alcohol) is a threshold amount.
2. The number of drinking occasions in a given span of time: how often an individual drinks.
3. The frequency of heavy intoxication: how often an individual drinks five or more drinks.

Two additional risk factors must be mentioned:

4. The behavioral signs of intoxication observed by others; friends, parents, authorities.
5. The number of warnings about excessive drinking given by others.

The last two items are not, strictly speaking, risk factors in themselves; they are rather visible indicators of the previous three factors. Since people are often able to compensate for (and disguise) the amount they drink, these indicators are useful for measuring the extent of drinking problems.

For a college student, examples of warning incidents might include complaints from the residence hall adviser, comments from teachers, and suggestions from friends that a visit to the student health service might be in order. Warning incidents should indicate to the individual that the consequences of his or her drinking have reached a level intolerable to friends and social contacts, but often these signals are dismissed or ignored. To further complicate matters, a young drinker may reach a consumption level of five or six drinks per occasion without adverse effects, even though this level is statistically associated with high risk. Even when problems begin to occur, they are often attributed to causes other than drinking.

Factors that traditional alcohol programs often concentrate on, such as the individual's "perception of responsibility to oneself and others" and "attitudes toward drinking," are not only difficult to measure, but also have a very low correlation with alcohol problems. The five factors listed above are statistically associated with alcohol problems and are good indicators of risk. They provide reference points for beginning the investigation of local problems and for developing an alcohol program addressed to areas of high risk.

The research studies discussed in this chapter and the previous one all support some general conclusions about college drinking that can also be used to help focus a campus alcohol program:

- Heavy drinkers experience more problems with alcohol, and the occasional bouts of drunkenness produced by six or more drinks dramatically increase the likelihood of adverse consequences.
- Men drink more and have more problems than women.
- Members of fraternity organizations drink more and have more problems than other students.
- Drinking levels and problem levels generally increase with academic class standing (freshman to senior).

Figure 3–4 illustrates graphically the relationship between drinking levels and problem levels.

The research results seem so conclusive that one might assume it would be relatively easy to identify local problems and establish an alcohol program. However, scientific data are not sufficient cause to change widely held and long-standing beliefs about alcohol. The kinds of drinking problems common to college youth differ from

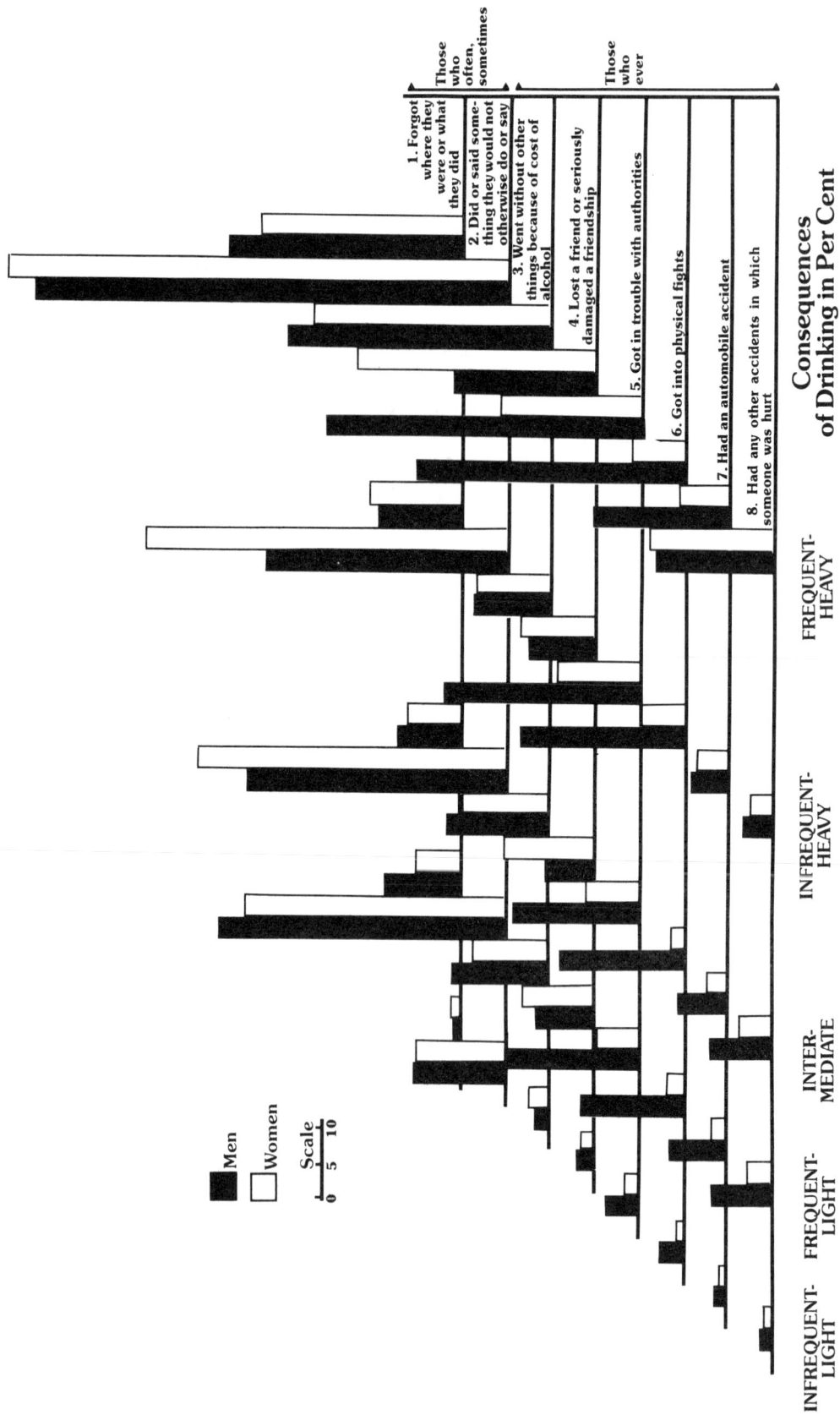

Consequences of Drinking in Per Cent

1. Forgot where they were or what they did

2. Did or said something they would not otherwise do or say

3. Went without other things because of cost of alcohol

4. Lost a friend or seriously damaged a friendship

5. Got in trouble with authorities

6. Got into physical fights

7. Had an automobile accident

8. Had any other accidents in which someone was hurt

Those who often, sometimes

Those who ever

Men

Women

Scale
0 5 10

INFREQUENT-LIGHT

FREQUENT-LIGHT

INTER-MEDIATE

INFREQUENT-HEAVY

FREQUENT-HEAVY

Figure 3–4. Consequences of drinking by sex and drinking typology.

those traditionally associated with alcoholism, so it is necessary to sensitize community members to the difference before they can perceive the existence of young adult problems. Even when certain problems are obviously present on campus, people often fail to recognize their extent or seriousness. For example, students and faculty alike may share the opinion that parties at which everyone gets bombed are acceptable and tolerable as long as nobody gets hurt. They need to be told about short- and long-range consequences of these events and their implications for community problems. Many problems are dismissed as simply manifestations of a stage of adolescence, and students themselves frequently express the belief that college is a place to enjoy life and let off steam (and therefore tolerate a certain level of drunkenness at social gatherings). Their attitude might change if they were aware of the persistence of drinking patterns learned in youth.

In short, one of the initial goals of an alcohol education program should be to increase public awareness about 1) the extent of problems associated with infrequent/heavy and frequent/heavy drinking, and 2) the risk levels associated with prolonged inattention to these problems. The first task of the program planners is therefore documentation of local problems, followed by interpretation of the results in the light of national statistics and distribution of this information throughout the

Table 3–2. Percentages of Subjects Experiencing Drinking-Related Behavior Problems (By Sex)

Drinking-Related Problem	Male		Female	
	N	%	N	%
Hangover	50	55.5	26	43.3
Nausea, vomiting	26	28.9	10	16.7
Driving after several drinks	53	58.9	21	35
Driving after drinking too much	25	27.8	8	13.3
Drinking while driving	38	42.2	7	11.7
Going to class after several drinks	7	7.8	1	1.7
Missing class after several drinks	4	4.4	0	0
Missing class due to hangover	21	23.3	5	8.3
Criticized for drinking	10	11.1	7	11.7
Gotten lower grade	5	5.6	1	1.7
Gotten into a fight	7	7.8	4	6.7
Thought you had a problem	2	2.2	5	8.3
Damaged property, pulled fire alarm, etc.	9	10	0	0
Forgotten what happened when drinking	23	25.6	12	10
Done something you have regretted	28	31.1	13	21.7
Had trouble with the law	10	11.1	1	1.7
Had trouble with the school	4	4.4	1	1.7
Involved in accident	8	8.9	4	6.7

Source: A.G. Little, "Drinking Patterns and Drinking-Related Behavior Problems of Wake Forest University Undergraduates," Department of Education, Wake Forest University, 1980. Table 4, p. 25.

community. Problem documentation and publication will help motivate community members to seek solutions to the alcohol-related problems they find intolerable.

A simple, five-page survey was used to document the drinking problems at a small coeducational university of 3,400 students, with the results shown in Table 3–2. The survey, conducted by one graduate student, identified twenty common problems students experienced as a result of drinking. The campus had been widely considered traditionally oriented and relatively trouble-free, but the results of the survey stimulated sufficient interest to lead to the creation of an alcohol education program. In the conclusion of the survey report, the author stated that "Any university which intends to attack the problem of alcohol abuse can establish an alcohol awareness program once the extent of the problem is defined. Models of other programs should

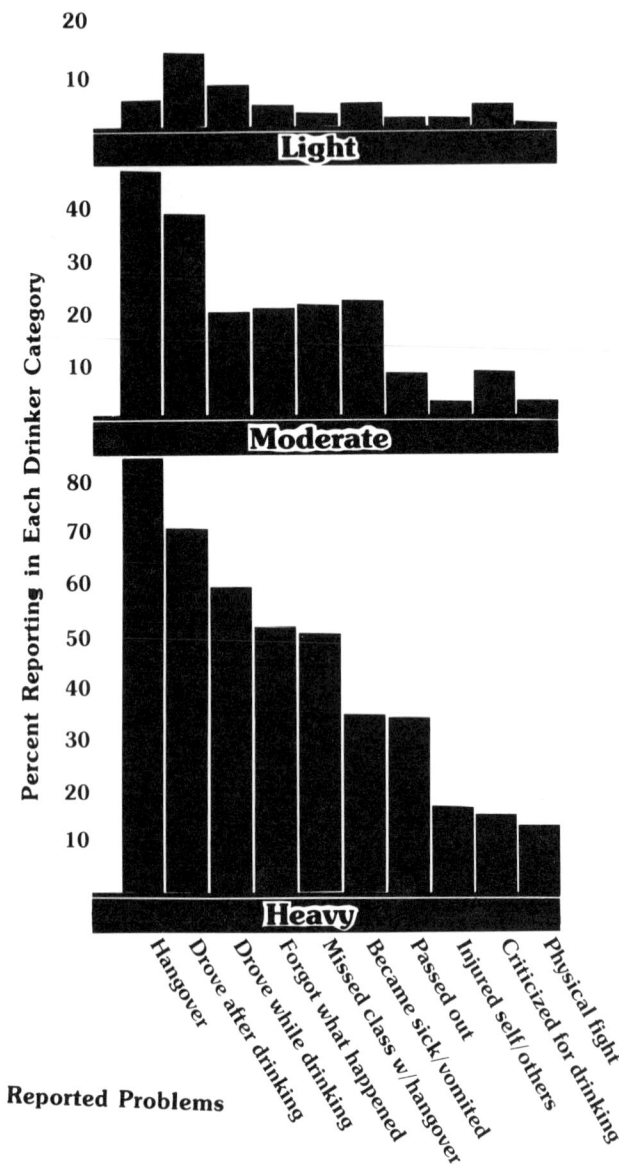

Figure 3–5. Levels of student consumption related to self-reported problems. (Source: Mills, Pfaffenberger, and McCarty 1981.)

be examined and adapted to meet the specific needs of the students of the university" (Little 1980: 22).

Figure 3–5 illustrates the relationship of consumption to problems reported by students in a survey at the University of North Carolina, Chapel Hill (Mills et al. 1981). The statistics show clearly that heavy drinkers have more problems than moderate drinkers; moderate drinkers have more problems than light drinkers; and light drinkers have more problems than abstainers.

Thought Questions

1. Can you recall any statements made recently by students, staff members, or faculty that reflect the attitude that alcohol problems are not serious on your campus?

2. What information, from local or national data sources, would help change this attitude?

3. Do you know anyone who drinks heavily, but maintains that they are not a "problem drinker" because they never drink in the morning and can stop whenever they wish? What kind of information would be useful for raising awareness in this case?

References

Burt, M.R., and M.M. Biegel. 1980. *Highlights from the Worldwide Survey of Nonmedical Drug Use and Alcohol Use among Military Personnel: 1980.*
Bethesda, MD.: Burt Associates, Inc. Sponsored by the Department of Defense.

Clark, W.B., and D. Cahalan. 1976. "Change in Problem Drinking over a Four-Year Span." *Addictive Behavior* 1: 251–259.

Deluca, J.R., ed. 1981. *Fourth Special Report to the U.S. Congress on Alcohol and Health.* Washington, D.C.: U.S. Department of Health and Human Services, DHHS Publication No. (ADM) 81–1080.

Jessor, R.; J.A. Chase; and J.E. Donovan. 1980. "Psychosocial Correlates of Marijuana Use and Problem Drinking in a National Sample of Adolescents." *American Journal of Public Health* 70: 605–613.

Johnston, L.D.; J.G. Bachman; and P.M. O'Malley. 1980. *Highlights from Student Drug Use in America 1975–1980.* The University of Michigan Institute for Social Research, report sponsored by The National Institute on Drug Abuse.

Little, A.G. 1980. *Drinking Patterns and Drinking-Related Behavior Problems of Wake Forest University Undergraduates.* Winston-Salem, N.C.: Department of Education, Wake Forest University. M.A. Thesis.

Mills, K.C.; B. Pfaffenberger and D. McCarty. 1981. "Guidelines For Alcohol Abuse Prevention on The College Campus." *Journal of Higher Education* 52: 399–414.

Polich, M.J. and B.R. Orvis. 1979. *Alcohol Problems: Patterns and Prevalence in the U.S. Air Force.* R-2308-AF, Santa Monica, CA.: RAND Corporation.

Rachal, J.V.; J.R. Williams; M.L. Brehm; B. Cavanaugh; R.P. Moore; and W.C.

Eckerman. 1975. *A National Study of Adolescent Drinking Behavior, Attitudes and Correlates.* Prepared for National Institute on Alcohol Abuse and Alcoholism, Report number PB-246-002; NIAAA/NCALI-75/27. Springfield, VA: U.S. National Technical Information Service.

Rachal, J.V.; L.L Guess; R.L. Hubbard; S.A. Maisto; E.R. Cavenaugh; R. Waddell and C.H. Benyud. 1980. *Adolescent Drinking Behavior, Volume I, the Extent and Nature of Adolescent Alcohol and Drug Use: the 1974 and 1978 National Sample Studies.* Sponsored by the National Institute on Alcohol Abuse and Alcoholism, and the National Institute on Drug Abuse. Durham, N.C.: Center for the Study of Social Behavior, Research Triangle Institute, Project No. 23U-1322.

Wechsler, H., and M. McFadden. 1979. "Drinking among College Students in New England, Extent, Social Correlates and Consequences of Alcohol Use." *Journal of Studies on Alcohol* 40: 969–996.

Additional Readings

Cahalan, D., and I. Cisin. 1968. "American Drinking Practices: Summary of Findings from a National Probability Sample, 1. Extent of Drinking by Population Subgroups." *Quarterly Journal of Studies on Alcohol* 29: 130–151.

DeRicco, D. 1978. "Effects of Peer Majority on Drinking Rate." *Addicitive Behaviors* 3: 29–34.

Dyer, A.; J. Stamler; O. Paul; M. Lepper; R. Shekelle; H. McKean; and D. Garside. 1980. "Alcohol Consumption and 17-year Mortality in the Chicago Western Electric Company Study." *Preventive Medicine* 9: 78–90.

Fillmore, K.M. 1974. "Drinking and Problem Drinking in Early Adulthood and Middle Age." *Quarterly Journal of Studies on Alcohol* 35: 819–840.

Jessor, R. and S. Jessor. 1975. "Adolescent Development and the Onset of Drinking: A Longitudinal Study." *Journal of Studies on Alcohol* 36: 27–51.

LaPorte, R.; J. Cresanta; and L. Kuller. 1980. "The Relationship of Alcohol Consumption to Atherosclerotic Heart Disease." *Preventive Medicine* 9: 22–40.

Margulies, R.Z.; R.C. Kessler; and D.B. Kandel. 1977. "A Longitudinal Study of Onset of Drinking among High School Students." *Journal of Studies on Alcohol* 38: 897–912.

Meyer, A., and J. Henderson. 1974. "Multiple Risk Factor Reduction in the Prevention of Cardiovascular Disease." *Preventive Medicine* 3: 225–236.

Polich, J.M.; D.J. Armor; and H.B. Braiker. 1980. "Patterns of Alcoholism over Four Years." *Journal of Studies on Alcohol* 41: 397–416.

Smart, R., and G. Gray. 1979. "Parental and Peer Influences as Correlates of Problem Drinking among High School Students." *The International Journal of the Addictions* 14: 905–917.

Wiley, J. and T. Camacho. 1980. "Life-Style and Future Health: Evidence from the Alameda County Study." *Preventive Medicine* 9: 1–21.

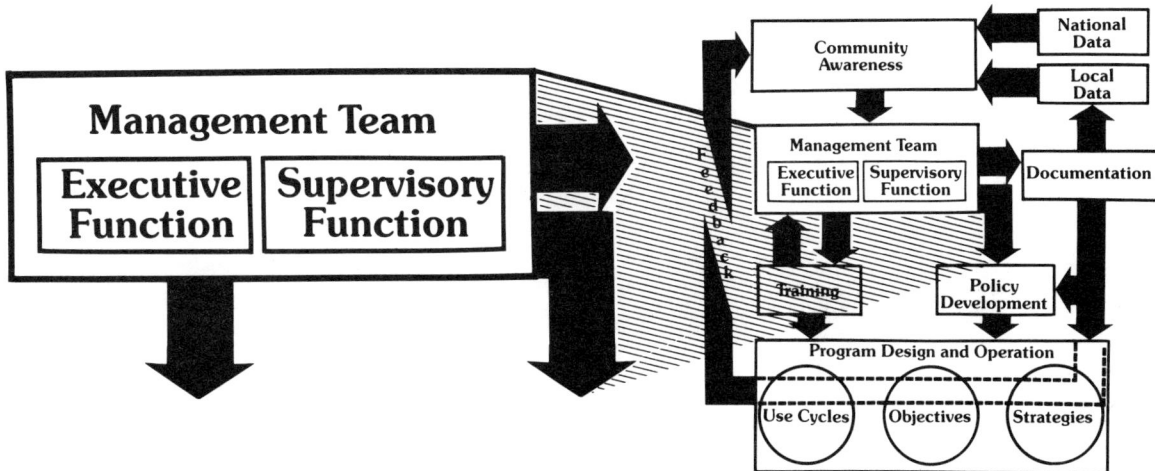

Management Team

Executive Function | **Supervisory Function**

Community Awareness

National Data

Local Data

Management Team

Executive Function | Supervisory Function

Documentation

Feedback

Training

Policy Development

Program Design and Operation

Use Cycles | Objectives | Strategies

Chapter 4

THE SYSTEM MODEL
Beginning a Program

In Chapter 1 you were introduced to a model of the problem-specific management system. This chapter described the components of that system, their functions, and their interrelationships.

Figure 4–1 illustrates the way the model works. Notice that the system begins and ends with "community awareness." An alcohol program should be operated by and for members of the community, for it derives its strength from the application of their collective energies to the solution of aggregate problems. A community will allow itself to be organized to solve problems only if its citizens are convinced that problems actually exist. Therefore the first step in the model requires raising community awareness by publicizing local and national data about alcohol problems.

The impetus for an alcohol program can come from a number of sources, and

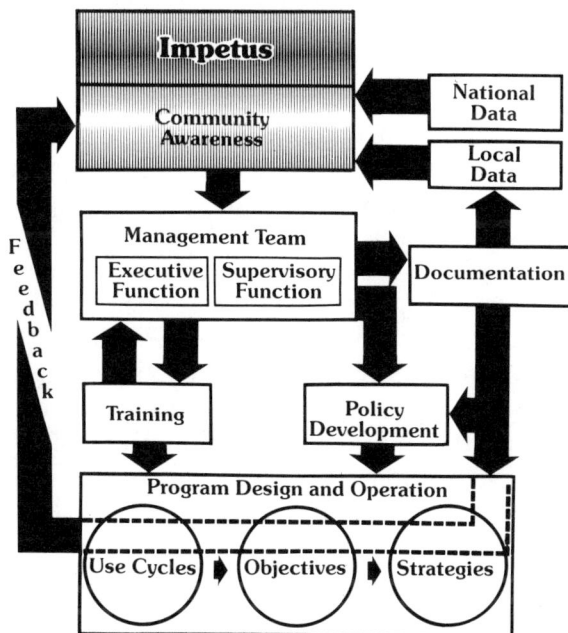

Figure 4–1. The problem-specific system: impetus.

41

these will be covered later in this chapter, but the model assumes the existence of a few individuals with sufficient problem awareness and motivation to launch the project. Typically, these people become part of the management team, serving either on the planning committee, the working committee, or both.

Every program needs direction, and in this model it is supplied by the two committees on the management team. The *planning committee,* composed primarily of community leaders, performs the "executive function"—guidance, support, and coordination of program activities. The "supervisory function" is performed by the *working committee,* which is responsible for the day-to-day operation of the program. In very small communities, membership on these committees may be almost identical, but on a college campus (even a small one) this situation rarely occurs, for reasons that will become obvious.

The working committee is also in charge of designing and implementing the documentation plan for the program. "Documentation" includes identification of alcohol-related problems (local data sources), specification of solutions (policy, program design), and measurement of the program's impact on those problems (feedback). The importance of documentation cannot be overemphasized, for it insures that program activities will be focused on specific problems of community concern and provides a mechanism for informing the community about program progress. It is one of the ways the program opens channels of two-way communication with the community.

One of the products of this dialogue with community members is a *policy statement,* which is essentially a blueprint of the program and a description of the community drinking environment. This document must be developed through a consensual, participatory process, otherwise the program will not reflect the community's collective intentions. Obviously, local conditions may alter over time, and the program may therefore change, so a policy statement cannot afford to be a static document; it must be a *working paper,* subject to modification and updating as the need arises.

Training is the formal process by which members of the community are taught skills in program management and operation. Management training must be initiated soon after the organization of the management team; operations training should take place only after the program has begun to take its final shape.

The operational phase of the program is a product of all the previous steps discussed above, and it is in this stage that the strength of the system becomes apparent. Program activities are carefully targeted at specific problems; they are tailor-made for local conditions and carried out by members of the community. If some strategies are unsuccessful, the system is sufficiently flexible to rebound with more effective ones. The overall documentation plan provides for the measurement of the impact of these strategies and for reporting this information to the community, thereby creating a closed loop that recycles itself as long as necessary to reduce the targeted problems.

To summarize, the key steps in program development are:

1. Organization of a management team that will support, guide, coordinate, and supervise the program.
2. Devising a documentation plan to assess the level and extent of community alcohol problems and whether program activities affected these problems.

3. Developing a consensual policy statement to formalize the program's existence.
4. Training the management team and peer educators to manage and operate the program.
5. Designing and implementing strategies to reduce documented alcohol problems.

Of course, programs do not start all by themselves; they are usually initiated by a few highly motivated individuals concerned about the human and financial costs of alcohol problems. A single, dedicated individual from the faculty, administration, staff, or student body can provide the push to start a program. This individual is often a college mental health counselor or a health educator, since people in these positions are usually the most aware of the extent of campus alcohol problems. The impetus frequently comes from the student affairs office or from a student-run organization (such as a fraternity, sorority, or student union). A faculty member involved in alcohol studies can initiate a program by offering a course in alcohol education. Since alcohol research is conducted in departments of psychology, sociology, anthropology, and public health, the opportunities for such courses on a given campus are more numerous than one might expect.

The Planning Committee

An alcohol program will never get off the ground if it does not have the support and approval of the college authorities, and it will not run efficiently if important segments of the college community are not represented on the management team. The function of the planning committee is to provide guidance, support, and coordination for the program—it is a kind of executive body. It should therefore have a representative from the chief executive's office (president, chancellor, or whatever title is used) to show that the program has won official sanction from the highest authority. This task is not as easy as it may appear, however. By lending official approval to the program college administrators are admitting that alcohol problems do exist on their campus, and they know that parents and alumni can react adversely to that admission. Nevertheless, if it can be demonstrated that ignoring alcohol problems will cost more in the long run than trying to manage them directly, most administrators would agree to lend their support to an alcohol education program.

It is equally important to have student representatives on the planning committee, since they are the only people who can provide the student viewpoint about alcohol use, alcohol policy, and alcohol problems. They can help keep the program grounded in reality.

Other members of the committee should represent important aspects of campus life to help coordinate the program's activities with other college functions. For example, if one of the program's goals is reduction of the number of social events devoted exclusively to drinking, representatives of the residence hall association and the interfraternity council can help coordinate program strategies with their respective organizations. Similarly, representatives from the housing office, residence hall advisers staff, student union, health service, counseling center, student affairs office, and mental health clinic could all serve useful coordinating functions on the planning

---

Table 4–1. Planning Committee

Representatives from:	Could provide:
Student body	Student support, guidance
Chancellor's office	Official sanction, moral and financial support
Student affairs (Dean of men) (Dean of women)	Official sanction, moral and financial support
Campus security office	Coordination with security function
Student union	Coordination with entertainment function, provide meeting space, staff help, and equipment
Housing office (R.A. staff)	Coordination with living activities, training opportunities
Residence hall association	Coordination with social events
Chaplain's office	Support, source of volunteers
Student health service (nurse, doctor, health educator)	Expertise, personnel
Mental health center (psychologist, social worker)	Expertise
Faculty	Personnel, authority within the college structure

---

committee. In addition, they could also provide meeting space, training opportunities, personnel, and possibly financial support. Table 4–1 is a list of typical committee members and their probable contributions.

Obviously the planning committee is rather large and ungainly, but since it is concerned with coordination and support, not operation of the program, it can afford to be larger and more loosely organized than the working committee. It also does not need to meet as frequently as the working committee.

The Working Committee

Committees have a poor reputation for getting things accomplished, but a small, carefully chosen committee can be more effective and efficient in performing some tasks than other types of organizations (corporate hierarchy, military chain of command, etc.). The task of the working committee is to design and supervise the operation of the alcohol education program, consequently it must be smaller and more task-oriented than the planning committee. Generally, it is wise to restrict the membership to no more than seven people—a small number reduces scheduling problems; an uneven number prevents deadlocks in case of disagreements. The various skills and abilities needed on the working committee are described below, but remember that one person may be able to serve in several roles.

The program director is a member of the working committee (and usually serves on the planning committee as well). The director should be a full-time professional employee of the college, and typically someone from the student health service or student affairs office fills this position. However, at least one very successful program was directed by an enthusiastic graduate student (paid by the university). The three most important qualifications the director must have are: 1) knowledge of health education processes; 2) organizational ability; and 3) strong interpersonal skills. Organizational and interpersonal talents are probably as important as knowledge of the field, because the director must convince people to participate in alcohol education projects, persuade college administrators to provide financial backing, coordinate diverse projects, and direct the day-to-day operation of the program. Someone skilled in the "art and science of volunteerism" is needed for this job.

Since the working committee must design and conduct the documentation phase of the program, it should include an individual with evaluation skills. A faculty member would be a natural choice, but a student with experience in surveys and social measurement techniques could also serve in this capacity. The evaluator is responsible for coordinating the problem identification survey and for the development of ways to measure program impact.

The training function is also the duty of this committee, so the membership should include several trainers—people skilled in group process and organizational development. Once again, they need not (and probably should not) be faculty members, since they will be training student volunteers. Indeed, there is some evidence that people learn better from their peers because of role identity.

Most program strategies involve public communications, therefore a media consultant would be a valuable member of the working committee. People with experience in graphic design, layout, broadcasting, and other media-related activities are good candidates for this position.

Student volunteers with unspecified skills are also important members of the working committee, particularly if they are chosen for their energy, enthusiasm, and creativity. They frequently generate the most original ideas for alcohol projects and activities and also serve as a sounding board for project proposals from other committee members.

Finally, it is profitable to have representatives of the student groups that have been targeted for attention in the program. For example, if one of the goals of the program is to reduce problems associated with residence hall parties, a member of the residence hall association on the committee could make the task much easier. Similarly, if fraternity groups are targeted, representatives of the fraternities should serve on the committee.

This chapter has attempted to explain how the system model works and how to start an alcohol education program. The chapters that follow will explore the components of the model in much greater detail.

Thought Questions

1. Can you identify the people on your campus who should serve on a program planning committee?

2. How would you go about convincing college authorities to lend their support to an alcohol education program?

3. Is there an individual on your campus who would make an ideal program director?

4. Among your friends and associates, can you identify those with the talents and skills needed to implement an alcohol program?

References

Dennison, D., and T. Prevet, 1980. "Improving Alcohol-Related Disruptive Behaviors through Health Instruction." *The Journal of School Health:* 206–208.

Gonzalez, G.M. 1978. "What Do You Mean—Prevention?" *Journal of Alcohol and Drug Education* 23: 14–23.

Kristein, M. 1977. "Economic Issues in Prevention." *Preventive Medicine* 6: 252–264.

Rozelle, G. and G. Gonzalez, 1979. "A Peer-Facilitated Course on Alcohol Abuse: An Innovative Approach to Prevention on the College Campus." *Journal of Alcohol and Drug Education* 25: 20–30.

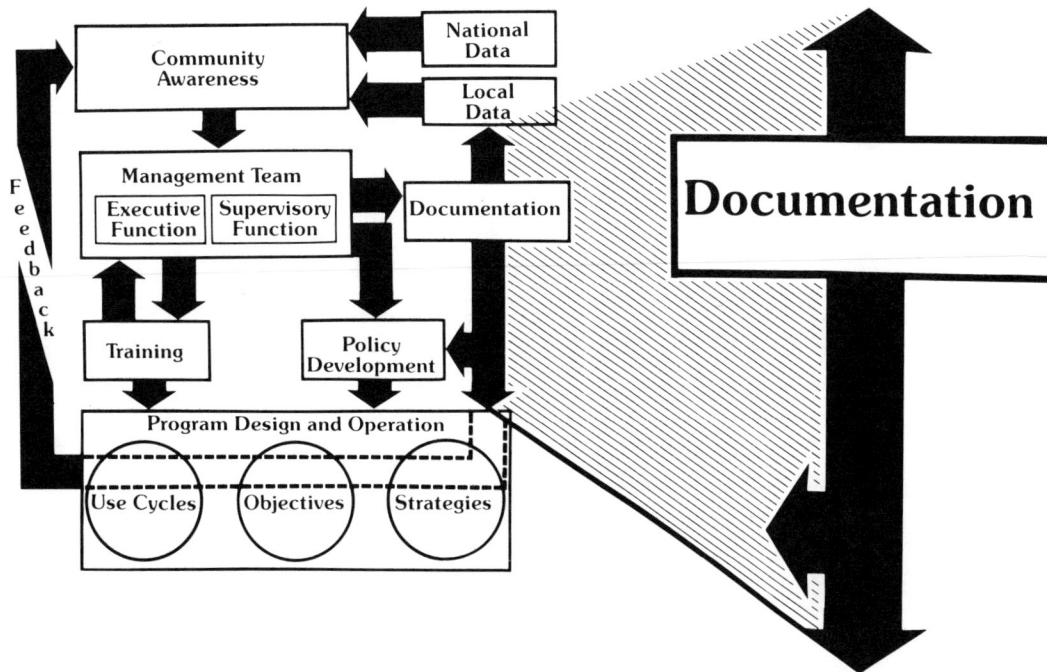

Chapter 5

DOCUMENTATION

In a problem-specific alcohol program, documentation consists of gathering information about drinkers and their habits, problems they experience (or cause), potential solutions to these problems, and the impact of the program on problem levels. Documentation makes it possible for program planners to set realistic goals, select appropriate strategies to reach these goals, and, most importantly, to measure whether the program accomplished its goals.

There are three types of information that programs need in order to operate and each type is relevant to an aspect of program function. The types of information are:

1. Information about alcohol-related problems: the nature of the problems, groups likely to experience problems, and the circumstances surrounding problem occurrence.
2. Information about solutions to alcohol-related problems: characteristics of the solutions, target groups, and expected outcomes.
3. Information about the effectiveness of the program in reducing problem levels.

Although collecting, organizing, and reporting information about the community and its drinking patterns could become an expensive proposition, a considerable amount of descriptive evidence can be gathered economically if you follow five basic principles.

Principle 1. Documentation is not an end in itself. An alcohol education program is not organized primarily to do social research, so program planners should determine the utility of the information they seek before they set out to collect it. Can the data be used to inform the community, clarify a problem, point to a solution, or identify a risk group? If not, it does not need to be collected.

Principle 2. There is no ideal documentation strategy—institutions and planning requirements differ too widely. Each documentation strategy must be tailor-made for the individual program and locale.

Principle 3. Documentation is not a one-time enterprise, but an ongoing, systematic method for monitoring community trends. It is an integral part of an institutional program. A typical program might include a yearly survey of drinking among incoming students, examination of monthly admissions to the student health service for new alcohol problems, and a semiannual review of damage reports from residence halls. A well-conceived program will respond to changes in the community, and a dynamic information-gathering strategy enables a program to adjust to those changes.

Principle 4. Documentation is not exhaustive scientific research or formal evaluation. Formal research has extremely rigid methodological requirements, and usually involves before-and-after measurements, isolation of control groups, random sampling, complicated statistical analyses, and other attributes of scientific investigation.

By contrast, program documentation simply accumulates information about the community. It does not have to employ high technology to explore the local drinking environment. A community alcohol program needs current, useful information about drinking and its associated problems. Documenting the number of local drinking-driving arrests each holiday season by examining monthly arrest records at the police station reveals more about community problems than an extensive statistical analysis of the reasons students give for drinking. A program can exist and produce services without a formal evaluation, but it cannot accomplish its goals without an adequate assessment of the community.

Principle 5. A documentation plan should also include some provision for assessing the results of particular activities and strategies while they are in progress or before they are applied campus-wide. The assessment should be designed for a quick analysis to allow midstream changes in program activities.

Part of the documentation process is called "needs assessment." A need is a problem in search of a solution, but every need is conditional upon something: the need for food is conditional upon the desire to stay alive (hunger strikers have no "need" for food). The need for an alcohol program is conditional upon the desire to reduce problems associated with alcohol use. Some needs depend upon social values, and these values are often idiosyncratic. In the last decade, for example, we have witnessed changes in our national values about the quality of the environment. The values of our culture toward clean air, clean water, and freedom from exposure to hazardous waste have changed drastically with our new awareness of pollution levels and our awareness of the limited capacity of the earth to store our garbage. William Rorabaugh, in his book *The Alcoholic Republic, an American Tradition*, argues that the right to drink (and the right to get drunk) in the United States is tightly interwoven with Americans' basic perceptions of the values of freedom and liberty.

> I believe that the stress of change was felt most keenly by the rising generation, that is, by those Americans born during or just after the Revolution, who came of age about 1800. Nowhere was that stress greater than on the nation's college campuses. College students, an admittedly elite minority, had to face crises that were both institutional and intellectual. Although colleges continued to emphasize curriculums designed to train youths to be ministers, students found that religious retrenchment meant that their degrees no longer entitled them to positions in the ministry. The proportion of graduates entering the ministry declined from one-third in the half century before 1770 to one-sixth in the decade after 1800. This decline in positions for graduates was accompanied by a growing belief that the college's traditional

role, that of educating an elite class, was in conflict with the Revolutionary concept of equality. Students steeped in ideals of liberty and equality had contempt for institutions whose outmoded curriculums, old-fashioned teachers, and predilection for training clergymen were survivals from colonial times.

This post-Revolutionary generation of students indulged in unprecedented lusty drinking. One spirits-loving collegian informed the president of Dartmouth "that the least quantity he could put up with...was from two to three pints daily." Worse than the amount of imbibing was the atmosphere that surrounded it, for students mixed their daily bouts of intoxication with swearing, gaming, licentiousness, and rioting. Consequently, college officials strengthened rules against the consumption of alcohol. Whereas the College of William and Mary in 1752 had warned students to drink hard liquor with moderation, after 1800 most colleges banned spirits altogether. At Union College, for example, the fine for bringing spirits onto campus was set at $1 in 1802, raised to $3 in 1815, and altered to a fine or suspension in 1821. Such regulations proved ineffective because students resisted the authority of college officers whom they no longer respected. A series of disturbances at the University of Virginia led one irate gentleman of the Old Dominion to suggest that "the place ought speedily to be burnt down as a horrible nuisance." Perhaps this Virginian got the idea from Princeton, where the students were suspected of setting fire to the main college hall. In any event, drunkenness and rioting had become ways for students to show contempt for institutions that failed to provide them with a useful, up-to-date, republican education (Rorabaugh 1979: 138–140).

Some experts suggest that any attempt to modify our values about drinking may uncover values that should not be tampered with. It is not unusual for alcohol advertisements in college newspapers to emphasize nonacademic values. The ads suggest that the values related to college education are secondary to the values associated with having a good time. These ads also link drinking values to the high levels of alienation and stress imposed by the institution and society at large. The comradarie achieved through social drinking can relieve anomie and stress. (see DeFoe and Breed, 1979).

Needs are also conditional upon cultural standards. The Environmental Protection Agency spends most of its research dollar on establishing standards for clean air and clean water. What standards could be used for alcohol consumption or for acceptable problem levels? Chronic alcoholism has always been the standard of unacceptability, but modern research has revealed disturbing information about young adult drinking and its associated problems, and the new data require a revision of the old standards. There is, however, no standard upon which every institution, group, or program can agree.

The administrative bureaucracy in most institutions of high learning is like a hibernating grizzly bear—it will not move until it has to, or is forced to. The definition of a problem depends upon the perception of a discrepancy between some ideal state and the actual state of affairs. If current drinking levels are accepted as normal and permissible, there is no discrepancy. There is no problem and no need. There will be no alcohol program.

Officialdom will begin to act when they perceive the discrepancy between the *image* of collegiate life and the *actuality* (based on drinking values). When those discrepancies lead to disruption of the college's mission, the sleeping bear may become restless. How do we wake it?

First, problem levels must be documented and made public. The public's awareness of acute problem levels is the first leverage point for awakening those in high places. If a well-designed (and therefore credible) documentation shows that problem levels exist and are connected to current drinking practices and traditions, it has begun to establish the need for a program. Next, reasonably priced, small-scale program activities are carried out and reported upon (in some published format). This step certifies progress toward problem reduction, and thereby sets the stage for more ambitious projects. All these activities are directed toward trying to persuade the institution, the community, and its members to adopt a new set of values. In order to accomplish the task, the new values must be seen as both beneficial and necessary to the survival of the community. They, too, are conditional. All of the documentation methods in this chapter involve direct contact with members of the community who drink or who deal with alcohol-related problems. Relevant data from the documentation enables program planners to talk intelligently about alcohol use and alcohol problems to community groups during different stages of the project, and to promote alcohol education as a means for developing communitywide solutions to problems. Documentation is therefore an advocacy tool because it can be used to raise community consciousness. It is also a planning tool and an indispensable first step in the interactive process of setting project goals.

To illustrate these functions, it is useful to look at an example from environmental science. A stream biologist and a crew are hired by members of a town council because they have received complaints that the drinking water is polluted. Citizens complain that the water tastes acidic and looks cloudy. Local fishermen have noticed dead fish in the river. The paper mill thirty-four miles upstream is the only suspected source of pollution, but it has been in operation for eight years without any previous episodes of pollution.

The stream biologist and the crew must first perform a *quality assessment* of the water and attempt to pinpoint the source of the problem. They would probably investigate factors such as the degree of water cloudiness, the number of suspended particles, the amount of dissolved oxygen, and the number of dead fish in the river.

The team would examine the water before it reached the paper mill and after it passed the site. They must establish a link, if any exists, between the activities of the factory and the nature of the damage to the community's water supply. Often paper mills use corrosive salts in their manufacturing process. These salts consume oxygen in the water needed to support wildlife, and can also cause cloudiness. If the team finds that the amount of dissolved oxygen decreases after the river passes the plant they would have reason to suppose that the paper mill was at fault. They could prepare an action proposal for the town council.

The information from documentation would be an *advocacy tool* for the town council. They could approach the factory management with this data and negotiate a solution to the problem. Perhaps the factory would change its processing methods. The factory management might suggest ways to increase the oxygen content of the water. An alternative water supply for the community could also emerge from these negotiations.

Like the stream biologists, an alcohol education team attempts to measure the problems associated with drinking. Often community members become concerned about alcohol-related problems because of complaints from others in the community.

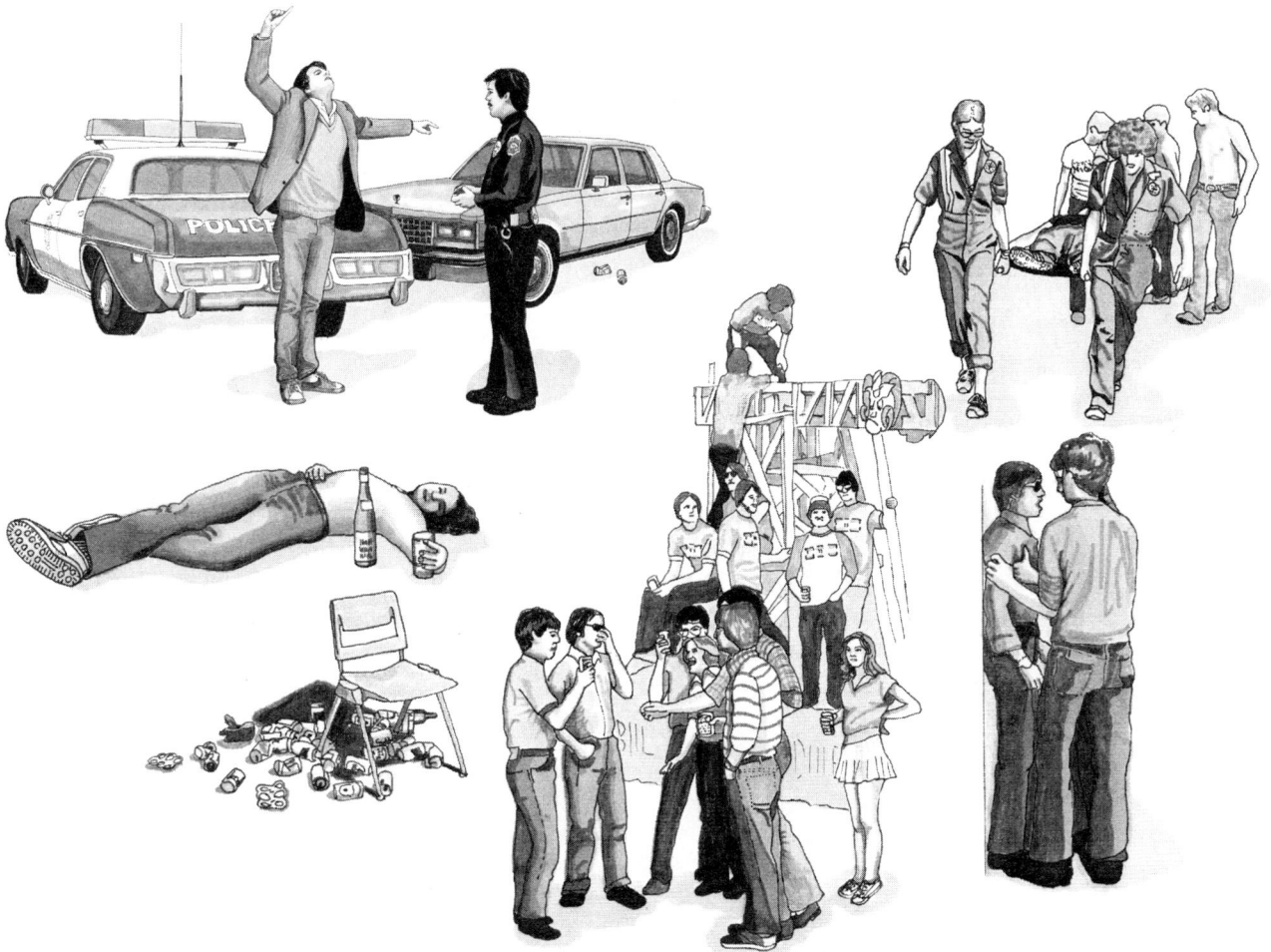

Figure 5–1. Some problems associated with drinking.

Town residents might complain about the noise from fraternity drinking parties. A teachers' group might be concerned with the amount of litter around a high school gym after Friday night dances. A college residence adviser may have to account for damage to the residence hall that occurs over weekends. Documentation helps establish the link between drinking and community problems and provides a focus for programs designed to solve those problems.

In summary, a documentation will help you to:

- Raise awareness in the community about the extent and nature of alcohol-related problems;
- Design an up-to-date program that is relevant to the current drinking patterns and alcohol-related problems in your community;
- Plan how to distribute program resources most effectively to minimize these problems; and
- Clearly specify the type of information that the program is supposed to deliver to the community.

In addition to the functions listed above, documentation will help you to avoid the two most common obstacles to program success: organizational barriers and planning barriers. *Organizational barriers* occur when the program does not have official support or sanction from community leaders. Often these leaders are simply uninformed about the structure and goals of the program. They usually assume that all alcohol education programs involve the identification and treatment of people who have serious drinking problems. Documentation will provide information that can be used to inform them about the program's purpose and thereby establish a sanctioned program base. Later activities will elicit participation by community members, but before they can be asked to get involved you must be able to describe the nature of the problem they are supposed to solve.

Planning barriers are the most common obstacles encountered and are the most likely to hinder program growth in its early stages. Planning barriers occur when program goals are not written out and made public. Specific goals are needed in order to choose appropriate program strategies, but more importantly, clear goals enable one to assign responsibilities, organize group activities, and select target audiences. Clear goals will therefore help you decide a variety of questions: Should peer educators be used to conduct media campaigns on alcohol-related injuries? Should they try to promote a change in the beer sales laws? Should they begin alcohol education classes in the junior high school? Should they try to establish a transportation service for drinkers at isolated parties? All of these program decisions require specific objectives before any action can (or should) be taken.

Figure 5–2. Methods for documenting alcohol problems.

Documenting Problems

There are five basic methods for documenting alcohol problem levels:

1. Reviewing published sources.
2. Analyzing institutional records and documents.
3. Surveying students about alcohol use, alcohol-related problems, and beliefs and attitudes about drinking.
4. Surveying "key informants" in the university system.
5. Informally interviewing concerned community groups.

PUBLISHED SOURCES

A review of published sources should begin with a library search of published articles on alcohol use and student drinking. Several journals regularly print articles that are relevant to alcohol education, for example:

The Journal of Studies on Alcohol
The Journal of Alcohol and Drug Education
The Journal of the American College Health Association
The Journal of Higher Education
American Journal of Public Health.

These articles can provide ideas for program activities, and because they present the results of special alcohol studies, they are a source of detailed information about individual attitude and behavior patterns related to alcohol and drug use. The articles may discuss newly discovered normative influences on drinking, such as changes in advertising legislation or modifications of drinking laws. Many articles offer information about sociocultural factors that can be instrumental in changing attitudes toward drinking.

National and local statistics about the production, sale, and distribution of alcohol beverages are also important data sources. The local economic impact of the alcohol beverage industry is often directly related to local levels of consumption. Attempts to reduce problem levels through alcohol programs may meet with resistance from groups who derive their income from alcohol sales. For example, college towns usually have a disproportionate number of bars and taverns and heavy keg sales, so alcohol retailers tend to be a powerful influence in the community. College newspapers derive some of their revenues from beer advertising. Major breweries' advertising budgets directly allocated to college campaigns annually exceed four hundred million dollars (Impact, 1981). Recently, one college town received national notoriety when it was revealed that distributors delivered 27,000 cases of beer there each week (the student population is only 20,000).

Reports of alcohol-related incidents frequently appear in local newspapers. While these events have timely interest, they are generally not useful as documentation sources. Occasionally, however, local reports can turn up a new and reliable data source that program planners had overlooked.

A visit to city hall can yield data on the total population of the community and the ratio of students to residents. City records also contain the number of licensed liquor outlets, the number of bars and taverns, and often the number of businesses that cater specifically to student needs. A call to the police station, or better yet a visit to the police public information officer, can result in information about the most frequent points of friction between police and students. The public information officer can identify "hot" spots in the community where party noise is a problem, areas where arrests for disorderly conduct are most frequent, and perhaps a list of the roads and highways where students are most likely to be arrested for drinking and driving offenses. Sometimes a public information officer will be willing to attend a meeting of the planning committee and offer suggestions about solutions. Police departments in college towns are becoming increasingly aware that alcohol-related problems occupy a large amount of their time and effort.

INSTITUTIONAL RECORDS AND DOCUMENTS

Records are particularly useful in documenting problem levels, and documents such as grant applications, evaluation reports, informal surveys, and health reports can be rich sources of information. These items are readily available to program planners, but it requires some imagination to use them effectively.

Dr. Jack McKillip, who structured the evaluation of the Southern Illinois Alcohol Education Program (McKillip 1980a and 1980b), reports that college administrators were impressed with some very simple but elegant data at the start of their program. The evaluation team made phone calls to city clerks around the state of Illinois to find out the number of licensed liquor outlets per 1,000 residents in nine target cities and in Carbondale, the home of the university. Carbondale had the highest density of alcohol vendors in the state: 4.9 liquor licenses per 1,000 adults, compared with the next highest community with 3.5.

University records are also good sources of information. Many schools keep monthly damage reports for each residence hall, and some record the number of alcohol-related incidents reported to campus police. Student affairs offices frequently have records on the number of student disciplinary cases that involve alcohol.

Descriptive information must often be acquired from multiple sources. Admissions statements from the student health service, the mental health service, the counseling service, and the student legal service often ask whether or not the visit is related to alcohol use, and therefore is part of their statistical record. If these services do not include such information, they can frequently be persuaded to add it.

Working with the admissions office, program planners can also get information on the following characteristics of the student body: distribution by class standing; distribution of females and males; places of residence; and membership in fraternities, sororities, and similar social organizations. Local studies on campuses have found that alcohol consumption and alcohol problems vary as a function of each of these characteristics.

STUDENT SURVEYS

One of the most common methods for gathering data is the student survey. The Student Alcohol Survey included in this chapter (Appendix 5–A was developed by Dr. Dennis McCarty at the University of North Carolina at Chapel Hill. It has been used in a variety of programs sponsored by the National Institute on Alcohol Abuse and Alcoholism, and shows consistent results when given year to year.

The Student Alcohol Survey was designed to count the incidence of problems and identify their antecedents. It includes items to measure the quantity and frequency of alcohol use, the occurrence of alcohol-related problems, and the attitudinal antecedents of alcohol use.

An alcohol survey usually takes the form of a written set of questions to which randomly selected members of the community respond. An alcohol use survey gathers information about:

- How much and how often students drink;
- The maximum amount that is consumed at any one time;
- The type of beverages consumed;
- The positive and negative consequencs that result from drinking;
- The most important reasons given for drinking;
- The outside influences that affect drinking behavior;
- The drinker's beliefs and attitudes toward drinking and its consequences; and
- The characteristics of the drinker in terms of age, sex, race, religion, economic status, grade point average, beverage preference, type of drinking environment preferred, and so on.

In short, a survey provides organized information about alcohol use within a given population. It can also be a vehicle for passing information to the respondents. For example, a survey conducted at freshman orientation could measure prevailing attitudes about alcohol in the incoming class, but it might also ask if they are aware of the campus alcohol education program and describe what they might expect from participation.

Remember that a student survey is only one source of information about drinking; it is not the only source for reliable data. A survey is often simply one step in the process of organizing observations of drinking and its consequences, and it may be preceded by other information-gathering techniques: observations, interviews, examination of existing records, or any of the other methods covered in this chapter. A survey is primarily a research tool that allows the investigator to examine systematic relationships between specific items, or variables, on the survey. For example, a survey can provide information about the relationship between the amount of alcohol consumed and the extent of alcohol problems. An investigator could explore the relationship between religious affiliation and positive and negative attitudes toward intoxication.

The most important information that a survey can provide that other methods may not yield is an estimate of the quantity of alcohol consumed. However, researchers have discovered that survey estimates of alcohol consumption levels do not always correspond with data from other sources. Students who conduct direct observations of drinking at parties will often remark that more alcohol seems to be consumed than is reported. Self-reports of alcohol consumption on national surveys also seem to account for only 40 to 60 percent of the amount of alcohol sold through retail outlets. Older, more experienced drinkers may report lower levels of consumption than their actual level, especially if the survey is distributed by their employer! On the other hand, young drinkers may overestimate the extent of their drinking because it is seen as an indication of "adult status."

The drinking of any beverage that contains ethyl alcohol can be measured along at least two dimensions: quantity (how much?) and, frequency (how often?). One drink is approximately one-half to three-quarters of an ounce of *ethanol* (pure, or absolute, alcohol). Because 100 percent ethanol is so strong it can severly burn the throat and tongue, it is diluted for consumption. The dilute forms are sold as beer, wine, fortified wine, brandies and liqueurs, and distilled spirits ("hard liquor"). Table 5–1 is taken from the Rand Corporation study of drinking in the Air Force, and gives an excellent summary of how to estimate the average amount of alcohol in beer, wine, and liquor. The table shows that a single drink contains approximately half an ounce of pure alcohol, regardless of the type of beverage consumed.

Once the amount of alcohol that an individual consumes at one time is determined, an estimate of the total volume of alcohol consumed per day, or per week or month can also be calculated. For example, if an individual drinks three twelve-ounce beers at a sitting, an average of one and one half times per week, the average ethanol consumption is .309 ounces per day. If two mixed drinks are usually consumed at one sitting, twice a month, it results in an average of .057 ounces of ethanol per day. Adding the two averages yields .366 ounces per day.

The Rand Air Force data indicted that 73 percent of their respondents drank less than one ounce of absolute alcohol per day (Polich and Orvis 1979). However, 3.6 percent of the sample drank more than five ounces per day, and they were the high risk group.

Whatever survey a program uses, estimates of *per capita alcohol consumption* should be gathered. If at all possible, consumption should be examined for trends across beverage type and age, and the information converted into an index of the absolute amount of alcohol consumed per person per month. To permit analysis by population groupings, the survey should include information on cetain important characteristics of the respondent, such as age, sex, race, class standing, fraternity or sorority membership, and living area. These data will be used to identify target groups

Table 5–1. Ethanol Content of Typical Drinks			
Item	*Beer*	*Wine*	*Liquor*
Size of typical drink (fluid ounces)	12.0	4.0	1.0
Ethanol content per ounce	.04	.12[a]	.43
Ethanol content of 1 drink (fluid ounces)	.48	.48	.43

[a]Where fortified wine (sherry, port, etc.) was the person's usual wine, the content was assumed to be .18 rather than .12.

Source: M.J. Polich and B.R. Orvis, *Alcohol Problems: Patterns and Prevalence in the U.S. Air Force,* R-2308-AF. Santa Monica, CA: RAND Corporation, 1979.

for program activities. The survey should also incorporate questions about willingness to participate in alcohol education activities and the types of program activities students prefer. In future surveys respondents could be asked about the program activities that they have participated in over the past school year.

A student alcohol survey is extremely useful for documenting drinking and problem levels. However, as a standardized instrument it may not be sensitive to local conditions. Information grounded in the realities of the community situation may not be as extensive as that provided by a survey, but it is probably more crucial to the planning process. This kind of information can often be gathered from key informants.

KEY INFORMANT SURVEY

A survey of key informants is similar to a student survey, but is much more economical and provides results more quickly. Key informants are members of university officialdom—campus security, staff, student health physicians, housing officers, or fraternity advisers—who deal closely with students, especially students with problems. Since the key informant group is smaller than the student body, it is easier to survey, but it can give a representative picture of alcohol use on campus and also provide some ideas for solutions. Dr. Jack McKillip, who refined this method, suggests that the key informant technique can be supplemented by structured telephone interviews of students, if necessary (McKillip 1980a).

The first area of inquiry covered by a key informant survey involves the significance of alcohol use on campus and includes questions about the following areas:

1. How important is alcohol use on campus?
2. How would you characterize drinking-related problems on campus?
3. What are the most persistent, damaging, and potentially harmful alcohol problems in the university community?
4. How well developed are current campus resources for reducing problem levels?
5. Where do you turn for help when you observe problems? Where do you refer students with serious drinking problems?
6. What do you think are the most pressing needs for inservice training?
7. What are appropriate goals for an alcohol education program?
8. How long have you been with the university? How much direct contact do you have with students?
9. How would you evaluate the university's current methods for dealing with alcohol-related problems? Are you a part of this process? Would you be willing to participate in the future?

To guide responses in the first area of inquiry, Dr. McKillip recommends using the ranking sheet shown in Table 5–2, which places alcohol problems in the context of other kinds of student problems. The ranking sheet can also be used to pinpoint trouble areas on campus. If residence advisers (RAs) in a residence hall give alcohol problems a significantly higher frequency rating than RAs in other halls, their dorm could become a target site for an alcohol project.

**Table 5–2. Questions Concerning Student Alcohol Abuse,
Key Informants Survey**

Based on your experience in working with students, rank the following problems according to their frequency of occurrence among students (1 = most frequent, 12 = least frequent):

_____ health related/medical

_____ emotional

_____ family/marriage

_____ sexual

_____ legal

_____ academic

_____ career

_____ alcohol

_____ interpersonal

_____ financial

_____ drugs (other than alcohol)

_____ other (please specify):_____

Source: J. McKillip, "Assessing the Need for Alcohol Education Programming on the College Campus." (Paper presented at the Southern Illinois University, Conference on Program besigns for the Prevention of Alcohol Problems on Campus, Carbondale, Illinois, August 5–7, 1980). Table 2, p. 8.

In order to get an overview of the existing referral network on campus, and to estimate potential demand on alcohol program resources, key informants can be given the checklist shown in Table 5–3. Their opinions about program direction and resource development are also useful for program planning. They could be asked open-ended questions about their own interests (and level of commitment) to alcohol program efforts. Using the questionnaire in Table 5–4 they can provide valuable information about appropriate goals for an alcohol education program. Data from this instrument are also useful for alerting university administrators to the fact that the program's focus is likely to be different from that which they expected. Their reactions will reflect their perceptions about program needs (values).

Finally, a key informant survey should gather information about the respondents:

Table 5–3. Questions Concerning Referrals of Students with Alcohol-Related Problems, Key Informants Survey

Check the following agencies you have contacted for information about alcohol use and abuse by students. To which agencies have you referred an individual with an alcohol problem? (Check all that apply.)

	Sought Information	*Referred Student*
A. Alcohol education project	_____	_____
B. Counseling center	_____	_____
C. Clinical center	_____	_____
D. Student health service	_____	_____
E. County community mental health center alcohol program	_____	_____
Other: (please specify)	_____	_____
_____		
_____		

Source: J. McKillip, "Assessing the Need for Alcohol Education Programming on the College Campus (Paper presented at the Southern Illinois University, Conference on Program Designs for the Prevention of Alcohol Problems on Campus, Carbondale, Illinois, August 5–7, 1980). Table 4, p. 11.

the amount of interaction that they have with students, the length of time they have been in their current positions, and the number of students they deal with personally each month. This section of the key informant survey can identify potential members of the management team.

At Southern Illinois University (SIU), key informants were asked to indicate the percentage of time they spent with students who had a problem with alcohol and the percentage of the students they see professionally who have alcohol problems.

Overall, 80 percent of the key informants labeled the problem of alcohol use among students as "serious." About 5 percent of their professional time was spent with students having problems with alcohol. They estimated that at least one in six students compound their personal problems by alcohol use. Residence advisers are closer to students on a daily basis than any other professional, and the RAs at SIU reported spending a great deal more time with students with alcohol problems than did others on campus.

GROUP INTERVIEWS

The group interview is a rapid and low cost method for identifying the more immediate problems associated with drinking. The interview is usually conducted by one or two students (peers) in a group of not more than twenty participants. The participants could be a college class or a group of people meeting to seek solutions to common problems (e.g., excessive noise and litter from dorm parties).

Interviewers can ask rather direct questions about the extent of alcohol use, but

Table 5–4. Questions Concerning Appropriate Goals for Campus Alcohol Programming, Key Informants Survey

Below is a list of goals with which the alcohol education project could be concerned. Please indicate how much you feel each goal should be emphasized in designing the alcohol education project:

		No Emphasis	Some Emphasis	Major Emphasis
A.	To teach the total effect of alcohol on the human system.	(1)	(2)	(3)
B.	To teach objective facts about alcohol.	(1)	(2)	(3)
C.	To help people see that drinking involves consequences.	(1)	(2)	(3)
D.	To develop a sense of pride in having a strong body and a wholesome mental attitude.	(1)	(2)	(3)
E.	To provide scientific information about how alcohol affects the body.	(1)	(2)	(3)
F.	To present abstinence as an attainable goal.	(1)	(2)	(3)
G.	To stop all forms of excessive drinking.	(1)	(2)	(3)
H.	To develop an attitude of respect for the rights of those who have opinions different from one's own concerning alcohol.	(1)	(2)	(3)
I.	To know why and where to seek competent aid on alcohol-related problems.	(1)	(2)	(3)
J.	To interest people in seeking satisfaction from life by meeting life's problems effectively.	(1)	(2)	(3)
K.	To teach people that alcohol is harmful at all times for everyone.	(1)	(2)	(3)
L.	To provide objective information about current problems of alcohol use (and abstinence) in modern American society.	(1)	(2)	(3)
M.	To help people gain better understanding of how drinking patterns and the occurrence of alcohol problems vary in different segments of American culture.	(1)	(2)	(3)
N.	To help develop realistic attitudes about drinking without much concern for the laws about drinking age.	(1)	(2)	(3)
O.	To teach the nonproblem users of alcohol as well as the problem ones.	(1)	(2)	(3)
P.	To teach people about responsible use of alcohol and not just about abuse.	(1)	(2)	(3)

Source: J. McKillip, "Assessing the Need for Alcohol Education Programming on the College Campus," (Paper presented at the Southern Illinois University, Conference on Program Designs for the Prevention of Alcohol Problems on Campus, Carbondale, Illinois, August 5–7, 1980). Table 5, p. 12.

typically begin by asking about the nature of the group and some of the problems commonly encountered. The tone should be friendly and helpful, and the interviewers should attempt to elicit lists of specific incidents and problems that have occurred recently.

The interview is usually conducted by two peer educators. One facilitates questions and responses and the other records the information from the group on a blackboard or notepad. Interestingly, groups that receive written summaries of the interview are more likely to participate in subsequent program planning sessions and alcohol education activities. A suggested group interview format and example are included in Appendix 5–B.

Documenting Solutions

The first step in documenting solutions is the compilation of lists of existing and potential resources and services available to the program. Program planners can develop a resource directory of agencies and individuals who provide alcohol-related services to the university community. For each of these agencies and individuals, the directory should include information on professional orientation, services provided, capacity to serve students, fee structure (if any), and the characteristics of the students who are currently being served. This catalog is critical for identifying possible areas of coordination and cooperation between the alcohol program and existing community services. By the same token, it identifies interest groups who may feel that the program is a threat to their existence.

A statement of program goals outlines the project's intent and direction, and includes specific behavioral objectives for the participants as well as broadly stated philosophical goals. It may also cover the program's assmptions and historical background.

The description of target groups would include characteristics such as age, class standing, sex, and place of residence. A review of the services provided embraces the substance of the program (for example, media campaigns, policy sketches, training sessions, and any other projects carried out under the auspices of the program). Materials and facilities can be characterized by location and relative access by students. There is no need for a lengthy description of the physical facilities unless the physical setting is crucial to the project (as in the case of a nonalcoholic tavern in the student union).

The program personnel are perhaps the most important element in a service program. A review of the personnel should include an analysis of the level of expertise and training necessary to accomplish program tasks. An outline of the relationship of the alcohol program to other programs in the university emphasizes the role of the program within the institutional structure. A prevention program may have innovative components that complement the content of other programs. For example, peer lectures about the problems encountered by the expectant mother who drinks may be unique to the college, but nonetheless relevant to a great number of married students.

Part of the documentation of solutions is a detailed description of the alcohol education program—a candid, month-by-month narrative of what the program did, and its apparent effects and outcomes. A journal of the project can be viewed as another tedious piece of paperwork, but it need not be. The information required to document a program can be gathered quite simply if it is organized before the project gets underway.

The types of information required to describe a program are fairly simple:

1. Program goals and objectives;
2. Target groups for services;
3. Services provided (the substance of the program);
4. Materials and facilities used in service delivery;
5. Personnel;
6. Relationship of the program to other programs in the community;
7. Special constraints on the program;
8. Costs of the program; and
9. An estimate of the program's success at problem reduction.

An alcohol program's training project on handling drunk students may parallel inservice staff training that has been an established part of the student affairs training schedule. A prevention program may supplement other programs by guiding students who have minor problems toward relevant advice in an area of their concern; job counseling, time management, or sexual counseling. A program's ability to coordinate services with other agencies is perhaps its most intangible and most important quality, and therefore the most important fact to document adequately.

Program descriptions should also cover constraints and obstacles that projects must overcome to survive. A project to reduce drinking problems in fraternities will have difficulty gaining acceptance by the target group. At a college steeped in a sports tradition, a project to reduce drinking at weekend football games will need to overcome enormous resistance. A program based on commuter campus must find methods to communicate with students who usually do not remain on campus after classes. All the techniques the program develops to overcome these obstacles must be recorded.

The costs of a program should be a matter of public record. An estimate of program "penetrability" can be obtained by dividing the number of students contacted by the number of dollars used to develop and deliver a service. The cost of a poster campaign, when compared to the number of students exposed to its specific message, can be surprisingly small. The cost of a workshop (including training, promotion, materials, and time) in relation to the number of students affected can be very expensive.

Finally, a program description should contain an estimate of its impact on targeted problems. However, this element of the description leads into a much deeper discussion, which is more appropriate to the next section of this chapter, Program Evaluation.

Program Evaluation

Critics of prevention programs claim that preventive services are unlikely to yield results. Outcomes are delayed, program services yield nothing tangible, and the connection between an investment and problem reduction is difficult to demonstrate. The only way to answer the skeptics is by thorough program evaluation. Evaluation, in

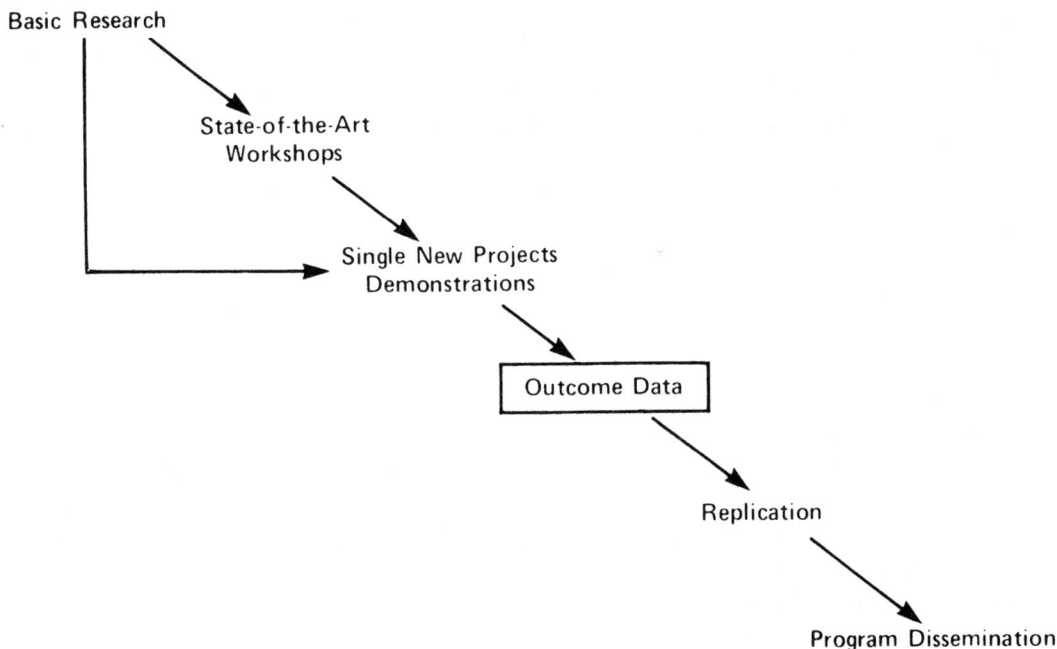

Figure 5–3. Continuum for prevention program development and evaluation. (Source: U.S. Department of Health and Human Services 1981.)

the most rigorous terms, connects particular service strategies to the reduction of specific problems. The U.S. Government's Alcohol Drug Abuse and Mental Health Administration's (ADAMHA's) prevention program guidelines for 1979 to 1982 attempt to organize the complicated evaluation process. The guidelines emphasize that it is not necessary for an original program idea to pass through all of the phases shown in Figure 5–3, but most ideas should be tested with outcome data from field tests before further distribution. The ADAMHA guidelines state:

> Basic prevention research attempts to document the existence of relationships between particular conditions and events (e.g., marital disruption, alcoholic parents, death in the family, or laws and regulations) and dysfunctional behaviors (e.g., poor school performance, vandalism, or alcohol- or drug-related problems). Basic research can also document behavior change. Does promoting more positive health-related behaviors result in more functional, healthy behavior and less dysfunctional behavior (e.g., improving feedback mechanisms which assist the person in determining whether he or she is becoming intoxicated and result in more accurate decisions about ability to drive)? Such research does not represent full-scale intervention but helps document the existence of relationships which would support the funding of intervention projects in an area. Basic prevention research can also include proposals for interventions which are breaking new ground and for which the intervention strategy has not been sufficiently developed to accomodate the more rigorous evaluation designs required for demonstration (U.S. Department of Health and Human Services 1981: 28).

Scientific evaluation of alcohol education programs is expensive. Typically, control and service target groups are identified, and the target group is then subjected to the activity that is designed to reduce a specific problem. The control group receives, ideally, equivalent exposure to a service, but not one aimed directly at the problem in question. The program evaluators must ensure that the control group and the target group are equivalent in numerous ways. Before and after measures are taken in both control and service groups. Evaluators may measure changes in knowledge and attitudes through surveys, or they may arrange complex behavioral observations of drinking at parties. They may try to gather "naturalistic data" on problem levels or drinking patterns by monitoring party expenditures for alcohol or counting the number of liquor bottles in trash cans each weekend.

To complicate matters further, evaluation of a prevention program differs from the evaluation of a treatment program. This is important because many evaluation techniques have been developed in treatment programs. Treatment activities are directed at a specific target group and the behavioral outcomes can easily be listed: abstinence from alcohol, improved job status, greater social contacts, and so forth. The evaluator of a prevention program must gather information on some general effect in the population at large or specific information on a general section of the population. In both cases, the quality of sampling procedures will dictate the quality of the evaluation results. In neither instance can those under test be easily identified. Specifying all of the methods that can be used to evaluate a program is beyond the scope of this text, but recent texts on program evaluation are readily available. (For example, see Weiss 1972 and Guba and Lincoln 1981.) Even without the necessity for a formal scientific evaluation of the program, a qualified evaluator should be a working member of the team. A professional evaluator can develop methods and strategies appropriate for the locale and program.

The evaluator must be involved in the planning process and therefore cannot be an outside consultant. An evaluator can conduct formal interview studies before and after a program, and carry out observations at private parties or scheduled drinking situations. Often the evaluator will use *unobtrusive measures* (observations made without the knowledge of the participants). A survey of drinking habits interrupts the life of the participant, but observations of the amount and type of beverages consumed at parties do not (see Guba and Lincoln 1981).

The process of observing, recording, and analyzing human behavior without the knowledge of those who are observed is particularly useful for alcohol studies. When drinkers are aware of being observed, they often modify their consumption according to the perceived expectations of the observer. Generally, older drinkers consume less and younger drinkers consume more, but the influence of the observer is not very predictable. Unobtrusive measures can be contrived for a wide range of situations. For example, students can observe the physical traces of a party by surveying the amount of litter, the number of liquor bottles, or the extent of damage to windows and doors at the party site. Joy Moser, in a treatise on the prevention of alcohol-related problems on an international level, suggests that counting cars in a tavern parking lot may indicate the incidence of drinking and driving (Moser 1981). She further suggests that the vigilance of local police in monitoring drunk driving can be inferred from the distribution of blood alcohol levels at arrest. If most blood alcohol levels are high (greater than .15 percent) it implies that only grossly intoxicated drivers are detained.

Public records can also be used to estimate the impact of a program. Statistics on drunk driving arrests are not very responsive to program effects (because the numbers are small), but records of disciplinary actions, dismissals, suspensions, or grade changes in a particular group on campus may be a good measure of program impact. Private records of student organizations, such as the cost of alcohol purchases compared with alternative beverage purchases, can indicate the influence of party planning workshops.

In order to conduct formal evaluation studies, Southern Illinois University targeted alcohol education programs at specific residence halls. The evaluation methods were, technically speaking, quasi-experimental nonequivalent control group designs.

At SIU, four residence halls were selected from a group of nine for study. Each hall had 110 undergraduate males. Two halls were designated as experimental halls and two as control halls. Extensive activities were conducted in the experimental halls during the last half of a semester. The control halls did not receive any direct services, but their residents could participate in projects and activities available on other parts of the campus.

The evaluators first compared the damage to residence halls before and after program activities. They also conducted before and after surveys of student drinking, including measurement of the amount and type of beverages consumed, knowledge about program activities, and alcohol-related behaviors. Behavioral observers recorded the extent of alcohol consumption for one hour on Thursday and Friday evenings once a month for four months. Observations during the first two months were designated as pretests and observations during the last two months were designated as post-tests. The observers recorded two measures: (1) the number of students entering the residence hall carrying alcohol; and (2) the proportion of people drinking in each residence hall.

Between the pre- and post-tests the experimental dorms were exposed to four major projects from the alcohol education peer group on campus. They received special invitations to attend a three-hour alcohol film festival in the student center. There were also two one-hour educational sessions conducted in each of the two residence halls. At the same time, each person in the experimental group received a packet of printed information about alcohol.

The evaluation indicated that damage to the two experimental halls was an average of $447.00 less than in the other seven halls in the complex. On the average, 13.5 percent of the people entering each of the residence halls during the pre-test observational hours carried alcohol. The proportion was statistically higher on Friday than on Thursday night, and higher between 8 and 10 PM than between 6 and 8 PM. Figures for the experimental and control halls did not differ before the intervention, but they did afterward. Only 8.7 percent of those observed entering the experimental halls carried alcoholic beverages, but 18.4 percent of the controls did carry them. In addition, the proportion of those observed drinking declined significantly after the interventions in the experimental halls. The observations of drinking in the control halls showed no change.

Measures of consumption, measures of purchase, and measures of damage can all be used to reflect program impact without the knowledge of those being observed. In the SIU study evaluators examined student willingness to advise strangers (over the telephone) whether to drive while intoxicated and to assist them in seeking alternative transportation. In this substudy, no differences were measured between the experimental and control groups, but this outcome was expected because no program components were aimed directly at the drinking driver.

Sometimes simple observations of the number of people at a party, the number of open containers at a football game, or the number of injuries following a rock concert can be used as indicators of program effects. A creative evaluator can also record the emergence of new behaviors introduced by alcohol project activities: the number of alternative beverages offered at a party; the number of parties with creative, nonalcoholic themes; the number of guests who are willing to remain sober so that they can drive; and even the number of people who are willing to take the keys from a drunk who is about to drive.

Evaluation is necessary in order to develop systematic methods to solve problems, and to insure that programs, in general, improve their effectiveness. But evaluation is not a prerequisite for beginning a local program. A small program that is just starting out would waste its limited resources attempting to set up a formal evaluation while failing to meet the need for training and other activities. Even the simplest program can impress observers and win broader support through careful documentation and planning. A formal evaluation can eventually follow a well-organized beginning.

Thought Questions

1. For problem documentation, can you name ten "key informants" in your own college?

2. What institutional records and documents would be useful for documenting problems?

3. Can you list several agencies (or individuals) who provide alcohol-related services at your college?

4. Do you know anyone on the faculty (or in graduate school) who could provide professional evaluation advice?

5. Can you think of any "unobtrusive measures" you could employ in documentation on your own campus?

References

Campbell, D.T., and J.C. Stanley. 1966. *Experimental and Quasi-Experimental Designs for Research.* Chicago: Rand McNally College Publishing Co.

Cooper, A.M., and M.B. Sobell. 1979. "Does Alcohol Education Prevent Alcohol Problems?: Need for Evaluation." *Journal of Alcohol and Drug Education.* 25: 54–63.

DeFoe, J., and W. Breed. 1978. "The Problem of Alcohol Advertisements in College Newspapers." *Journal of the American College Health Association.* 27: 195–199.

Guba, E.G., and Y.S. Lincoln. 1981. *Effective Evaluation.* San Francisco: Jossey-Bass Publishers.

Green, L.W. 1977. "Evaluation and Measurement: Some Dilemmas for Health Education." *American Journal of Public Health.* 67: 155–161.

Impact: Marketing, Financial, and Economic News and Research for the Wine and Spirits Executive. December 1981.

McCarthy, D. 1978. *The Student Alcohol Survey: User's Manual.* San Francisco: URSA Associates.

McCarty, D.; M. Poore; K. Mills; and S. Morrison. In press. "Direct Mail Techniques and the Prevention of Alcohol Abuse among College Students." *Journal of Studies on Alcohol.*

McKillip, J. 1980. "Assessing the Need for Alcohol Education Programming on the College Campus." Paper presented at Southern Illinois University Conference on Program Designs for the Prevention of Alcohol Problems on Campus, Carbondale, Il, August 5–7.

McKillip, J. 1980b. *Evaluation Report for SIUC Alcohol Education Project 1978–1980.* Report submitted to Illinois Department of Mental Health and Developmental Disabilities, Division of Alcoholism.

Moser, J. 1981. *Prevention of Alcohol-Related Problems: An International Review of Preventive Measures, Policies and Programs.* Toronto, Canada: The Alcoholism and Drug Addiction Research Foundation.

Polich, M.J., and B.R. Orvis. 1979. *Alcohol Problems: Patterns and Prevalence in the U.S. Air Force.* R-2308-AF, Santa Monica, CA: RAND Corporation.

Rorabaugh, W.J. 1979. *The Alcoholic Republic, an American Tradition.* New York: Oxford University Press.

U.S. Department of Health and Human Services, 1981. *ADAMHA Prevention Policy and Programs 1979–1982.* DHHS publication No. (ADM) 81–1038. Rockville, MD.

Weiss, C.H. 1972. *Evaluation Research-Methods for Assessing Program Effectiveness.* Englewood Cliffs, NJ: Prentice-Hall.

Appendix 5–A

The Student Alcohol Survey

INTRODUCTION

This survey requests information on six areas; 1) your awareness of alcohol education; 2) your drinking habits and experiences; 3) your opinions about alcohol; 4) your beliefs and information about alcohol; 5) the drinking habits of friends; and 6) demographic information. The items in this survey have been prepared so that they can be answered easily. For most items, circle the number that corresponds to your response. Make your answers as clear as possible. Sample items illustrate how questions should be answered.

A. Sale of alcohol to individuals less than 21 should be permitted.

Strongly Moderately Slightly Neither Slightly Moderately Strongly
Disagree 1 2 3 4 5 6 7 Agree

If you strongly favor the sale of alcohol to those less than 21, you should circle "7" to indicate strong agreement with the statement.

Disagree 1 2 3 4 5 6 (7) Agree

Conversely, if you saw good points and bad points but felt the bad points were a little more important, you might disagree slightly. Indicate your feelings of slight disagreement by circling "3".

Disagree 1 2 (3) 4 5 6 7 Agree

Other response scales are similar, but may use different end points. For example:

B. In my opinion, drinking is...(Circle one answer for each pair of adjectives.)

Very Moderately Slightly Neither Slightly Moderately Very

Bad 1 2 3 (4) 5 6 7 Good
Unpleasant 1 2 3 4 5 (6) 7 Pleasant
Harmful 1 2 (3) 4 5 6 7 Beneficial

With items like this, it is important to respond to each pair of adjectives. Thus as the example illustrates, you would rate drinking on all three scales— "bad–good," "unpleasant–pleasant," "harmful–beneficial." To make the rating circle the number that best represents your response.

The Campus Alcohol Education Service has conducted workshops in residence halls, fraternities and sororities. In addition, to promote responsible drinking, the Service has distributed posters and book marks, advertised in the newspaper and produced public service messages on radio. The questions in this section ask about your experience with and evaluation of these services and materials. Indicate your response to each question by circling the appropriate number.

1. Before you received this survey, did you know about the Campus Alcohol Education Service (CAES)?

No 1
Yes 2   01

2. Have you attended any of the alcohol education workshops sponsored by CAES?

No 1
Yes, most recently last spring 2
Yes, most recently this fall 3   02

3. "When you say beer ...," a description of the Campus Alcohol Education Service (CAES) printed on heavy yellow paper has been distributed on campus and with orientation materials. Have you read this brochure and, if so, was it informative?

No, I have not read "When you say beer ..." 1
Yes, I read the brochure; it was *not informative* 2
Yes, I read the brochure; it was *informative* 3   03

70

4. A second CAES pamphlet, "Dealing With a Drunk Person" provides advice on how to help very intoxicated individuals. Have you read this pamphlet and, if so, was it informative?

No, I have not read "Dealing With a Drunk Person" . 1
Yes, I read the pamphlet; it was *not informative* 2
Yes, I read the pamphlet; it was *informative* 3   04

5. In cooperation with the *Daily Tar Heel*, CAES is sponsoring public service advertisements that provide information about alcohol. Have you read these ads and, if so, were they informative?

a) Advertisement titled—"Which Will Sober You?" A comparison of the effectiveness of coffee, cold showers, and time on sobering up.

No, I have not read "Which Will Sober You?" 1
Yes, I read the ad; it was *not informative* 2
Yes, I read the ad; it was *informative* 3   05

b) Advertisement titled—"The Socializers." Recipes for mixed drinks with half the usual alcohol.

No, I have not read "The Socializers" 1
Yes, I read the ad; it was *not informative* 2
Yes, I read the ad; it was *informative* 3   06

c) Advertisement titled—"What's the Difference?" A description of the quantity of alcohol in one beer and one mixed drink.

No, I have not read "What's the Difference?" 1
Yes, I have read the ad; it was *not informative* 2
Yes, I read the ad; it was *informative* 3   07

6. This fall CAES, in cooperation with Chapel Hill radio station WCHL, has produced public service radio announcements. Football and basketball players give a short message about alcohol and responsible drinking. Have you heard these announcements on WCHL and, if so, did you like them?

No, I have not heard the announcements 1
Yes, I have heard the announcements;
I did not like them 2   08

Yes, I have heard the announcements;
I liked them 3

7. How likely are you to enroll in a course on alcohol?

Very Moderately Slightly Neither Slightly Moderately Very
Unlikely 1 2 3 4 5 6 7 Likely   09

8. How likely are you to attend a CAES workshop held in your residence hall or at a convenient location on/off campus?

Unlikely 1 2 3 4 5 6 7 Likely   10

Drinking

The next set of questions is concerned with your drinking habits and experiences. Even if you do not drink, it is important to answer these questions. Circle the appropriate number to indicate your response.

Beer

9. Beer glasses and pitchers vary in size. When responding to these items try to estimate quantities in terms of 12 oz. bottles or cans of beer.

a) During the *last 4 weeks*, on how many days did you drink beer?

beer frequency: 0 1 2 3 4 5 6 7 8 9

never — one day — two days — three days — 1 day/wk — 2 days/wk — 3 days/wk — 4 days/wk — 5 days/wk — 6-7 days/wk   11

b) What was the *greatest* number of beers you drank on one day during the *last 4 weeks*?

12 oz. beers
greatest #: 0 1 2 3 4 5 6 7 8 9+

zero — a six pack — nine or more   12

71

c) On how many days in the last last 4 weeks did you drink the number of beers indicated in question 9b?

frequency; greatest #: 0 1 2 3 4 5 6 7 8 9
(never, one day, two days, three days, 1 day/wk, 2 days/wk, 3 days/wk, 4 days/wk, 5 days/wk, 6-7 days/wk)

13

d) During the last 4 weeks, how many bottles, cans or glasses of beer did you usually drink on the days that you drank beer?

12 oz. beers, usual #: 0 1 2 3 4 5 6 7 8 9+
(zero, a six pack, nine or more)

14

Wine

10. Wine glasses vary in size. We assume that the average wine glass holds 4 oz. and a bottle of wine contains 6 glasses.

a) During the last 4 weeks, on how many days did you drink wine?

wine, frequency: 0 1 2 3 4 5 6 7 8 9
(never, one day, two days, three days, 1 day/wk, 2 days/wk, 3 days/wk, 4 days/wk, 5 days/wk, 6-7 days/wk)

15

b) What was the greatest number of glasses of wine that you drank on one day during the last 4 weeks?

4 oz. glasses of wine, greatest #: 0 1 2 3 4 5 6 7 8 9+
(zero, a fifth)

16

c) On how many days in the last 4 weeks did you drink the number of glasses of wine in question 10b?

frequency, greatest #: 0 1 2 3 4 5 6 7 8 9
(never, one day, two days, three days, 1 day/wk, 2 days/wk, 3 days/wk, 4 days/wk, 5 days/wk, 6-7 days/wk)

17

d) During the last 4 weeks, how many glasses of wine did you usually drink on days that you drank wine?

4 oz. glasses of wine
usual #: 0 1 2 3 4 5 6 7 8 9+
(zero, a fifth)

18

Liquor

11. Most mixed drinks contain 1.5 oz. of liquor (bourbon, gin, rum, scotch, vodka, etc.). Thus, there are about 5 drinks in a half-pint and 10 in a pint.

a) During the last 4 weeks, on how many days did you drink liquor?

liquor, frequency: 0 1 2 3 4 5 6 7 8 9
(never, one day, two days, three days, 1 day/wk, 2 days/wk, 3 days/wk, 4 days/wk, 5 days/wk, 6-7 days/wk)

19

b) What was the greatest number of drinks that you drank on one day during the last 4 weeks?

1.5 oz. of liquor
greatest #: 0 1 2 3 4 5 6 7 8 9+
(zero, a half-pint)

20

13. The next items examine the good and bad things that sometimes happen during or after drinking alcohol. Circle the best response.

How many times during the last month have you:

Scale: none (0), once (1), twice (2), 3 times (3), 4–5 (1/wk) (4), 6–10 (2/wk) (5), 11–14 (3/wk) (6), 15–22 (4–5/wk) (7), 23+ (6–7/wk) (8)

	none	once	twice	3 times	4–5 (1/wk)	6–10 (2/wk)	11–14 (3/wk)	15–22 (4–5/wk)	23+ (6–7/wk)	
a) enjoyed drinking with friends?	0	1	2	3	4	5	6	7	8	34
b) had a hangover?	0	1	2	3	4	5	6	7	8	
c) performed poorly on a test or important project?	0	1	2	3	4	5	6	7	8	
d) tried to stop someone from drinking too much?	0	1	2	3	4	5	6	7	8	
e) had a minor injury while drinking? (e.g., cut, sprain, or burn)	0	1	2	3	4	5	6	7	8	38
f) been to "keg parties"?	0	1	2	3	4	5	6	7	8	
g) been in trouble with the police or residence hall authorities because of your drinking?	0	1	2	3	4	5	6	7	8	
h) been very drunk?	0	1	2	3	4	5	6	7	8	41

How many times during the last month have you:

	none	once	twice	3 times	4–5 (1/wk)	6–10 (2/wk)	11–14 (3/wk)	15–22 (4–5/wk)	23+ (6–7/wk)	
i) damaged property while drinking?	0	1	2	3	4	5	6	7	8	42
j) sipped alcoholic drinks to slow the effect of alcohol?	0	1	2	3	4	5	6	7	8	
k) pulled a false fire alarm while drinking?	0	1	2	3	4	5	6	7	8	

c) On how many days in the *last 4 weeks* did you drink the number of drinks indicated in question 11b?

frequency, greatest #: never (0), one day (1), two days (2), three days (3), 1 day/wk (4), 2 days/wk (5), 3 days/wk (6), 4 days/wk (7), 5 days/wk (8), 6–7 days/wk (9)

0 1 2 3 4 5 6 7 8 9   21

d) During the *last 4 weeks*, how many drinks did you *usually* drink on days when you drank liquor?

1.5 oz. of liquor   a half-pint

usual #: zero (0) ... 0 1 2 3 4 5 6 7 8 9+   22

12. During the last year, how frequently did you drink...

Scale: never (0), less than 1/mo (1), 1/mo (2), 2–3 days/mo (3), 1–2 days/wk (4), 3–5 days/wk (5), 6–7 days/wk (6)

	never	less than 1/mo	1/mo	2–3 days/mo	1–2 days/wk	3–5 days/wk	6–7 days/wk	
a) in a bar in town?	0	1	2	3	4	5	6	23
b) at a campus party?	0	1	2	3	4	5	6	
c) at sporting events?	0	1	2	3	4	5	6	
d) while riding in a car?	0	1	2	3	4	5	6	
e) with meals?	0	1	2	3	4	5	6	27
f) alone?	0	1	2	3	4	5	6	28
g) at a residence hall party?	0	1	2	3	4	5	6	
h) in a restaurant?	0	1	2	3	4	5	6	
i) at a fraternity party?	0	1	2	3	4	5	6	31
j) at your parents' home?	0	1	2	3	4	5	6	
k) in your place of residence?	0	1	2	3	4	5	6	33

Scale for items l–bb:

	none	once	twice	3 times	4–5 (1/wk)	6–10 (2/wk)	11–14 (3/wk)	15–22 (4–5/wk)	23+ (6–7/wk)	
l) tried to stop someone who drank too much from driving?	0	1	2	3	4	5	6	7	8	
m) gotten into an argument while drinking?	0	1	2	3	4	5	6	7	8	46
n) gotten into a physical fight while drinking?	0	1	2	3	4	5	6	7	8	
o) stopped drinking in order to sober up before going home?	0	1	2	3	4	5	6	7	8	
p) vomited from drinking?	0	1	2	3	4	5	6	7	8	
q) driven a car after having several drinks?	0	1	2	3	4	5	6	7	8	50
r) eaten food while drinking to slow the effects of alcohol?	0	1	2	3	4	5	6	7	8	
s) missed a class because of a hangover?	0	1	2	3	4	5	6	7	8	
t) passed out from drinking too much?	0	1	2	3	4	5	6	7	8	
u) had a nonalcoholic drink instead of an alcoholic drink?	0	1	2	3	4	5	6	7	8	54
v) drank more than you meant to?	0	1	2	3	4	5	6	7	8	55
w) been criticized by a friend, a date or your spouse because of your drinking?	0	1	2	3	4	5	6	7	8	56
x) gone to parties where only alcohol was served?	0	1	2	3	4	5	6	7	8	
y) thought you might have a problem with your drinking?	0	1	2	3	4	5	6	7	8	58
z) let a friend drive or help you home because you were not sober?	0	1	2	3	4	5	6	7	8	
aa) not remembered what happened while you were drinking?	0	1	2	3	4	5	6	7	8	
bb) had your sexual performance negatively affected because of your drinking?	0	1	2	3	4	5	6	7	8	61

14. A party giver may serve alcohol in a variety of ways and guests may drink in different ways. Consider each of the following items and indicate how likely or unlikely you are to act in that manner. Circle the number corresponding to your answer. These items can apply to those those who drink and those who do not.

As a *host* how likely are you to:

a) have activities other than drinking alcohol as the primary focus of parties you host?

Very Unlikely 1 Moderately 2 Slightly 3 Neither 4 Slightly 5 Moderately 6 Very 7 Likely   62

b) provide food if alcohol is served at your party?

Unlikely 1 2 3 4 5 6 7 Likely   63

c) have nonalcoholic drinks available at your party?

Unlikely 1 2 3 4 5 6 7 Likely   64

d) offer a nonalcoholic drink to someone who has had too much to drink?

Unlikely 1 2 3 4 5 6 7 Likely   65

74

e) provide transportation or overnight accommodations for those unable to drive safely after drinking?

Very Moderately Slightly Neither Slightly Moderately Very
Unlikely 1 2 3 4 5 6 7 Likely   66

As a *guest* how likely are you to:

Strongly Moderately Slightly Neither Slightly Moderately Strongly

f) decide before you go to a party how many drinks you will have?   Unlikely 1 2 3 4 5 6 7 Likely   67

g) drink to feel comfortable meeting and talking with other guests?   Unlikely 1 2 3 4 5 6 7 Likely   68

h) eat while drinking to slow the effects of alcohol?   Unlikely 1 2 3 4 5 6 7 Likely   69

i) drink nonalcoholic drinks at a party?   Unlikely 1 2 3 4 5 6 7 Likely   70

j) let a friend drive you home if you are not sober?   Unlikely 1 2 3 4 5 6 7 Likely   71

                    blank   72
                    2301   73–76
                                77–80

_____

END CARD

_____

Opinions

The opinions and feelings you have about alcohol, alcoholism, and drinking are also of interest to us. The next items provide information on those issues.

15. Indicate the extent to which you agree or disagree with each of the items. There is no correct or incorrect response. Your feelings will provide the best answer. If you really are not sure, you may use the midpoint of the scale for your response.

Strongly Moderately Slightly Neither Slightly Moderately Strongly

a) People should be permitted to drink as much as they want   Disagree 1 2 3 4 5 6 7 Agree   01

b) I could have an alcohol problem if I continue my current level of drinking   Disagree 1 2 3 4 5 6 7 Agree   02

c) The campus setting at this university encourages drinking.   Disagree 1 2 3 4 5 6 7 Agree   03

d) Most of my friends drink at least once a week.   Disagree 1 2 3 4 5 6 7 Agree   04

e) There is strong pressure to drink socially on this campus.   Disagree 1 2 3 4 5 6 7 Agree   05

16. In my opinion, my drinking only one or two alcoholic drinks (beer, wine, or liquor) at a party where most others are drinking is...(Respond to each pair of adjectives.)

Very Moderately Slightly Neither Slightly Moderately Very

a) Bad   1 2 3 4 5 6 7 Good   06
b) Unpleasant 1 2 3 4 5 6 7 Pleasant   07
c) Harmful   1 2 3 4 5 6 7 Beneficial 08

17. In my opinion, my drinking soft drinks (and only soft drinks) at a party where most others are drinking is... (Respond to each pair of adjectives.)

a) Bad   1 2 3 4 5 6 7 Good   09
b) Unpleasant 1 2 3 4 5 6 7 Pleasant   10
c) Harmful   1 2 3 4 5 6 7 Beneficial 11

18. In my opinion, my drinking 6 or more drinks (beer, wine, or liquor) at a party where most others are drinking is... (Respond to each pair of adjectives.)

a) Bad   1 2 3 4 5 6 7 Good   12
b) Unpleasant 1 2 3 4 5 6 7 Pleasant   13
c) Harmful   1 2 3 4 5 6 7 Beneficial 14

19. In your opinion, are the next statements likely or unlikely to be true at a party where most people are drinking? In the items below, "alcoholic drinks" refer to beer, wine or liquor.

a) I feel that most people who are important to me prefer that I have no more than one or two alcoholic drinks.   Unlikely 1 2 3 4 5 6 7 Likely   15

Very Moderately Slightly Neither Slightly Moderately Very

b) I feel that most other students at this university prefer that I have no more than one or two alcoholic drinks.   Unlikely 1 2 3 4 5 6 7 Likely   16

c) I feel that my friends at the party would disapprove if I had 6 or more alcoholic drinks.   Unlikely 1 2 3 4 5 6 7 Likely   17

20. Do you, your parents, and your close friends drink? Circle the one response for each person that best describes their drinking.

Don't know/N.A. Non-drinker Drinks infrequently Light drinker Moderate drinker Heavy drinker Problem drinker

a) Father   1 2 3 4 5 6 7   18
b) Mother   1 2 3 4 5 6 7   19
c) Closest friend 1 2 3 4 5 6 7   20
d) Me   1 2 3 4 5 6 7   21

Beliefs

This set of items examines what you know and think about alcoholic beverages.

21. Alcohol is:

a stimulant 1
a depressant 2
both a stimulant and a depressant 3
don't know 4

22

22. Drinking milk before drinking an alcoholic beverage will:

have no effect on the absorption of alcohol 1
speed up the absorption of alcohol 2
slow the absorption of alcohol 3
don't know 4

23

23. The alcohol in one drink is usually metabolized (destroyed by the body) in:

a half hour or less 1   24
about one hour 2
about two hours 3
don't know 4

24. A 4 oz. glass of wine contains approximately the same amount of alcohol as:

one-half a beer (6 oz.) 1   25
one beer (12 oz.) 2
two beers (24 oz.) 3
don't know 4

blank   27

25. To sober up more quickly, you can:

drink coffee 1   26
take a cold shower 2
do nothing but wait 3
don't know 4

26. In your opinion, are the feelings and events listed likely or unlikely to occur at a party where most people are drinking and you have six or more drinks (a six pack of beer, a bottle of wine, or a half-pint of liquor)? If you do not drink, would these happen if you were to drink that much?

After drinking six or more drinks, I would. . . .

	Very Unlikely	Moderately	Slightly	Neither	Slightly	Moderately	Very Likely	
a) feel part of the group	Unlikely 1	2	3	4	5	6	7 Likely	28
b) remain in control of the situation	Unlikely 1	2	3	4	5	6	7 Likely	29
c) have a good time	Unlikely 1	2	3	4	5	6	7 Likely	30
d) injure myself	Unlikely 1	2	3	4	5	6	7 Likely	31
e) be asked to drink more	Unlikely 1	2	3	4	5	6	7 Likely	32
f) forget worries or problems	Unlikely 1	2	3	4	5	6	7 Likely	33
g) feel good	Unlikely 1	2	3	4	5	6	7 Likely	34
h) be drunk	Unlikely 1	2	3	4	5	6	7 Likely	35
i) act foolishly	Unlikely 1	2	3	4	5	6	7 Likely	36

	Very Bad	Moderately	Slightly	Neither	Slightly	Moderately	Very Good	
j) In my opinion, feeling part of the group is	Bad 1	2	3	4	5	6	7 Good	37
k) In my opinion, remaining in control of the situation is	Bad 1	2	3	4	5	6	7 Good	38
l) In my opinion, having a good time at a party is	Bad 1	2	3	4	5	6	7 Good	39
m) In my opinion, injuring myself at a party is	Bad 1	2	3	4	5	6	7 Good	40
n) In my opinion, being asked to drink more at a party is	Bad 1	2	3	4	5	6	7 Good	41
o) In my opinion, forgetting worries or problems at a party is	Bad 1	2	3	4	5	6	7 Good	42
p) In my opinion, feeling good at a party is	Bad 1	2	3	4	5	6	7 Good	43
q) In my opinion, being drunk at a party is	Bad 1	2	3	4	5	6	7 Good	44
r) In my opinion, acting foolishly at a party is	Bad 1	2	3	4	5	6	7 Good	45

77

Biographical Information

The last section of the survey requests information on personal history items, such as sex, race, and place of residence. Each item has been related to differences in drinking habits and opinions. The information is necessary so that these influences can be controlled when the answers from all respondents are examined.

For each item, circle the number which indicates the best response for you.

27. What is your sex?

Female 1   *46*
Male 2

28. What was your age on your last birth-day? (fill in blank) _____   *47–48*

29. How do you describe yourself? (Circle the best response.)   *49*
American Indian or Alaskan Native 1
Asian or Pacific Islander 2
Black/Afro American 3
Hispanic or Mexican American 4
White, not of Hispanic origin 5
Other 6

30. What is your marital status?   *50*
Never married 1
Currently married 2
No longer married 3

31. How are you classified by the University?   *51*
Freshman 1
Sophomore 2
Junior 3
Senior/5th Year Student 4
Graduate Student 5
Not a student 6

32. Are you a full-time student?   *52*
No, not a student 1
No, a part-time student 2
Yes 3

33. Which of the following best describes the grades you have received since you enrolled at this University?   *53*
Not a student 0
Mostly A's 1
About half A's and half B's 2
Mostly B's 3
About half B's and half C's 4
Mostly C's 5
About half C's and half D's 6
Mostly D's or below 7

34. What is the religious preference of each of the following persons? (Circle one number in each column.)

	You (54–55)	Father (56–57)	Mother (58–59)
Baptist	01	01	01
Congregational (U.C.C.)	02	02	02
Episcopal	03	03	03
Jewish	04	04	04
Latter Day Saints	05	05	05
Lutheran	06	06	06
Methodist	07	07	07
Muslim	08	08	08
Presbyterian	09	09	09
Quaker (Society of Friends)	10	10	10
Roman Catholic	11	11	11
Seventh Day Adventist	12	12	12
Unitarian-Universalist	13	13	13
Other Protestant	14	14	14
Other Religion	15	15	15
None	16	16	16

78

35. How often do you attend church services or participate in the activities of religious organizations?

Never	1 or 2/yr	Less than 1/mo	1 to 3/mo	1/wk	2 or more/wk
1	2	3	4	5	6

60

36. What is your best estimate of your parents' approximate income last year?

61

Less than $5,000 ... 1 $25,000–$29,999 ... 6
$5,000–$9,999 ... 2 $30,000–$34,999 ... 7
$10,000–$14,999 ... 3 $35,000–$39,999 ... 8
$15,000–$19,999 ... 4 $40,000 or more ... 9
$20,000–$24,999 ... 5   Not applicable ... 0

37. What is the highest level of formal education obtained by your parents? (Circle one number in each column.)

	(62) Father	(63) Mother
Less than high school	1	1
Some high school	2	2
High school graduate	3	3
Technical school	4	4
Some college	5	5
College degree	6	6
Some graduate school	7	7
Graduate degree	8	8

38. Do you currently have a job?

64

No ... 1
Yes, work study ... 2
Yes, part time ... 3
Yes, full time ... 4

If yes, how many hours per week do you usually work? (fill in blank)

_____ # hours   65–66

39. Are you currently a member or a pledge of a fraternity or sorority?

67

Yes, currently a member ... 1
Yes, currently a pledge ... 2
No, but may join later ... 3
No, I am not a member ... 4

40. With whom do you live?

68

By myself ... 1
Roommate(s) ... 2
Spouse ... 3
My parents ... 4
Other relatives ... 5

41. Where do you live?

69

North Campus Co-ed Residence Hall ... 1
North Campus Single Sex Residence Hall ... 2
South Campus Residence Hall ... 3
Granville East/West ... 4
Granville South ... 5
Odum Village ... 6
Fraternity/Sorority House ... 7
Rented Apartment ... 8
Other off-campus residence ... 9

Thank you for completing the survey. Please place the completed survey in the self-addressed envelope and mail. If you are on campus, use campus mail to return the survey.

Blank   70–72
2302   73–76
        77–80

Use this space for any comments you would like to make.

A codebook and computer program (in SAS) have been developed for the Student Alcohol Survey. They are available at cost ($4.00 for the codebook and $3.50 for the program) by writing to:

Librarian
Center for Alcohol Studies
Room 335 Wing B Medical School Building 207H
The University of North Carolina
Chapel Hill, North Carolina 27514

SOURCE: McCarty, D. 1980. "Student Alcohol Survey." In D. McCarty; S. Morrison; J. Ward; M. Poore; L. Mason; J. Whiteside; and K.C. Mills. *Campus Alcohol Education Service—Second Year Evaluation Report*. Unpublished manuscript. Center for Alcohol Studies, School of Medicine, University of North Carolina at Chapel Hill.

Appendix 5–B

Group Interviews

Interview questions are broken into two parts, 1) questions regarding the type and cost of problems experienced and 2) questions about the conditions and participants in the drinking situation. The interviewer/facilitator should also try to get some ideas about solutions from the group as well. These questions are simply *suggestions,* and you will need to apply the ones that are appropriate in a given situation.

Questions about the nature of the group:
—What is your living (or work or friend) group like?
—Who are the members? How many?
—How many males and females are in the group?
—What are their ages? Class standing? Other indicators of social status?
Are most of the group members from a similar family background?
—Are there definite cliques that form within the main group?
—Are members of the subgroups identifiable by some other characteristic? Hobbies, outside activities, etc.?
—Do the subgroups usually get together to drink?
—Where do the subgroups congregate to drink?

Questions about drinking behavior:
—How often do your friends consume beer, wine, or liquor?
—What is the preferred beverage?
—What is the most a member of the group will drink at any one event?
—When does the group drink? Morning? Afternoon? Evening?
—How many days a week do drinking and parties regularly occur?
—Are there individuals who seem to drink more than others?
—How often are parties arranged?

Questions about the consequences of alcohol use:
—Can you tell me about some things that happen to your group when they drink?

—Can you tell me the *best* things that have occurred while people have been drunk?
—Can you tell me the *worst* thing that has happened when people were drinking?
—Has anyone ever passed out from drinking?
—Has anyone ever been arrested for drinking and driving? How often does this occur?
—Has anyone ever been assaulted while drinking?
—Has anyone ever consumed enough to be taken to the hospital?
—Has a doctor (or wife, or friends, or employer, or teacher) suggested that anyone might cut down on their drinking?
—Have you ever observed property damage while people in your group have been drinking? Fires?
—Have you ever seen anyone injured when they have been drinking?
—Have you ever witnessed arguments or fights while the group was drinking?

Beliefs:
—Does the group look up to a member who can "hold his liquor?"
—Do most of your friends drink?
—Does your circle of friends have a better time when they drink?
—Is alcohol almost a necessity in order to have a good party?
—Do group members seem to feel more important when they have had a few drinks?
—Do your friends feel that drinking and driving is allowable for short distances?
—Does the group designate a nondrinker at each party who can drive?
—Are nonalcoholic beverages served at most parties?

Attitudes:
—Does your group promote drinking as an acceptable activity?
—Does drinking, as an activity, ever receive negative comments?
—Are most members of the group too polite to refuse a drink if offered by a superior?

81

—How does your group feel about people who become very drunk, but cause no damage or harm?

—Do you think that your group condones petty pranks that occur during a party?

—Does the group have an opinion about alcohol advertising?

Situations:

—What contexts or settings does your group drink in? Please be specific: Bars? Apartments? Cars? At work? Residence Hall? At games? Anywhere?

—What reasons are usually given for throwing a party? After work? Weekends?

—Are outsiders invited or encouraged to attend?

—When is the maximum amount of alcohol likely to be consumed?

—How many days of the month do you have beer in your residence? Wine? Liquor?

Next the interview moves on to minor alcohol problems. The interview flows smoothly if the interviewer can inquire about *categories* of problems.

Health Problems:

—How often do group members experience hangovers?

—Has anyone in your group taken an alcohol overdose and required hospitalization? Passed out from drinking too much?

—Has anyone in your group injured themselves while intoxicated?

—Has any person in your group experienced reactions to alcohol or to drug use that may not have occurred otherwise?

Property Damage Problems:

—Has anyone broken windows or door while drinking?

—Have you witnessed false alarms or fires?

—Have you seen furniture damaged during parties?

Legal and Arrest Problems:

—Has anyone in your group been arrested for disorderly conduct?

—Has anyone in your group been arrested for drinking in public?

—Has anyone in your group been arrested for drinking and driving?

—Has anyone in your group been arrested for fighting or assault?

—Has anyone in your group been arrested for violent crime while intoxicated?

Financial Problems:

—Has your group incurred outstanding debts for party expenses?

—Has anyone in your group had to pay fines for drinking-related arrests?

—Has your group incurred any legal fees for drinking or drug use actions?

Problems at Work:

—Do some people report that drinking makes studying easier?

—Is there extreme competitiveness in your institution?

—Are nonalcoholic drinks provided at dorm parties?

—Have you seen tardiness or absenteeism as a result of drinking or hangovers?

—Has anyone in your group been reprimanded or expelled because of repeated alcohol problems?

Problems with Friends:

—Have you witnessed arguments as a result of drinking or drug use?

—Is there an increase in conflict situations or fights after a party?

Family Problems:

—Do people in your group talk about parents with alcohol problems?

—Have individuals in your group mentioned that they would not like their parents to find out about their drinking?

Personal Problems:

—Do people in your group report a difficulty with studying because of too much partying? By self? By others?

—Do any of your friends complain of depression or feelings of helplessness after drinking?

—Has anyone become involved in an unwanted pregnancy while drinking?

Finally, the interview must cover *prevention activities* that have been thought about or implemented as a part of social activities in the group.

How often are you likely to decrease overconsumption by...

providing an activity other than drinking as a focus of a party?

promoting nonalcoholic beverages?

providing high protein food, such as cheese or meat snacks, if alcohol is served?

purchasing alcohol consistent with the number of drinkers?

setting limits for guests who overconsume?

How often are you likely to reduce legal and financial problems by. . .

caring enough to prevent a friend from driving after drinking?

forcefully taking keys away from a friend about to drive while drunk?

providing transportation or overnight accommodations for those unable to drive safely?

How often are you likely to reduce casualty problems by. . .

clearing a party environment of safety hazards before guests arrive?

arranging for alternative transportation?

How often are you likely to reduce problems of litter and noise by. . .

providing trashcans and incentive to use them for party goers?

providing indoor areas where drinkers can party without disrupting neighborhood residents?

EXAMPLE: INTERVIEW OF COLLEGE RESIDENCE HALL PERSONNEL

The planning committee meeting was held in mid-January with the residence director, eight residence advisers (RAs) and several dorm officers and hall residents present. Questions produced the following results:

1. What are some of the alcohol-related problems that you have in your dorms?
   a. Verbal aggression and excessive noise.
      1) Shouting matches between dorms.
      2) 80 percent of an RA's job is turning down noise, often in early morning hours.
      3) When residents have been drinking they do not follow the advice of the RA to turn down the noise, but also are very apologetic the next day saying, "I'm sorry, but I was drunk." There is a tendency to believe that being drunk excuses their behavior.
   b. Personal injury.
      1) Approximately 15–20 incidents per semester according to the residence director.
      2) These occasionally come as a result of mixing alcohol and drugs.
   c. Dorm damage.
      1) Kicking everything in sight.
      2) Throwing objects.
      3) Pulling objects off walls (i.e., bulletin boards)
      4) Urinating on RA's doors.
2. What are some observations that you have made about the residents' drinking behavior?
   a. That drinking happens occasionally when the person is alone; that not all drinking happens within a social context in our dorms.
   b. That residents place emphasis on the behavior of drinking, not on the consequences. In other words, they drink to drink, not to get drunk.
   c. Homesickness and low grades often lead to depression, but there was perception of alcohol as an antecedent or consequence of residents' depression.
   d. The most common reason for drinking is "force of habit."
   e. Residents show good responsibility in drinking and driving. It often happens that if a group is driving off campus to drink, they will draw straws to see who stays sober to drive home.
   f. Sophomores tend to have the most problems (alcohol and non-alcohol-related), of any class.
3. What do you think are the solutions to these problems you have described?
   a. Show people they can have a good time without getting drunk.
   b. Relate vanity and drinking, especially showing males that women are often turned off by drunk men.
   c. Dispel feelings that being drunk excuses behavior.
   d. Use breathalyzer at mixers, but only with instruction that would minimize incentive to "drink a lot to blow high."

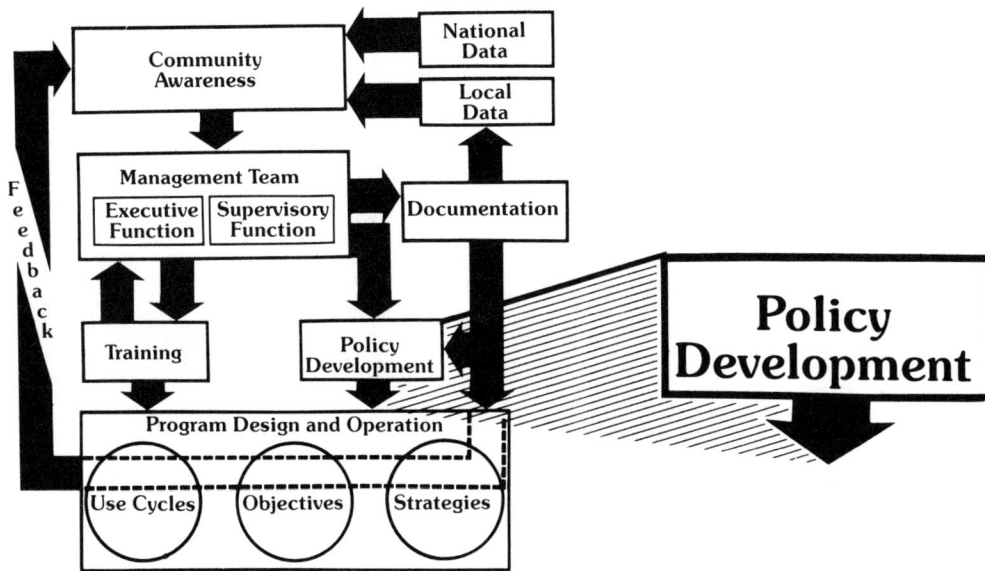

Chapter 6

POLICY DEVELOPMENT

OBJECTIVES

When you have finished this chapter, you should be able to:

1. Differentiate between traditional alcohol policies and the type of policy appropriate for a problem-specific alcohol program;
2. Describe the functions that a policy statement serves in an alcohol program; and
3. Outline the relationship of policy development to other elements of the management system.

Alcohol policies are not new; their earliest manifestations developed from legalistic attempts to reduce the availability of alcohol by restricting hours of sale, where it can be sold, the type of containers it can be sold in, and the minimum age of the purchasers. Also, some policies effectively raised the price of alcohol by specifying high luxury taxes. The most extreme example of a restrictive alcohol policy in the United States was the Eighteenth Amendment, which prohibited the manufacture, transportation, and sale of alcoholic liquors except for sacramental purposes.

Alcohol policies derived from a purely medical perspective are relatively new by comparison. Typically, they set conditions under which individuals with alcoholism or other serious drinking problems can obtain help without damage to personal life or career. Company alcohol policies are a good example of this type of policy; they are usually integrated with other employee assistance programs, establishing procedures and guidelines for employees (with supervisory participation and approval) to be referred to a treatment agency. Medically derived policies are designed to identify the problem drinker early in his or her drinking career and to clear the path for early treatment (psychotherapy, Alcoholics Anonymous, hospitalization, etc.). These policies focus on the individual drinker and are not considered preventive in nature.

Most previous attempts to deal with alcohol-related problems have fluctuated between the extremes of over-restraint and simple neglect. The latter attitude is particularly common among colleges and universities that fail to institute alcohol programs for fear of impinging on the rights of the individual student drinker.

> For too long alcohol use on the American college campus, though recognized as an integral part of student social life, has been subject to an ongoing policy of benign neglect. Though the code and attitudes of former eras have no relevance to present-day social custom and habit, little effort has been made to confront either the challenge or the problem of alcohol use by student citizens of the academic community (BACCHUS 1981: 8).

Literature from the BACCHUS[1] program outlines four broad principles for policy development. Using these principles, policymakers can balance situational conditions,

---

[1]Boost Alcohol Consciousness Concerning the Health of University Students (BACCHUS) is a national organization that is affiliated with the Education Commission of the States, the National Football League, the Distilled Spirits Council of the United States, and the Campus Alcohol Information Center, University

health considerations, and safety responsibilities against the rights of individual drinkers.

1. Every individual has the right to make a rational decision whether or not to use alcohol beverages without being subject to interference or pressure from any other individual or group;
2. The moderate use of alcohol can be part of a physically, socially, and psychologically healthful lifestyle for adults;
3. The excessive use of alcohol, far from being the "norm" it might appear to be at times, is an unacceptable social practice; and
4. Individuals with alcohol addiction problems should be encouraged to recognize their condition and to seek help.

An effective policy statement sets up the mechanisms for comprehensive alcohol education. A good example may be found at the University of Rhode Island, where program leaders developed a policy specifically constructed to define the mechanisms for data collection, training programs, and special projects, and also set budgets for alcohol education activities.

Policy formulation is a management task carried out by members of the executive committee and—or the planning committee. A rough sketch of the policy statement should be worked out long before any program activities begin, and must be developed with input from students, staff, faculty, and members of the college administration. The consensual process is the most critical feature of policy development—balancing rights and responsibilities cannot be accomplished without it:

> A campus committee on alcohol education should establish as its goal a realistic alcohol beverage policy. The committee should reach a consensus on the issues surrounding responsible decision-making about alcohol. Once a consensus has been reached, the policy should be transplanted into specific guidelines about the use and misuse of alcohol beverages that are safe and healthful. The many influential forces on campus, such as the administration, fraternities, sororities, clubs, professional organizations and sporting events, should be used to reinforce the policy guidelines so that students are motivated to adopt them as their standard of behavior about alcohol beverages. (BACCHUS 1981: 5).

If policymakers do not connect simple alcohol consumption with alcohol-related problems, they will never convince the community that a prevention program is necessary. In the past, this connection has been obscured by a lack of good data, but access to better information has begun to change attitudes worldwide:

> Recognition that alcohol consumption can have a wide variety of consequences has led policy-makers in some parts of the world to consider a whole range of preventive

---

of Florida, Gainesville. Among other items, BACCHUS publishes a pamphlet "The BACCHUS Handbook, A Guide for Community Action to Promote Responsible Decisions about Drinking." For more information write to:

BACCHUS
P.O. Box 1197
Washington, D.C. 20013

measures and their broader implications in terms of percentages of populations concerned, priority targets, determination of high risk groups, effectiveness and cost of measures, and possible disadvantages, such as the increase in other problems (Moser 1981: 17).

A consensual policy is therefore a necessary, integral part of a prevention program, and must be based on information about the extent and nature of alcohol-related problems in the community concerned. The shape and direction of the policy will depend on whether community leaders have accurate information about problem levels. In the last five years, a large number of colleges and universities have begun formal efforts to collect, analyze, and report data about local drinking patterns and their consequences, but seldom have these efforts been linked to a need for policy development.

Historically, alcohol education programs on American college campuses have been fragmented, poorly funded, and generally without clear goals and objectives. This situation is due partially to conflicting advice from experts about *what* to prevent and *how* to prevent it. Rarely have the experts relied on local problem documentation as a basis for their recommendations, preferring instead to form an intuitive assessment of local needs. Programs based on intuition and guesswork usually fail to receive community support and therefore fail to change drinking patterns. These programs also fail to develop comprehensive policy statements, which contribute to their fragmentation and lack of direction: "...Unless there exists a clear policy on prevention of alcohol-related problems, programs providing information and education are likely to produce conflicting results" (Moser 1981: 171).

The creation of a policy statement for an alcohol education program is a way to formalize and perpetuate the changes it is designed to achieve. Incorporating program goals, activities, procedures, and recommendations for the future in a policy statement helps insure the program's continued existence. **A policy statement is also a formal declaration of community values, norms, and traditions regarding drinking; it defines the rights and responsibilities of the drinker and balances them against the needs of the community as a whole.**

Alcohol policy statements are not a new idea on college campuses, but their integration with alcohol education programs is a relatively novel idea. At some institutions, policy statements consist of a single paragraph placing the responsibility for a drinker's actions solely on the individual:

The University will establish no policy or regulation that sanctions either the use of alcoholic beverages or any action which contravenes State or Federal Law regarding their purchase or consumption.

The Alcoholic Beverage Control Laws as amended in 1967 (G.S. 18-90.1) make it unlawful for any minor under 21 years of age to purchase alcoholic beverages which contain more than fourteen percentum (14%) of alcohol by volume. The University will cooperate in the enforcement of this statute.

The University discourages the drinking of alcoholic beverages, drunkenness, and other abuses of alcoholic beverages. Being under the influence of alcohol is considered a serious breach of conduct, and students who violate these standards are subject to appropriate disciplinary action. (Record of the University of North Carolina at Chapel Hill 1981: 143–144).

At other institutions, policy statements are long documents specifying intricate procedures for the registration and planning of any party held on campus, and often include complex rules governing where, when, and how students are permitted to drink. Both kinds of statements are difficult for students to follow, and even more difficult for the authorities to enforce. By contrast, a well-balanced policy is concise, sets forth realistic guidelines so that voluntary compliance is possible, and concentrates exclusively on documented problems. It is helpful at this point to examine in detail the ways a policy statement functions in the overall management system. A policy statement:

1. *Insures consistency* by stating program goals and the activities corresponding to those goals;
2. *Informs* the public about the program and its function;
3. *Establishes procedures and guidelines* for documenting problems;
4. *Recommends program activities* for the present and future;
5. *Outlines current laws and regulations* regarding alcohol and specifies individual responsibilities under the law; and
6. *Provides for revising and updating* policy to meet changing conditions.

Consistency

A policy statement helps insure that a program's goals and its activities are in agreement. Public declaration of aims and means opens both to public scrutiny. Since these aspects of the program were presumably the product of community participation, the match of goals and activities should be sound. Related to this issue is the need to insure that goals and activities are focused on specific problem areas. In this respect, the statement may contain a list of high risk areas, groups, or situations targeted for immediate action. A planning committee at a major university spent a semester documenting this kind of information and then produced a policy statement specifying objectives and strategies targeted at specific problems. For example, they had determined that drunk driving was a particularly acute problem in the remote South Campus area, and their statement pointed out this fact and recommended measures to reduce the problem.

It is clear that a policy statement is an important tool in the hands of the planning committee, but like any tool it can become dull and blunted if it is not sharpened and oiled frequently. The planning committee has an obligation to review the statement to make sure that is is up to date, applicable to current problems, and consistent with the aims of the institution.

Information

Many of the people who must deal with alcohol problems on college campuses still believe that alcohol programs must be primarily concerned with detecting student alcoholics or promoting prohibition of alcohol. By reporting documented problem levels and risk areas and by publicizing program goals specifically targeted on problems, a policy statement can help change outmoded beliefs about the function of alcohol programs.

Traditional policy statements frequently go to great lengths to specify where alcohol can be consumed (in residence hall lounges but not in rooms, on the lawns but not on the steps, not at building entrances, etc.). Students usually ignore these restrictions, and their generally unenforceable nature damages the credibility of anyone associated with formulating the regulations. Policy statements that attempt to regulate a student's right to drink (as an adult) are generally disregarded.

On the other hand, an effective policy statement informs students and all members of the university community about the rights and responsibilities associated with drinking. The *On Campus Review,* a publication sponsored by the U.S. Brewers Association, recently reported on the development of a residence hall policy at the Washington State University at Pullman (1981):

> Students who drink outside the residence halls are held accountable for their behavior in the halls in the same way as students who drink in their rooms or at a floor party. Irresponsible drinking is considered unacceptable. Drinking is not an excuse for irresponsible behavior; thus Standards Boards are expected to take judicial action against hall residents who behave irresponsibly after drinking too much.
>
> Additionally, individual residents are held accountable for the actions of their guests. In cases where guests of students drink irresponsibly and exhibit inappropriate behavior, the guests will be asked to leave the hall. The university police will be called by residence staff in cases where guests fail to comply with requests of the staff. Students whose guests drink or behave irresponsibly will be subject to judicial action by the Hall Standards Board (p. 146).

This policy is reinforced by guidelines for party planning:

> A "Party Organizer's Responsibility Statement" also must be signed by the main organizers. This lists general areas of responsibility and liability and includes the following statement:
> "I (we) the undersigned individuals accept and understand the responsibilities which we incur as the persons responsible for organizing the floor party scheduled on (date) on (floor) in (name) residence hall.
> "Furthermore, we understand that residence hall, university, or civil discipline proceedings may be brought against us if we disregard the parameters set forth in the Washington State University residence hall alcohol policy" (p. 146).

A complete copy of the Pullman policy is included at the end of this chapter in Appendix 6.

In other words, an effective policy concentrates on the adverse consequences of drinking, not on the regulation of individual freedoms. This emphasis reflects the "environmental approach" to problem reduction—by altering the conditions surrounding known problem situations, the likelihood of problem occurence is reduced. Under these principles, a policy statement may legitimately include guidelines for party planning that include suggestions for security, provisions for cleanup, the limits of safe occupancy for buildings, and specify who is responsible for costs of damages if they occur.

Documentation

A coordinated data reporting system keeps a program focused on documented problems and not on individual drinking problems. Coordinated documentation of current problems is the best way to insure that a program stays up to date and relevant to community needs. By way of example, the Washington State University policy quoted above also included procedures for documenting problems arising from parties:

> Another requirement is that each floor party must be evaluated. A form for this purpose is completed and signed by an attending staff member, party coordinator and the Head Resident within one week after the event. Along with general comments, six questions are answered.
>
> 1. Were any alcohol policy infractions noted at the party?
> 2. How well controlled was the event in terms of how it was set up and run?
> 3. Was any irresponsible drinking evident? If so, what was done?
> 4. Was any irresponsible behavior noted? If so, what?
> 5. Were there any damages?
> 6. Recommendations for improvement?
>
> These written evaluations provide a continuing means of pinpointing where additional work may be needed in particular halls. They serve a useful purpose not only for Head Residents and Resident Advisers in carrying out their roles, but for structuring the educational programs that are required at least twice a semester.

A policy statement may also specify methods for collecting information from campus police, the student health service, the student mental health service, the hospital emergency room, residence hall advisers, and the interfraternity council. These procedures could thereby insure that data are gathered from diverse sources on a regular schedule. In practice, a single individual is usually given the responsibility of organizing and reporting the results to the executive and planning committees.

Program Activities

A policy statement may also outline immediate and long-term program activities (such as training projects, community awareness campaigns, alcohol education workshops, etc.) and make provisions for further policy development. In this way, policy development becomes an instrument for program continuity and builds in an element of flexibility by providing for policy change in the future.

The range of possible activities is limited only by the imagination and creativity of the program planners, but alcohol programs around the world are excellent sources for program ideas. A number of international organizations are currently developing policies and programs to reduce alcohol-related problems. Most of these programs depend on a policy statement to declare and reinforce their program goals.

Legal Parameters

Every state, province, and local government in North America has laws to control the sale and distribution of alcohol in its many forms. Since a policy statement is an official university document, it must be consistent with state and local laws. For example, the provisions of a policy statement cannot contradict the state's Dram Shop Law, which may contain complicated, obscure, or even generally unknown provisions.

> Dram shop liability was introduced into American law in the mid-1800's by temperance advocates attempting to close saloons and "dram shops." These early laws ("dram shop acts") typically provided that tavern owners be financially responsible (liable) for the support of families of patrons who had become "habitual drunkards." Often, the civil statute would be complemented by a criminal provision prohibiting the sale of alcoholic beverages to habitual drunkards or to persons of "known intemperate habits" (Mosher 1979: 773).

The early dram shop laws were largely symbolic, however, and aside from a few well-publicized cases, they had little real impact. However, in the twentieth century these laws began to be applied to the sale of alcoholic beverages to minors as well as to habitual drunkards. "Third party" liability cases extended the laws to cover compensation for automobile accident victims—they could sue tavern owners and similar "commercial servers" whose patrons had caused the accidents.

> A typical statute provides that a commercial server of alcoholic beverages be found liable for injuries caused by his patrons if the server sold or gave alcoholic beverages to the patron in violation of the law. A violation occurs if the patron is a minor, a habitual drunkard or someone "already" or "obviously" intoxicated when served (Mosher 1979: 775).

Eighteen states have dram shop laws, and in ten others the courts have used common law to impose civil liabilities on commercial servers of alcoholic beverages when "negligence" can be proved. Dram shop acts and common law precedents are important to colleges and universities because test cases are changing the definition of who is liable for a drinker's actions. In some states, the definition of the third party ranges from the traditional retail server to a more general category of "social hosts." While most states still limit liability to commercial vendors (e.g., tavern owners, retail clerks, waiters, and bartenders), the idea that *any* social host may be responsible for his or her guest's actions is gaining ground. A social host may be a fraternity, a residence hall government, a private citizen, or even a company providing alcoholic beverages for an employee party. In some cases, a university can legally be considered a social host.

Some courts have been willing to impose penalties on social hosts similar to those imposed on commercial vendors, especially if minors have been served. Through these cases the courts have declared that determining the age of a drinker is not an overly burdensome task for a social host. However, most courts have failed to address the question of liability for allowing adults to become intoxicated.

An innovative project in California uses the state's dram shop law, which incorporates third-party liability as an incentive for training bartenders. This project offers hotel and restaurant chains training programs for their bartenders to prepare them to recognize overly intoxicated drinkers. The program teaches bartenders how to detect signs of intoxication, how to "cut off" the drinkers, and how to estimate the amount of alcohol a drinker needs to reach an illegal blood alcohol level. The program is still in its early stages, but the response of bartenders has been so positive that several large companies have decided to continue their training. The fact that employees are properly trained to detect severely intoxicated persons could protect both the employees and their companies from a dram shop law suit (Mosher and Wallack 1979).

In clarifying legal responsibilities, a policy statement may address the question of host liability. The circumstances that determine liability vary from state to state, but social hosts can be held responsible for damages in most states if they fail to show reasonable discretion in serving an intoxicated person, if the person who was served was underage, or if someone was injured or killed as a direct consequence of the hosts' behavior.

For example, if an underage student attends a party where his age is not checked and the amount he drinks is not monitored, and he is later involved in a serious accident driving home because he is intoxicated, the social host can be held liable for the costs of damages resulting from the crash.

A policy statement can help individuals and institutions avoid legal problems by clarifying these liabilities. It may list the responsibilities of the social host and provide a set of guidelines to help avoid problems. For example, one policy statement suggested that party sponsors should:

- Provide a sanitary system for dispensing beverages;
- Have reasonable hours of service;
- Provide nonbreakable drink containers; and
- Designate someone responsible for implementing the guidelines.

Some laws seem to be written with arbitrary disregard of the consequences. In one college town it is illegal to drink alcohol on the public sidewalks. However, it is legal to drink beer or wine on the main street because that is a state highway and not under the jurisdiction of city law. Furthermore, public consumption on private property is not forbidden. Students can buy beer at a private convenience store and drink in the parking lot, but they cannot return to the store because it does not have a license for on-premises drinking. They may go from the parking lot to the street, but they may not carry an open beverage onto the sidewalk. If they remain undetected long enough to get to a school lawn, they are again safe. The school is state-owned and their behavior is therefore under the jurisdiction of state law. However, they cannot drink in any buildings on campus other than residences, for those areas are off-limits for alcohol consumption.

Some states prohibit the purchase of alcohol with state funds, which would include state college and university monies. In most states it is illegal for anyone to sell alcohol for cash or credit unless they are licensed to do so, therefore charging for individual drinks at a fraternity party would be in violation of the law. By reiterating these laws, a policy statement helps clarify and publicize the legal conditions surrounding alcohol sales.

A policy statement can also specify the legal rights and responsibilities of drinkers and outline the rights of those who choose not to drink or be exposed to alcohol use. A strong policy statement can even result in the establishment of nondrinking residence areas and the matching of roommates on the basis of drinking or nondrinking preferences. A policy statement might also include suggestions (based on balanced rights and privileges) by which tenants of a campus living area could reach agreement about the type and nature of parties they would permit.

A policy statement can help protect the rights of students, staff, and faculty who have drinking problems by describing the established judicial and medical referral procedures for those who are brought to the attention of the authorities. If existing procedures are inadequate, program planners may seek to change them and establish a more effective or humane policy.

In defining the legal environment, a campus policy statement may also point out that violations of the college code of conduct or state law cannot be excused simply because the violators were intoxicated at the time. Many campuses have policy statements that remind all citizens of the college community that they are responsible for the outcomes of their drinking behavior and that excessive drinking is not an excuse for doing something that an individual would not do otherwise.

Revision

In a sense, the built-in procedures for revising and updating a policy statement are more important than the content. Legal issues, party guidelines, damage responsibility, the specification of rights, or other specific features may be important parts of a policy statement in a particular situation, but provisions for soliciting community opinion and procedures for the continued collection of data on problems are always important. Policy direction may alter with fluctuating problem levels and changing community concerns. Such variation is healthy; it reflects community participation and consensus and insures that the policy will stay current with the changing norms and values of the community.

Why is the process of policy development so central to the problem-specific approach to alcohol problem management? A comprehensive, consensual policy will help your program avoid the "brushfire syndrome." Alcohol programs often channel resources into combating single problems—brushfires—and fail to address the broader, underlying problems—the source of the fuel. For example, a campus program might concentrate, semester after semester, on training residence hall advisers to deal with problems arising from dormitory parties. At first, students may be enthusiastic about the new program and work diligently to manage the previously uncontrollable parties in their dorms. But they will simply be fighting brushfires while the size of the fire campuswide is spreading. Eventually, even dedicated students will lose interest as it becomes increasingly apparent that their isolated efforts are not affecting the larger problem. A program without a comprehensive, communitywide policy statement is like a fire department that goes out to fight individual oil tank blazes while a refinery may be burning. An alcohol program must have an overall policy to guide its actions.

If it were possible to show that specific prevention strategies or a combination of measures would reduce alcohol problem levels, the task of creating a comprehensive policy would be simplified. Unfortunately, there is no guaranteed method, no panacea for all problems. For this reason, a policy statement should be a flexible, dynamic document that can reflect changes in the program as old or unsuccessful strategies are discarded and new ones are adopted. This flexibility, in turn, is based on community participation in the process of gathering data and developing a program addressed to local needs.

Thought Questions

1. Are you familiar with the local laws and regulations regarding alcohol use in your own community?

2. What sources would you use to compile a comprehensive list of such laws?

3. Has anyone of your acquaintance been cited or arrested for violation of an obscure ordinance?

4. Can you describe the areas in which documentation (Chapter 5) and policy development overlap and reinforce each other?

5. Have you observed examples of "brushfire fighting" on your campus?

References

Boost Alcohol Consciousness Concerning the Health of the University Students (BAC-CHUS). 1981. *Alcohol and the American Campus,* Washington, D.C., February.

Maloff, D.; H. Becker; A. Fonaroff; and J. Rodin. 1979. "Informal Social Controls and Their Influence on Substance Use." *Journal of Drug Issues* 9: 161–184.

Moser, J. 1981. *Prevention of Alcohol Related Problems: An International Review of Preventive Measures, Policies and Programs.* Toronto, Canada: The Alcoholism and Drug Addiction Research Foundation.

Mosher, J.F. 1979. "Dram Shop Liability and the Prevention of Alcohol-Related Problems." *Journal of Studies on Alcohol* 40: 773–798.

Mosher, J.F., and L.M. Wallack. 1979. *The DUI Project.* Sacramento, Calif: Department of Alcoholic Beverage Control, State of California.

Record of the University of North Carolina at Chapel Hill, 1981. *The Undergraduate Bulletin.* Number 918, Chapel Hill N.C.

Roman, P.M. 1980. "Employee Alcoholism and Assistance Programs, Adapting an Innovation for College and University Faculty. *Journal of Higher Education* 51: 135–149.

Room, R., and J. Mosher. 1979/1980. "Out of the Shadow of Treatment: A Role for Regulatory Agencies in the Prevention of Alcoholic Problems." *Alcohol Health and Research World:* 11–17.

Washington State University at Pullman. 1981. "Policy Regarding Use of Alcoholic Beverages in Washington State University Residence Halls." *On Campus Review* 3, no. 2 (Spring/Summer): 1–4.

Whitehead, P.C. 1976. "Effects of Liberalizing Alcohol Control Measures. *Addictive Behaviors* 1: 197–203.

————. 1979. "Public and Alcohol Related Damage: Media Campaigns and Social Controls." *Addictive Behaviors* 4: 83–89.

Appendix 6

Policy Regarding Use of Alcoholic Beverages in Washington State University Residence Halls

The Washington State University residence hall alcohol policy places major responsibility for individual and group conduct upon the students who are involved in the use of alcoholic beverages.

Students who drink outside of the residence halls are held accountable for their behavior in the halls in the same way as students who drink in their rooms or at a floor party. Irresponsible drinking is considered to be unacceptable and students are held accountable for their behavior. Drinking is not an excuse for irresponsible behavior, thus Standards Boards are expected to take judicial action against hall residents who behave irresponsibly after drinking too much. Additionally, individual residents are held accountable for the actions of their guests. In cases where guests of students drink irresponsibly and exhibit inappropriate behavior, the guest will be asked to leave the hall. The University police will be called by residence hall staff in cases where guests fail to comply with requests of the staff. Students whose guests drink or behave irresponsibly will be subject to judicial action by the hall Standards Board.

Head Residents and Resident Advisors are expected to ensure that *all* students are aware of the alcohol policy, the rationale for the unacceptability of irresponsible drinking/behavior, and the consequences of such. Residence hall staff are expected to ensure that students who are planning and/or attending floor parties understand *in detail* the alcohol policy, their liability, and their responsibilities for appropriate planning, monitoring, post-function cleanup, behavior of guests, and payment for damages incurred at the party. After a resident hall has met the alcohol education expectations, the Head Resident may grant permission for floor parties to be held. It is the responsibility of the Head Resident to determine *when* a group is prepared to undertake the planning and execution of a floor party and to approve such a party.

Head Residents and Resident Advisers should not have to be directly involved in "policing" floor parties, rounding up people for post-function cleanup, or other particulars of function planning. Responsibility for a function is totally that of the students, and staff should be concerned primarily with ensuring adequate student planning, along with the evaluation of the planning and responsibility of students involved, after the function has taken place. Responsibility for student and guest behavior, for damage sustained by the residence hall during the function, and for post-function clean-up, should all be part of the provisions made in the student planning. Execution and implementation of the planning procedures should be done by the students and evaluated by the staff.

The giving of responsibility for student behavior to the students can only be achieved by the willingness, on the part of both students and staff, to cooperate with each other. Through the proposed guidelines and policy implementation, social function planning can be accomplished which will take full advantage of this willingness to cooperate, and which will facilitate the return to more realistic and satisfying roles for both staff and students.

Principle of "Shared Responsibility"

In residence halls on the Washington State University, access is officially granted only to residents and guests of residents. With this as a premise, the normal concept of "public" does not apply to the common areas of the residence hall (those other than the student rooms). Areas such as lobbies, elevators, and stairwells are public in the sense that they are "open to all" in the residence hall, but private in the sense that these areas are open exclusively to those in the residence hall, plus residents' guests. Rather than call these common areas in the residence hall "public spaces," a more appropriate designation would be "shared spaces," meaning a place commonly and normally used by all who have a right to be in the residence hall itself. Extending this concept further, it is reasonable to grant certain rights to a group of individuals who closely share a common living area, such as a residence hall section or corridor. Such rights would include using their shared space for special programs and functions as a majority of the individuals concerned sees fit. These rights would be accompanied by suitable and necessary responsibilities, of course, including financial, legal and social liabilities.

An apartment dweller or home owner is responsible for actions that occur in the space that is his/hers, but fully enjoys the privilege of having and using that space as he/she desires. In the residence hall, individuals taking similar responsibility of their shared space, by mutual consent, should be able to enjoy comparable privileges.

Residence Living Parameters

Residence hall staff and party planners are accountable for responsible planning and conduct of floor parties at which alcohol is served in addition to modeling responsible attitudes and behavior.

The Washington State University policy with regard to alcoholic beverages reads as follows: (WAC 504-20-025)

University regulations forbid illegal possession, illegal use, or sale of intoxicating beverages in University residence halls, fraternities, and other group houses. Intoxicating beverages may not be used in lounges, recreation rooms, conference rooms, and public areas of residence halls and University owned buildings.

In addition, the Department of Residence Living has set certain parameters regarding the use of alcoholic beverages in residence halls.

A. Open containers of alcohol are not allowed in public areas. Public areas are defined as areas within the residence hall which have 24 hour visitation and are open to anyone other than hall residents and their guests, e.g., lobbies, stairways, elevators, laundry rooms, etc.
B. Alcohol is not allowed in restrooms.
C. Alcohol is not allowed in transit (room to room) at times other than during an organized party. No drinking will be allowed in hallways, nor will loitering in the halls with alcohol be allowed during times other than those events scheduled and arranged as organized floor parties. Transit of open containers of alcoholic beverages between rooms is *not allowed* during coordinated room parties where students in several rooms on a floor or hallway get together and purchase intoxicating beverages for use in their individual rooms. In such cases, doors must be closed, and noise and other common courtesies and policies of the hall and

Washington State University must be adhered to by those participating in such coordinated room parties.
D. Kegs (or bulk beer in any form of container) are not allowed except under the provisions of an approved floor party.

Floor Party Parameters

In order for a floor party which involves the consumption of alcoholic beverages to be held in a residence hall, the following parameters must be met:

A. At least 2/3 of the floor must approve a floor party.
B. A non-staff member will be in charge of the party. Specific responsibilities will be assigned to each person (see appendix A—responsibility statement and appendix B—attorney general's statement on the liability of the party planner).
C. A Residence Living staff member is required at all parties. Staff members may drop in on parties, but may not be active participants unless they are included on the guest list.
D. Head Resident approval of planned parties is required and must be obtained at least 5 days before the event.
E. Time lines:
   1. Parties are allowed only on Friday or Saturday nights. Organized floor parties are not allowed on special weekends (e.g., Moms' Weekend, Dads' Weekend, Homecoming, Residence Hall Week, Orientation Week (from check-in to the first day of classes), Closed Week, and Finals Week).
   2. No party may last more than 6 hours and must be held between 6 p.m. and 2 a.m.
   3. Maximum number of people: 100.
   4. *Alphabetized* guest lists must be turned into the Head Resident *24 hours* before the event. A guest list is defined as all persons invited to the function—maximum of 100, excluding staff.
   5. All money must be collected 24 hours before the event. Washington State law prohibits the sale of liquor by the drink at parties such as floor parties. Chits or any form of script may not be used instead of cash.
   6. *A damage deposit must be turned into the Head Resident 24 hours before the event.*

The exact amount is to be determined by the Head Resident and depends upon the individual residence hall situation.

7. *Alcohol policy must be posted on floor bulletin boards.*

8. If a keg is used for the party, it may be brought into the hall *4* hours before the party begins. It must not be tapped until the start of the party and must be removed within *48* hours of the party. If it is not consumed at the party, it must be poured out when the party has ended.

F. Organization

1. Invitation of guests must be on an individual basis, (personally or word of mouth) no publicity or posters may be used.

2. Public areas in the residence hall which are designated private for purposes of the party must be marked accordingly.

3. Clean up should be done by *noon* the next day.

4. 20% of total money collected must be spent on food and/or non-alcoholic beverages.

5. Only one keg (either standard 15.5 gallon or pony keg of 7.5 gallon size) will be allowed at any one event. Special notation of intent to purchase a keg must appear on all party forms and must be approved when party plans are submitted *in advance* of the party.

6. The total amount of alcohol allowed at a party will be calculated as follows: 1 oz. per person per hour—1 oz. per person means: 1 oz. hard liquor, or 3 oz. wine, or 9 oz. beer. For additional information on blood alcohol concentration, see appendix E.

7. No more than 2 or 3 (depending on hall size) parties will be allowed per night in each residence hall, exceptions can be granted for Christmas and special occasions.

G. Responsibility

1. Party planners are responsible for monitoring all aspects of the party and are liable for any violations of the alcohol policy or hall rules, (see appendix A—responsibility statement).

2. There must be at least one security person on duty at all times to monitor entrances and exits to allow in only invited guests and to contain the party to a limited area. It is strongly recommended that a person from another floor or hall be hired to be in charge of security. Bartenders should know how to serve drinks and when not to serve drinks. They are responsible for party guests who become intoxicated, (see appendix C on bartenders responsibilities).

3. All floor residents are expected to enforce the regulations of the alcohol policy and/ or hall rules.

4. Individuals are responsible for their guests. When an entire floor is invited, the party planners are responsible for the group.

H. Violations

1. Any violations which cannot be corrected immediately by the residents, party planners, and/or security people will result in the party being shut down by residence hall staff.

2. Alcohol violations will be handled through Standards Board or the Head Resident.

3. Violations can also result in the suspension of the floor alcohol policy or the alcohol policy for the residence hall involved. Such suspension would prohibit all forms of floor parties or coordinated room parties.

I. Alcohol Education Policy

1. All residence halls wishing to have floor parties which involve the consumption of alcoholic beverages must provide an ongoing and comprehensive alcohol education program for their residents. This program may include information on other kinds of drugs as well, if so desired. Individual programs will be presented *not less than two times* each semester and shall include but not be limited to at least two of the following six areas:
   a. Responsible Drinking
   b. Responsible Hosting at Parties Where Alcohol is Served
   c. Alcohol and Its Effects on the Body
   d. Sociological Perspective of Alcohol Use (the role of social pressure and modeling)
   e. Decision-Making about Drinking
   f. Drinking and Driving

The Office or Residence Living will maintain a file of educational materials, programs, and names of resource persons on the topic. Contact the Area Director for the particular hall for further information (335-2611).

J. Evaluation

1. Evaluation of floor parties must be completed and signed by the attending staff member, party coordinator, and Head Resident no later than one week after the event (see appendix D—evaluation form).

K. General Statements

1. Anyone on the floor can initiate a party proposal.

2. Permission can be requested from the Director of Residence Living for exceptions to this alcohol policy for special occasions.

3. A signed statement from each resident, which indicates that they have read and understand the alcohol policy must be obtained by the party planners before a floor party may be held.

4. Persons under 21 years of age are not allowed to consume intoxicating beverages according to Washington State law. Persons who are under 21 and who are consuming alcoholic beverages at a floor party are subject to arrest in cases where the police are involved in handling behavior at the party.

5. Residence hall staff are not allowed to purchase alcoholic beverages for floor parties.

6. The attached floor party planning guide or a similar form developed by the hall should be used for planning (see appendix F).

7. Individual halls may set parameters for alcohol use within their halls which are more restrictive than this policy.

Source: Betas, G.A., B.J. Rexwinkel and other members of Department of Residence Living staff. 1981. "Policy Regarding Use of Alcoholic Beverages in Washington State University Residence Halls." Washington State University.

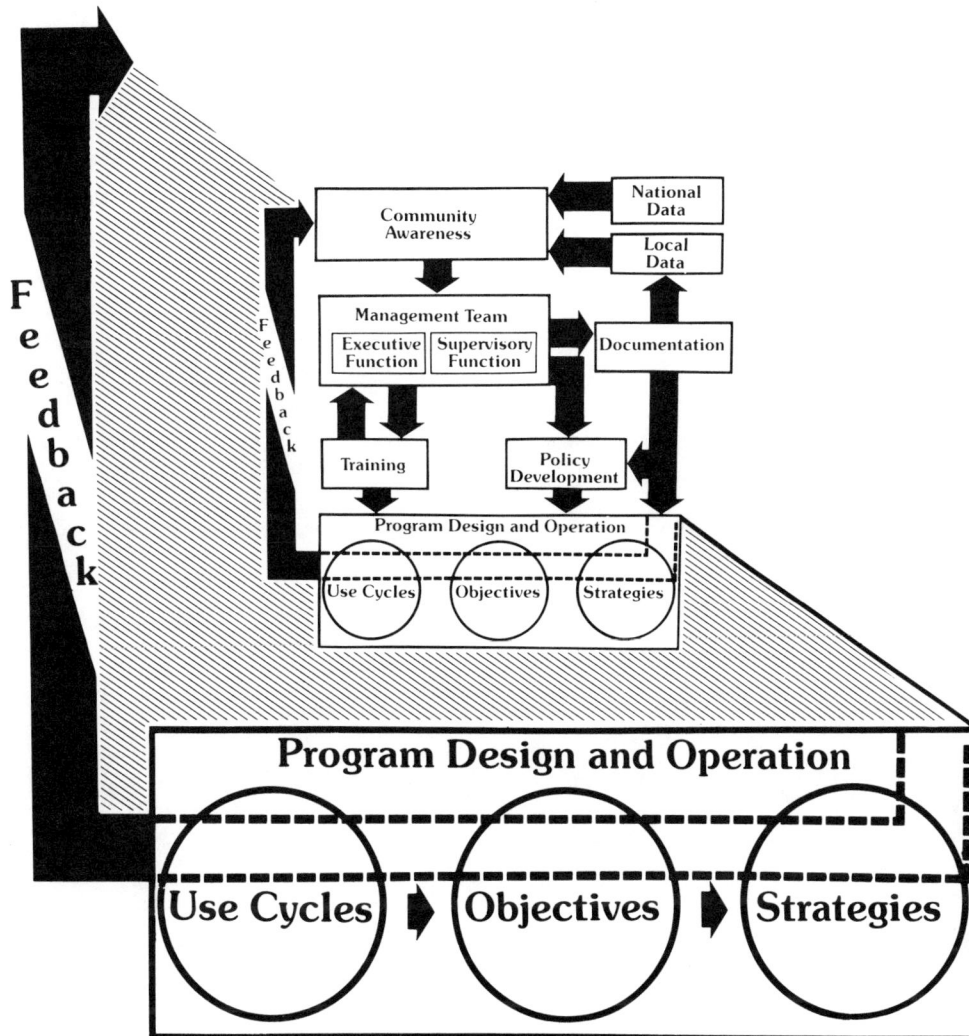

Feedback

Feedback

Community
Awareness

National
Data

Local
Data

Management Team

Executive
Function

Supervisory
Function

Documentation

Training

Policy
Development

Program Design and Operation

Use Cycles

Objectives

Strategies

Program Design and Operation

Use Cycles → Objectives → Strategies

Chapter 7

DESIGN AND OPERATION

This chapter outlines the process by which program planners target strategies to reduce alcohol-related problems. The visible parts of an alcohol program are its projects and activities, and in this respect many programs look alike. Anyone can show a film, hold a discussion, conduct a workshop, or produce a media campaign, but these strategies must be focused on specific problems and must be related to some overall plan of action. It may be tempting to rush into a project—especially if you are alarmed about a particular problem at your institution—but in order to achieve a lasting effect you should fit these projects into the overall development plan. Numerous strategies have had short-term success in a variety of communities, but alcohol-related problems usually seem to return. The reason why so many of these strategies failed is not because they were poorly designed or executed but because they were performed in isolation from the community and they were not internalized by the community or its leaders. The problem-specific system promotes the process of internalization of changes.

The Use Cycles

In order to learn the process of designing and operating an alcohol program, one first needs to understand the process by which people decide to drink and by which communities promote certain kinds of drinking behavior. Figure 7–1 is a diagram of the key parts of the individual alcohol use cycle. The cycle contains the factors that influence an individual's alcohol consumption, including personal, situational, and normative influences. Drinking *behavior* includes not only the act of consuming alcohol, but also how much, how quickly, and how often it is consumed. Drinking has biological and behavioral *consequences* that work in various ways (conscious and unconscious) to reinforce drinking behavior. Since immediate consequences of moderate consumption tend to be minor, even pleasant, the individual can be subtly encouraged to drink again. *Beliefs* and *attitudes* about alcohol are shaped in part by these early experiences and help to create a disposition to drink. The *decision* to drink, once made, is put into action by social pressure from friends and associates and triggered by a specific *situation*—a time, a place, the people present, and the availability of alcohol. Long-range consequences accumulate gradually and arise from repetitions of the cycle over time, and the individual is usually not aware of this process. Obviously, the components of the cycle tend to interact and reinforce one another.

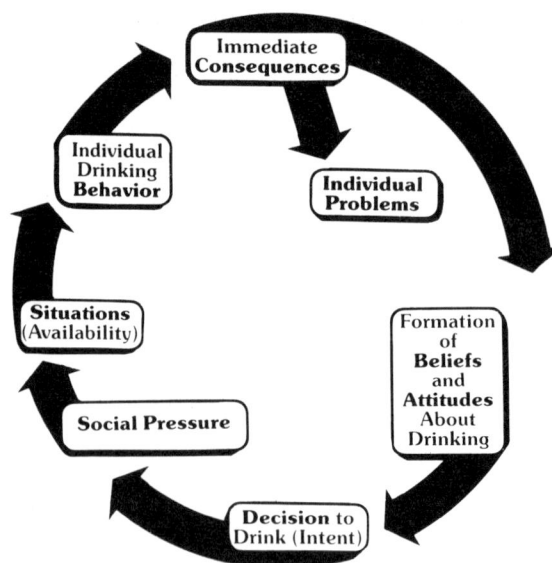

Figure 7–1. The alcohol use cycles: the individual.

Figure 7–2 pictures the alcohol use cycle as it applies to the community. Community *values* (generalized standards of behavior) and community *norms* (more specific expectations regarding behavior) are manifested in various ways with respect to alcohol. For example, in a university community the values and norms may reflect a high degree of tolerance for certain kinds of alcohol consumption. Indeed, there may even be a very strong *tradition* of drinking at particular times and places: end-of-semester parties, victory celebrations, get-acquainted beer busts, and so forth. The availability of alcohol and support mechanisms for its use interact with the community's values, norms, and traditons to create a drinking *environment* peculiar to each community. The drinking *practices* that occur in that environment may vary from subgroup to subgroup within the community, but taken on the whole, continue to feed into (and reinforce) the values, norms, and traditions. It is easy to imagine how this social process shapes the drinking patterns in communities over many years, as the values and norms of those who have lived before us become the basis for our current values and norms.

In Figure 7–3 the two cycles have been combined to show their interrelationship. This diagram illustrates the fact that individual drinking patterns are not usually self-generated, but depend heavily on the social context. Even if a person has no direct experience with alcohol, he or she will still hold certain beliefs and attitudes about drinking drawn from community values and norms. Once the decision is made to drink, the community drinking environment has a powerful influence on how, when, and where the individual will drink. Problems the individual has with alcohol become part of the aggregate problems of the community (unless the individual's problems deviate significantly from the community norms—e.g., alcoholism—in which case the person is treated in a special way).

In an alcohol management program, as one plans activities to influence beliefs, attitudes, behaviors (and values, norms, and traditions), it is apparent that many

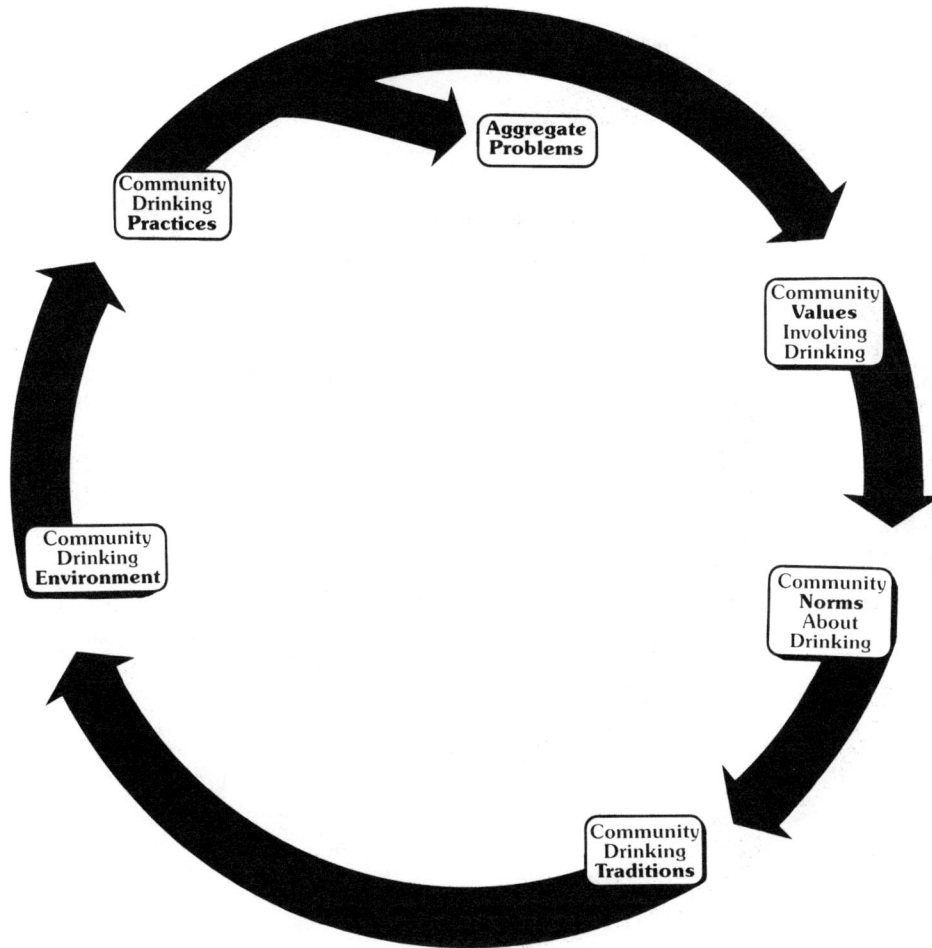

Figure 7–2.   The alcohol use cycles: the community.

alcohol-related problems are simply endpoints in a long and complex process involving a great number of people. A successful program must try to reach a large proportion of the community to reduce even the simplest problem. Although you can address these problems at any point in the alcohol use cycle with limited resources of time, money, and personnel; you must not attempt to invest too much in one area. The flow chart in Figure 7–4 depicts a scheme for achieving problem-reduction effectively and with an efficient use of resources. The strength of this system hinges on the application of the alcohol use cycles described above. It is from the use cycle that you choose specific problems to attack (through the process of community documentation and negotiation) and it is to specific points in the cycles that you target your strategies. In other words, your strategies provide the crucial link between problem identification and problem reduction. If the problem documentation indicates that alcohol-related litter is a persistent and outstanding problem in your community, then the program must reduce litter. If it shows that drinking and driving problems are significant, the program must reduce drinking and driving problems. The goal is not to try and change individuals one by one, but rather to strive for communitywide change.

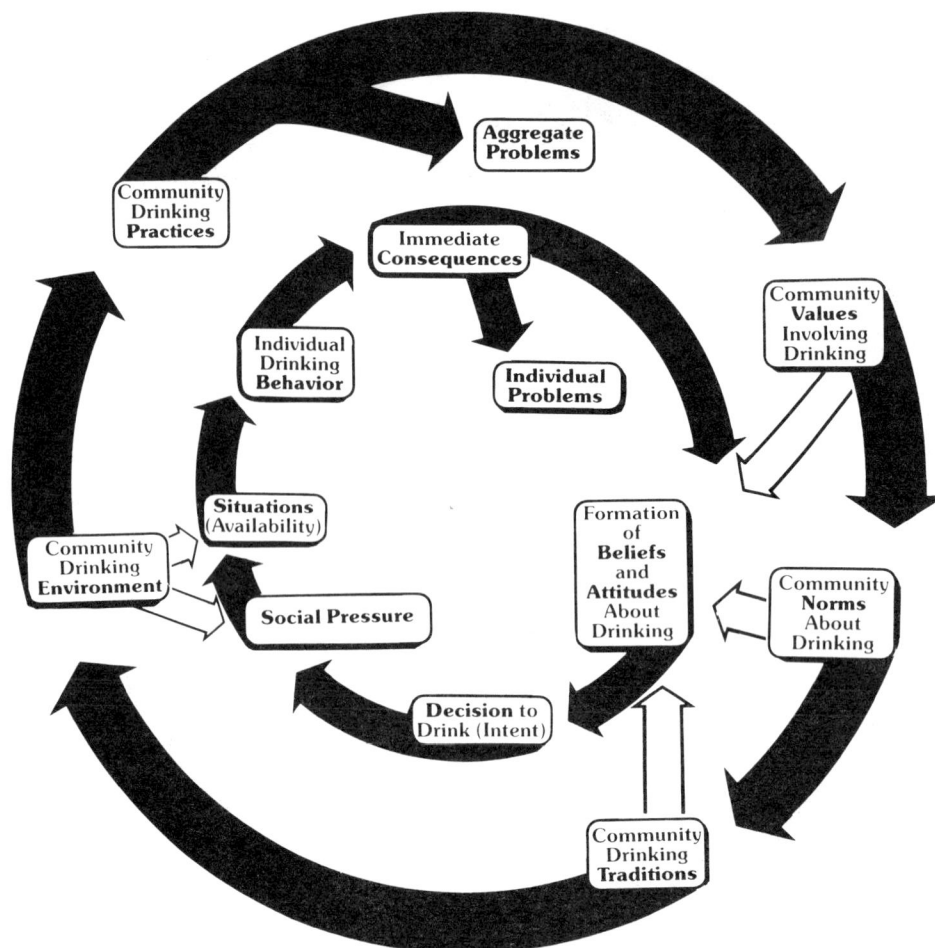

Figure 7–3.   The alcohol use cycles: the individual and the community.

Design Strategy

Program design depicted in Figure 7–4, begins with the specific set of problems identified through the documentation process. These problems are related to specific points in the use cycles. The next step is to set clear objectives for each problem: the degree of problem reduction that the program aims to achieve. When clear objectives have been formulated for each problem, program planners can select strategies (activities, project's policy statements) designed to intervene in the cycle and prevent problem occurrence. Several strategies may be used for a particular problem, and a combination of strategies is usually more effective than a single strategy.

Using methods tailored to the local audience and targeted at specific points in the use cycles, the program will change the way community members think about alcohol and drinking. This attitudinal change will be reflected in a measurable degree of problem reduction. To illustrate the way the program design model works, the remainder of the chapter is a case study that illustrates how a typical program might work.

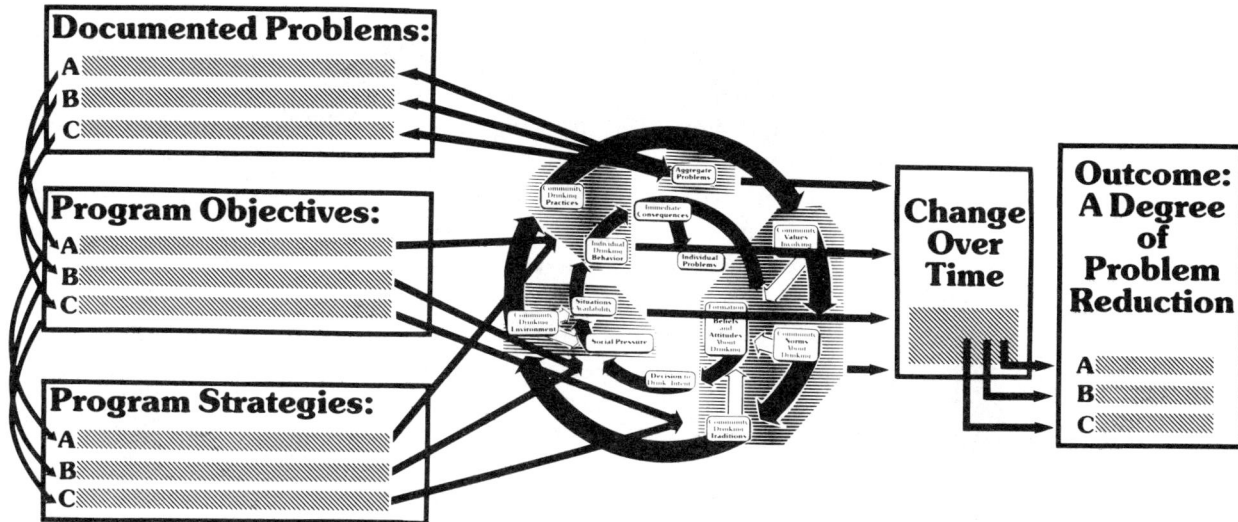

Figure 7–4. The relationship between objectives and strategies through alcohol use cycles.

Case Study

A member of the psychology department at a large university decided to offer a course on alcohol education after he observed a number of alcohol-related problems on the campus. The course was designed to focus on problem solving through direct participation of all forty students in the class, and employed the principles of problem-specific alcohol education. The goals of the course included:

1. Increasing the student body's awareness of the nature and extent of alcohol use at the university;
2. Expanding students' awareness of the nature and extent of alcohol-related problems on campus;
3. Designing and delivering alcohol education services to the student body;
4. Coordinating these services with other student services in order to expand and reinforce their effects;
5. Developing an alcohol policy for the university community; and
6. Reducing the significant alcohol-related problems on campus.

The first part of the course dealt with documentation and lasted three weeks. The class then implemented their documentation plan by mailing survey questionnaires to the student body and by conducting key-informant interviews. Since a majority of the students lived in the residence halls on campus, a special effort was made to document problems in the dormitories. The most common problems reported by residents of this target area were: driving after drinking, missed classes due to hangovers, arguments, and blackouts. Heavy drinkers reported twice as many problems as moderate drinkers.

Excessive consumption (drinking *behavior* in the use cycle) was thereby identified as a significant problem causing a number of adverse effects (hangovers, blackouts, arguments). Driving after drinking, a separate problem, was also targeted for action. In the next segment of the course the students studied the nature of the problems they had identified and began to set objectives for problem reduction. For example, with respect to driving after drinking they learned that at most parties where alcohol is served, about half of the guests will be driving when they leave, and those who choose to drink and drive are not likely to be criticized by others. Most people who drive while intoxicated do not anticipate any adverse consequences; they have probably driven home many times in that condition without arrest or accident, and their friends have done so as well. The prevailing *belief* (see use cycle) seems to be that there is minimal risk in driving while drunk, which leads to the *attitude* that drinking and driving is safe and acceptable, especially if one is not caught. Furthermore, people who decide to drive while drunk tend to ignore friends who urge them not to drive. Their behavior while intoxicated is particularly difficult to modify, and their friends may not wish to confront them in that condition because their reactions may be unpleasant or even violent.

In view of the apparent low risk involved (or at least the perceived low risk), the alternatives to driving after drinking are not very attractive. The basic alternative is simply not drinking when one intends to drive, but this means missing out on the social benefits of drinking. Arranging another mode of transportation may be inconvenient or expensive, and some individuals feel that asking a friend to drive is an admission that they "can't handle their liquor." These factors often combine with other elements of campus culture to create major problems at colleges and universities.

The students decided that one objective of their program would be to reduce by 50 percent the drinking-driving incidents reported on student surveys. With regard to the problem of excessive intoxication, the surveys showed students in some residence halls were getting drunk an average of twice a week, so the program objective in this case was reduction of reported intoxication in those dormitories to no more than twice a month. The class agreed that any significant reduction of either problem could be considered success. Once the target levels had been set, the class began to design projects to achieve these objectives. "Brainstorming" sessions in class yielded lists of possible strategies, and these lists were then reduced to one or two projects through a process of elimination based on an analysis of resource availability, cost-benefit comparisons, time availability, and other limiting factors.

Next, students were trained in presentation methods and group techniques to enable them to carry out their projects (they became "peer educators"). The class had chosen three types of activities for their program: workshops, demonstrations, and media campaigns. The workshops were an ideal method for demonstrating new beliefs, attitudes, and behaviors associated with drinking, or providing opportunities to practice new behaviors, and for learning new skills. Of course, attendance and participation depends to a great extent on the effectiveness of workshop publicity carried out beforehand. Most of the workshops were successful in drawing student participants; publicity was effective and the workshop topics were relevant to student concerns. For example, a workshop on bartending taught skills such as estimating levels of intoxication of party guests and reducing the alcohol intake of those already inebriated. In another workshop, participants learned emergency medical techniques for dealing with dangerously intoxicated individuals.

Demonstration of breath alcohol testing (the "breathalyzer" used by police) were

Figure 7–5. Case study strategies.

held in conjunction with dormitory parties. This activity was the most popular and well-received of all the strategies used in the program.

Media campaigns consisted primarily of posters, newsletters, and circulars distributed to target areas on campus. Some of these items were used to promote the program and enlist participants, but most of them were designed to alter prevailing beliefs and attitudes associated with the targeted problems. In addition, the class used a videotape about drinking and driving to stimulate discussions of the problem in various meeting contexts.

To minimize the problems of coordinating these diverse activities, and to use their resources most effectively, the class concentrated most of their projects on a single residence area with 700 male students. These students had been identified in the survey as the heavier, high-risk, drinking population that experienced more problems than students in other areas. Representatives from the class negotiated extensively with residence advisers, floor officers, area government officers, social chairpersons, and interested students about alcohol education services the class was prepared to provide. These negotiations were crucial for altering key residents' opinions about the unconventional nature of the program activities, and for scheduling program activities in conjunction with social activities in the dorms.

Because of the prevalence of drinking and driving indicated on the needs assessment and the potential risks associated with arrests and accidents, this problem was the focus of three activities: The videotape highlighting the problem of drinking and driving, demonstrations of breath alcohol testing, and a circular letter dealing with the incidence of drinking and driving on campus and suggesting ways to reduce the problem. The videotape was shown four times to a total audience of 207 students. Breathalyzer demonstrations were given at three keg parties and 325 students watched the demonstration. The letter was sent to all 700 men in the residence area.

The videotape, entitled "Until I Get Caught," was originally produced for the Public Broadcasting System (Maas 1978). Narrated by Dick Cavett, the film covers a number of research studies on alcohol's effect on driving ability and includes interviews with family members of people killed by drunk drivers. It examines legal and educational programs to reduce drinking and driving that have been tried in the United States and Europe. Finally the tape encourages people to take active steps to prevent friends from driving while intoxicated and urges communities to enforce drinking and driving laws more strictly. The last section of the tape is an excellent trigger for a thirty-minute discussion led by class members. Apart from the overall goal of reducing drinking and driving, the discussion had four objectives derived from the alcohol use cycle.

The participants would *individually* acquire:

1. new beliefs and attitudes about the effects of alcohol on driving skills; and
2. new beliefs about the consequences of drinking and driving upon the lives of others.

The participants would *collectively* acquire:

3. new social values and norms regarding the undesirability of drinking and driving; and
4. new social practices in which friends will stop friends from driving drunk.

In the breathalyzer demonstrations at parties, members of the class set up the instrument and encouraged interested guests to try it out at intervals during the evening. They also provided wallet-size blood alcohol concentration (BAC) cards to help the participants estimate blood alcohol from their body weight and number of drinks consumed. Party guests were usually tested several times over the duration of the party. The peer educators also explained the relationship between the rate of drinking and blood alcohol level, and provided simple tests of motor skills to demonstrate impairment at each level. (Note: Sometimes participants will try to use the breathalyzer as a game, and will compete to see who can "blow the highest." Because the goal of the demonstration is to illustrate the blood alcohol levels associated with moderate drinking, high blood alcohol concentrations are pointless and counter-productive. This kind of competition can be reduced by providing beverages lower in alcohol content to each person who takes the breathalyzer test and by setting 0.089gm/100 ml BAC as the absolute limit for participation.)

The demonstration served the overall goal of trying to reduce the incidence of drinking and driving, and had four specific objectives derived from the alcohol use cycle:

The participants would *individually:*

1. acquire new beliefs about the effects of blood alcohol level on perception and motor skills; and
2. learn ways to estimate their own levels of intoxication (observable impairment of varying degrees).

The participants would *collectively:*

3. acquire a social awareness of others' levels of intoxication; and
4. support the practice of estimating their friends' levels of intoxication in order to prevent them from driving drunk.

The third element of the program directed at the target residence area was a newsletter sent to each of the 700 male residents. The letter described the serious extent of the drinking-driving problem among students and suggested a simple test for estimating degree of impairment from alcohol called the "nystagmus" test (Burns and Moskowitz 1977). The person who conducts the test places his or her forefinger about fifteen inches from the drinker's eyes. The finger is then moved slowly in an arc to the side of the person's visual field. If the drinker is intoxicated, his or her eyes will usually jerk rapidly as they try to follow the moving target. If he or she is sober, eye movement will be smooth. Research shows that the test is accurate about 75 percent of the time when the drinker's blood alcohol level is above .089gm/100 ml blood (.089%). The letter encouraged students to use the technique to test their friends before they drive.

The letter had two objectives derived from the alcohol use cycle (aside from the overall goal of reducing the incidence of drinking-driving):

1. Students would learn to use the nystagmus procedure to test each other's level of intoxication before driving.
2. Students would acquire the belief that the test is a sensitive indicator of intoxication (and therefore would choose to use it.)

The alcohol use cycle is useful because it breaks alcohol use into discrete units and thereby helps in planning and evaluating each component of an activity. In the example above, the film/discussion was (appropriately) directed at changing student beliefs related to stricter enforcement of drinking and driving laws. In a questionnaire filled out by the film audience, students generally agreed that one drink could affect driving ability, and that specific driving skills could be affected by two drinks. They also indicated that they believed driving after two drinks was potentially harmful to oneself and others, and a majority said they would attempt to stop friends from driving drunk. However, they also indicated that they would not change their own drinking and driving behaviors. In order to affect this behavior, more participatory activities were necessary.

Evaluation of the breathalyzer demonstration showed that it was successful in increasing students' awareness of their blood alcohol levels and their knowledge about the number of drinks associated with specific levels. However, breath testing did not reduce drinking and driving by those who participated in the demonstration (as compared with those who did not try the test). Nor did the breath test convince participants that they were more susceptible to arrests or accidents after drinking.

People who received the circular letter were significantly more likely to try to estimate their own level of intoxication than those who received a letter without nystagmus information. The letter also encouraged people to try the breathalyzer demonstration at parties, and 29 percent of the individuals who received the letter tried the breath test. But although the letter was successful in increasing attempts to monitor personal blood alcohol levels, students were still unlikely to use the nystagmus test on their friends. (The gap from beliefs to action cannot be covered by information alone, but must be supplemented by practice in a social setting—perhaps a party game based upon the nystagmus test.)

In their other activities around campus, class members had similar levels of success in achieving their objectives. The workshops on bartending and emergency medical techniques did teach valuable skills to a fair number of students, but the class ultimately came to the realization that any significant reduction in alcohol-related problems would take much longer to accomplish than a single semester. Consequently they set about developing a comprehensive alcohol policy statement for the university and also created an executive planning committee composed of university officials (the class itself was the working committee). Their projects were replicated and expanded by subsequent alcohol education classes, but without official university involvement the program would have had no institutional life outside the classroom (and therefore could be terminated or simply die out at any time).

Summary

Chapters 1 through 7 of this handbook were designed to show the overall process by which an alcohol program can be planned, organized, and carried out, and therefore they have been of a general nature. The remaining chapters are far more specific, because they deal with training peer educators to carry out the program; particular design considerations (how to develop objectives, how to decide on the most effective and cost-efficient strategies); and an analysis of the alcohol use cycle.

Thought Questions

1. In your own institution, are you aware of community values, norms, and traditions that may affect the attitudes of incoming students toward alcohol use?

2. Are you aware of any beliefs and attitudes of your own that may have changed as a result of these values, norms, and traditions?

3. Can you think of any innovative strategies that could be used on your campus to intervene at crucial points in the use cycle?

References

Burns, M. and H. Moskowitz. 1977. *Psychophysical Tests for DWI Arrest.* NTIS no. DOT HS 802 424. Los Angeles: Southern California Research Institute.

Fishbein, M. and I. Ajzen, 1975. *Belief, Attitudes, Intention and Behavior: An Introduction to Theory and Research.* Reading, MA: Addison-Wesley.

Maas, J. 1978. "Until I Get Caught." Film produced by the Psychology Department, Cornell University and the New York State Commission on Alcoholism. Long Beach, Calif.: Southerby Publications.

McCarty, D.; M. Poore; K.C. Mills; and S. Morrison. "Direct Mail Techniques and the Prevention of Alcohol Abuse among College Students." In press, *Journal of Studies on Alcohol.*

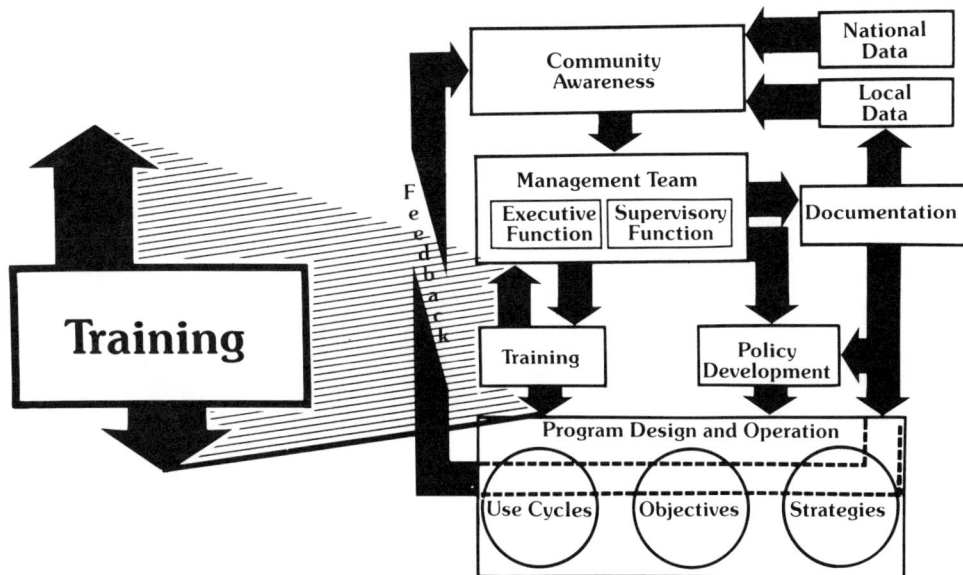

Chapter 8

DEVELOPING A TRAINING CURRICULUM

There is a story about two Indian tribes who lived on the same river, about five miles apart. The first tribe lived upstream and was a fishing community. The second tribe lived downstream and made their living farming. The upstream tribe occasionally lost some of its fishermen to the swift currents. They would be carried downstream eventually to be swept over the great waterfall. The downstream tribe, over the years, became adept at rescuing the lost fishermen and returning them to the upstream tribe. The upstream tribe, in return, would provide them with fish for use as food or fertilizer. The downstream tribe gained reputations as excellent lifesavers and good farmers. The upstream tribe earned a reputation for wet fishermen.

The lifesaving tribe put great stock over the years in training young braves to swim the river and become expert lifesavers. Their service was valuable to the welfare of both communities. It saved lives, generated income, improved public relations, and was satisfying to the participants. The upstream tribe knew how to fish well, but the tribal chiefs did not have the foresight to learn how to prevent the fishermen from falling into the river. They, too, needed a training program—perhaps on water safety.

Members of a college community who become alarmed at the increasing costs and damages of excessive alcohol use often want to rush out immediately and try to do something about the problem right away. The typical program that results from this impulse trains people to become lifesavers. Students are trained to confront other students with alcohol problems (those who have fallen in the river) and refer them to local treatment centers. The increasing number of victims brought in by the new "lifesaving" program places demands on treatment center resources, which leads to requests for increased budgets, better facilities, and more training for primary care specialists. Prevention activities are overlooked in the scramble to provide these resources for treatment of alcoholics.

Alcohol education programs are also called upon to train students in emergency techniques to treat people who have overdosed on alcohol or drugs. This concern for lifesaving training often displaces the need for comprehensive program planning and policy development. A training program can only be an effective tool for alcohol education if the training curriculum focuses on long-term campus needs as well as the more immediate (lifesaving) concerns.

In an alcohol education program committed to *problem reduction* participants must never lose sight of their role in minimizing *future* problems. The planning committee can use national and local data sources as a guide for identifying problems that have occurred in the past and are likely to occur again, and they must plan a training curriculum based on prevention of anticipated problems. A curriculum designed in this fashion teaches knowledge, skills, and techniques by which community members can intercede in the cycle and catch problems before they become unmanageable. Prevention, in other words, means not letting the fishermen fall in upstream.

A training curriculum must concentrate equally on immediate and long-term program needs. Resident advisers may need emergency medical training to save students who have become severely intoxicated, but they also need to know how to plan the semester's social activities so that problems of severe intoxication do not arise. Pledge training coordinators in fraternities need to know the local laws about drinking and driving, but they must also be aware of the role model they present to pledges with respect to excessive drinking.

Two kinds of training serve these short- and long-term needs: *management training*, which fosters growth and development of the program, and *operations training*, which concentrates on delivery of alcohol education services to the community. To some extent, this is an artificial differentiation, since there is considerable overlap between the two, but it is easier to explain them if they are examined separately.

Figure 8–1 illustrates the relationship of the two types of training to the program model. Management training deals with the organization, administration, and direction of an alcohol program. Operations training is concerned with the implementation of program strategies. Although program design and operation could be accomplished without the management superstructure, it would not insure program continuity and therefore could fail to have a long-term impact on campus alcohol problems.

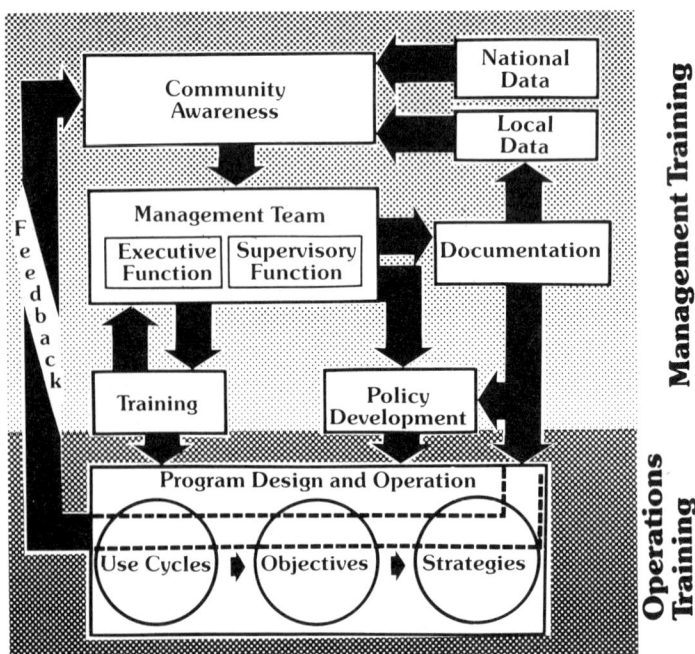

Figure 8–1. The problem-specific system: management and operations training.

The Management Team Should Be Trained To: **The Operations Team (Peer Education) Should Be Trained To:**

1. Interpret national data on student drinking for its local implications.

2. Interpret documentation of local problems to identify: the most significant problems, when and where they arise, which ones seem amenable to solution.

3. Target high-risk groups and high-risk situations in the community.

4. Select peer educators and train them to deliver services.

5. Develop written program goals.

6. Survey and analyze resources.

7. Manage the program budget.

8. Develop a network of key campus groups to help serve the program.

9. Set up formal procedures for policy development.

10. Report project successs and failures and decribe documented changes in problem indicators.

Design strategies (focusing on specific problems) that are likely to be accepted in the community, given prevailing norms, beliefs, and attitudes toward the problems and the proposed solutions.

1. Identify problems that are significant, relevant, interesting and solvable.

2. Examine the short-term and long-term manifestations of the problems and how they fit in the alcohol use cycle.

3. Write specific objectives for each project, spelling out exactly what the activity is supposed to accomplish.

4. Design activities to accomplish the objectives.

5. Carry out the activities as part of a team.

6. Evaluate the effectiveness of the activities in reaching their objectives.

7. Write reports summarizing the results.

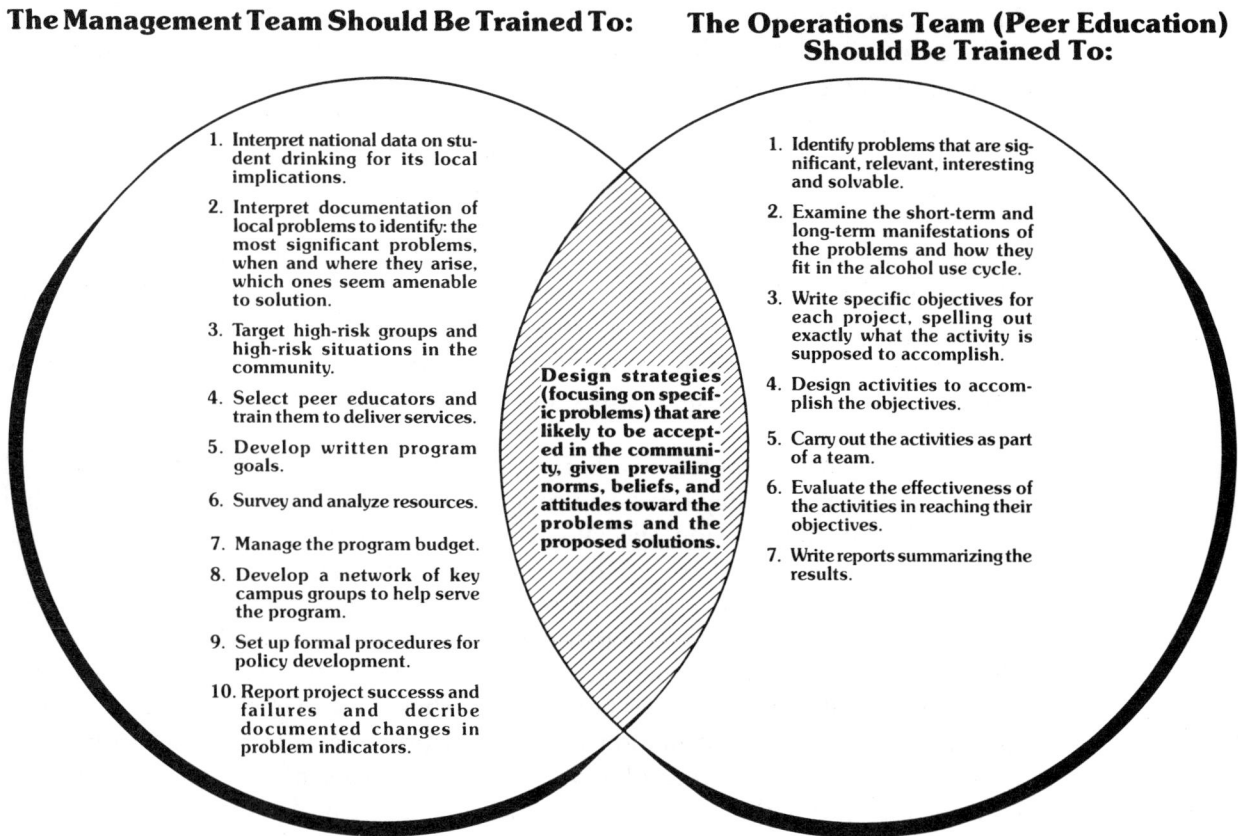

Figure 8–2. Management team roles versus operations team roles.

The overall goal of training is to provide a permanent organizational superstructure for the program so that it will not flounder after one or two years. Accordingly, the content of training exercises—especially for management functions—should consist primarily of organizational issues. A good analogy for this kind of training is found in the oriental adage: "If you give a man a fish, you feed him for one day; if you teach him to catch fish, you feed him for life." Training for management should therefore concentrate on methods for motivating volunteers, enlisting support from the power structure, budgeting, documenting problems, goal setting, and similar functions. Similarly, operations training should consist primarily of transferable implementation skills (team building, task assignment, group techniques, motivation, etc.) and secondarily of specific, service-related skills (how to demonstrate a breathalyzer, produce a poster, write an effective motivational advertisement, etc.). Figure 8–2 represents the functional relationship of the two kinds of training and the areas in which they overlap.

Management Training

The areas of responsibility of the management team are shown graphically in Figure 8–1: documentation, policy development, and training. Although it may seem paradoxical for management to train itself, the management team (see Chapter 4) must always include a few individuals with expertise in alcohol program development. These people may be health care professionals, faculty members in psychology (or related fields), individuals with experience in alcohol projects, or simply highly motivated people who have studied this book. These members of the team must train the others.

The first step in management training is teaching the system of problem-specific alcohol education. Not only must every member of the team learn the form and function of the program, they must also be convinced that it is an appropriate approach to alcohol education. This handbook should be helpful in accomplishing this phase of their training—especially the portions in which traditional methods are compared to the new approach. The assumptions on which the new method is based (Chapter 9) and the description of the distinctive nature of young adult alcohol problems (Chapter 2 and 3) should also be useful.

Once the management team is thoroughly familiar with problem-specific alcohol education and its goals, they can begin to learn the scope and nature of local alcohol problems. The documentation specialist on the Working Committee is the logical person to carry out this phase of their training. (Of course, this means that some documentation must already have been carried out, at least on a limited scale.) Appendix 8–A at the end of this chapter contains an example of the kind of report that could be used to educate the management team about local risk behaviors and risk groups. A report of this nature does not have to be based on an elaborate survey as long as it contains validated information about local drinking patterns and problems.

Appendix 8–B is a list of problems compiled by means of a simple questionnaire mailed to residence hall advisers (RAs). Since RAs must deal with student problems daily, they are an excellent source for this kind of information. Moreover, they are easy to survey because RAs are a relatively small group and usually are quite willing to respond if they feel the information will help promote solutions to these problems.

The planning committee can authorize and fund a thorough documentation at this point in the program if one has not already been made. Members of the working committee must be trained to carry out the documentation whenever it is carried out, and this task is best left to the documentation specialist on the team, since he or she can instruct the volunteers in the proper execution of the survey techniques that are being used. It is also the responsibility of this specialist to prepare one or more people to document program activities and progress. Unless the program is documented, it can neither grow nor advance, since there would be no basis for making decisions about which elements should continue and which should be terminated.

Next, the planning committee must analyze data from the local documentation to determine which problems are the most significant, how and where they arise, and which ones seem amenable to solution. From this analysis they should produce a list of the high risk groups and high risk situations that give rise to the problems. Portions of this handbook will serve as a guide in this process, especially the chapter on documentation, but team members with experience in this kind of analysis should help instruct the others on the team.

When the team has completed the task of problem identification, they can begin to formulate the program goals that will eventually be part of the policy statement. Research into previous local efforts to solve alcohol-related problems can be valuable for setting new program goals. Earlier programs may have employed strategies that worked for a while, but ended when funding ceased or when a key individual in the program left the institution. Previous policy statements may serve as a starting point for the management team as they begin to formulate a new, comprehensive statement.

National data, local data, previous programs and policies, and similar material comprise the content of the management training curriculum. But this information must be presented to the team in the context of the problem-specific system. In other words, they must be made aware of the fact that the content of the program will change over time; that current conditions, problems, and relationships in the community will not remain constant, and that they must therefore develop a flexible program that can adapt to these changes.

State and local alcohol laws are another important content area for training the management team. Not only will these laws and regulations dictate the direction of some program goals, their legal implications for the institution may convince the college administration to accept formal sponsorship of the alcohol education program. Appendix 8–C contains a summary of alcohol-related laws compiled for use in an alcohol program at a large university.

The management team must also study the existing community resources that are available to serve or supplement an alcohol education program. One or two members of the planning committee can be assigned the task of compiling a list of these resources and presenting their findings to the full committee. Since a well-chosen planning committee will represent a variety of administrative divisions and offices in the institution, each of them may have special knowledge of resources that the program can use. Examples of resources are: a university budget line for salary to pay a full-time health educator, college credit for alcohol education courses, or even the free use of a college conference center. One of the more obvious resource needs is a program budget, and it may be derived from one or many sources, depending on local conditions, organization, and accounting restraints.

Managing a budget is another skill that must be learned by members of the team. University administrative officers on the Planning Committee may have budgetary expertise, but if no one has sufficient knowledge in this area, it is imperative that an expert (such as a business professor or college budget officer) train the committee properly.

The ultimate product of management training is a formal program proposal. In addition to the supporting materials (documented problems, risk groups, laws and regulations, etc.), this document must contain recommendations to the institution's leaders for specific problem-reducing measures. This proposal is the core of the program policy statement, and both documents contain the same elements (see Chapter 6). The policy statement cannot be issued until all elements in the community have had a chance to make contributions to it, so the management team must meet with community members and help them develop a consensus on the issues. In this task the team could benefit from instruction in group dynamics and consensus-seeking techniques, and professionals in this area are usually present on college campuses (in departments of education, psychology, health, and counseling).

Finally, management training must include some instruction in techniques for mobilizing the community to participate in the program. This element of training is primarily, if not exclusively, for members of the Working Committee, since they are responsible for turning the plan into action. Most institutions have a number of experts in the fields of interpersonal communication, group motivation, and fund raising. They may be faculty members in psychology, education, or medicine, or they may be administrative personnel in the development office or in employee relations. These professionals are the logical trainers for this phase of the management curriculum, and they may even have materials already prepared to teach aspects of community mobilization. In part, the goals selected by the management team will dictate who will participate in the program and how they will contribute. If the goals emphasize raising community awareness, media campaigns to accomplish the task will require volunteers (peer educators) with skills in layout and graphics, journalism, or radio and TV announcing. If the goals require training exercises for various groups, it is necessary to recruit volunteers with expertise in the content areas needed (emergency medical training, bartending, etc.). In order to write and implement a policy statement using student input, people in student government, the campus legal office, and the interfraternity council could make available contributions.

In addition to the members of the management team, other individuals could receive management training if it would help implement the program. For example, area government officers in residence halls, faculty advisers to fraternal organizations, or campus security officers might promote the program better if they were included in management training.

There is a danger in using "experts" to train and staff the management team: frequently, professionals in specialized fields are biased toward particular strategies for problem reduction. These biases have often been responsible for the intuitively based programs of the past (see Chapter 1). Professional counselors, for example, may wish only to train students to identify and confront students with severe alcohol problems in order to get them into a counseling center. Public relations experts on the college staff may advocate elaborate media campaigns, and physicians may push for expanded alcoholic treatment facilities on campus. If these single-strategy advocates prevent the development of a multiple-strategy program, they have performed a disservice to the institution.

Generally, programs staffed by people with a wide range of skills are more likely to achieve program goals. The management team should be broadly based, composed of a cross section of the college community from trustees to students. Indeed, student participation is vital.

Operations Training

Operations training prepares student volunteers to carry out program services. In other words, they are trained to become *peer educators*. The term "educator" is here used in its broadest sense, that is, "one who conveys knowledge." Few traditional teaching methods are employed in most alcohol projects. More importantly, peer educators not only "educate" they also lead by example. They serve as role models for other students, and this function is just as important as the instructional part of their job. Indeed, it is doubtful whether beliefs and attitudes can be changed except through peer role modeling.

As with management training, operations training should emphasize process rather than content whenever possible. Teaching peer educators solely to produce workshops, for example, is a poor technique. In the first place, even if the workshops are effective, they are appropriate only for certain kinds of program objectives and they may not be as cost-effective as other strategies. Moreover, the universe of problems will not be affected by attention to the areas covered by workshops. If peers are trained to produce a variety of strategies, the program stands a much higher chance of success.

A training program must also emphasize the development of unique and innovative strategies to reduce problems. Strategies are limited only by the creativity of the peer educators—for example, a nonprofit, nonalcoholic pub in a residence hall basement was a very successful strategy at one college, and a T-shirt media campaign was successful at another college. In both cases, the projects were the products of the students' imagination and creativity. They thought up the strategies, and then learned how to carry them out. They were enthusiastic about the projects because they had developed the ideas themselves, and the student body in each locale responded well because the ideas were new and tailored to their local preferences and lifestyles.

Finally, peer training, like every other aspect of the alcohol program, must center around documented local problems. Some training programs provide a panoramic survey of alcohol information without putting it into a relevant problem context. For example, reams of information on the metabolism of alcohol are useless unless the trainee understands the implications of that data for determining an ovedose.

Program planners should be sensitive to another, often overlooked, aspect of peer training: personal growth and development of the peers. If their training is relevant to their everyday lives, and if it promotes development of their interpersonal skills, they will participate more wholeheartedly and the program will also grow and prosper. The connection between alcohol training and real life problems must therefore be made very clear to the trainees. Every training exercise should be designed around a particular problem area.

Training formats will vary with local conditions. In some institutions, peers have been trained in alcohol education classes (for which they earned college credit); in others, they have been prepared for their jobs in a series of short workshops supplemented by textual materials. Classroom training has several advantages: the instruction can be more complete and more systematic, and learning is rewarded with college credit.

Whichever format is used, the training method must be participatory. Most college instruction is carried out in nonparticipatory fashion; the students sit passively in a classroom and listen to the instructor talk about the subject. Course content tends to be heavily factual, and tests tend to measure factual recall. Peer training must not use this traditional method . Students should actively participate in the learning process, so the trainer's task is to design learning experiences that require the trainees' involvement. Factual information about alcohol can be learned individually (the last six chapters of this handbook are designed for individual learning); program skills and techniques should be experienced collectively. This experiential model implies the use of group learning techniques: discussions, "brainstorming," forcefield analysis, team building, and similar exercises. It would be best if the program could enlist the services of a faculty member or an interested graduate student with expertise in group dynamics; otherwise, there are a number of good sources from which training exercises could be developed. The bibliography at the end of this chapter contains a list of books that would be helpful in training peer educators, and incidentally, for designing participatory strategies for the program itself (games, simulations, role playing, etc.). Table 8–1 is an example of a short curriculum actually used in a university to introduce peer educators to the campus alcohol program.

Table 8–2 contains a list of objectives for peer training that can be used as a guide in setting up a training curriculum (modified, where necessary, to suit local conditions).

Table 8–1. A Four-Part Training Curriculum for Peer Educators/Students

I.   *First Week:* Introduction to alcohol-related problems in the community.
  1. Exercise in identifying feelings (may range from negative to positive) about alcohol-related problems.
  2. Group-building exercise.
  3. Brainstorming. Subject: groups that interact with the university, on and off campus.

II. *Second Week:* The university as part of a community.
  1. Ice-breaking exercise: get acquainted with each other and with guest speakers.
  2. Guest speakers (dean of students, vice-chancellor, university lawyer, chief of police, mayor, head of campus security): each has five minutes to give individual perspective on the problem.
  3. Questions to speakers:
    a. What led up to the positions they took?
    b. What are the responsibilities of community members?
    c. How does the university relate to the community?
    d. Law enforcement problems; what led to the problems, who is involved, etc.?
    e. Specifics of the laws and the implications for students.
  4. Group discussion following departure of speakers: What are the most significant problems uncovered in the meeting?

III. *Third Week:* Alcohol and the college campus.
  1. Group problem-solving activity: participants identify campus alcohol problems, suggest nominal solutions.
  2. Speaker: factual presentation of campus alcohol survey results.
  3. Speaker: description of the problem-specific approach to alcohol education.
  4. Questions and discussion: Problems uncovered by the survey; problem-specific approach to solutions.

IV. *Fourth Week:* Problems
  1. Movie "Until I Get Caught"
  2. Student legal aid service speaker
  3. Breathalyzer demonstration and impairment tests
  4. Discussion: dealing with attitudes and beliefs.

Source: Adapted from a curriculum by Lucie Minuto, Health Education Division, Student Health Service, University of North Carolina at Chapel Hill, 1981.

Table 8–2. Training Objectives for Peer Educators

Program Design Component	*Peer Educators Must Be Able to:*
Documentation of Problems	*Identify* places, events, and groups associated with problem occurrence. *Describe* community problems to community members. *Define* problems which community members agree are unacceptable.
Policy Development	*Assist* community members in reaching consensus on a community alcohol policy. *Seek out* a network of supporting programs and key people.
Program Design and Operation	*Analyze* community alcohol problems in terms of the alcohol use cycle. *Devise* objectives to reduce specific problems in specific areas. *Choose* target levels for problem reduction. *Communicate* objectives to the community. *Design* strategies, based on the objectives, to reduce problem levels. *Implement* strategies.
Documentation of Program	*Record* program activities as they occur. *Solicit* feedback from community members about program activities. *Measure* success of strategies against target levels. *Report* results of program to community members. *Revise* program objectives and strategies, based on evaluation of success or failure of parts of the program.

For example, students who help collect local data on alcohol problems can assist their peers in the interpretation of the information in order to single out problems for solution. Different teams of students can concentrate on different problems. They should be guided in this exercise by a trainer familiar with documentation and analysis. Similarly, the trainer can facilitate their analysis of the short- and long-term manifestations of their chosen problems and how these problems fit into the alcohol use cycle.

The succeeding chapters in this handbook can be used as a guide for trainees in writing objectives, choosing strategies, and evaluating results. A trainer who is thoroughly familiar with the problem-specific system can develop exercises to assist the operations team in learning how to carry out these tasks.

Part of the training curriculum is the actual experience of implementing the strategies they have developed—negotiating with the target audience, insuring attendance and participation, and modifying the activity to make it more effective. Once again, the trainer can be available as a "resource person," but the trainees must learn by doing, even if that means making a few mistakes. The satisfaction they will get from doing a job themselves will foster continued interest in the program.

Programs in which college students are allowed to take the initiative in creating their own strategies produce both high quality projects and excellent results. Peer educators suddenly become managers, artists, legal advisors, audiovisual technicians, editors, journalists, and local politicians. It is not uncommon for students in these programs to remark that the experience was the most exciting and valuable part of their entire college education.

Operations trainees need to be familiar with the overall structure of the alcohol program so they will understand where they fit in the organization and how their efforts will advance the program's goals. The previous chapters in this book should be helpful in providing such an overview. The remaining chapters supply some essential information about alcohol education techniques and an exposition of the alcohol use cycle (which contains factual content regarding alcohol and its biological and behavioral properties). The chapters on technique are useful for trainers as well as trainees, and contain examples of strategies that can be adapted to local conditions. The self-instructional units (Chapters 14 through 19) on the alcohol use cycle are a minicurriculum of alcohol information. They can be used individually or can be supplemented by group training exercises.

Thought Questions

Training requires the services of people with expertise in evaluation, education, business, law, organizational development, and other disciplines mentioned in this chapter. Can you think of individuals on your campus who could fill these training roles?

Books on Group Learning Experiences

Bertcher, H., and J. Gordon. 1972. *Techniques of Group Leadership*. Ann Arbor: Manpower Science Services.

Chesler, M., and R. Fox. 1966. *Role-Playing Methods in the Classroom*. Chicago: Science Research Associates.

Hill, W.F. 1969. *Learning Thru Discussion*. Beverly Hills, CA: Sage Publications.

Horn, R.E., ed. 1977. *The Guide to Simulations/Games for Education and Training*, 3rd ed. Cranford, NJ: Didactic Systems, Inc.

Livingston, S.A., and C.S. Stoll. 1973. *Simulations Games*. New York: Free Press.

Maier, N.R.F. 1963. *Problem-Solving Discussions and Conferences*. New York: McGraw-Hill.

Olmstead, J.A. 1974. *Small-Group Instruction*. Alexandria, VA: Human Resources Research Organization.

Sharan, S., and Y. Sharan. 1976. *Small-Group Teaching*. Englewood Cliffs, NJ: Educational Technology Publications.

Stadsklev, R. 1975. *Handbook of Simulation Gaming in Social Education* (2 vols.). Tuscaloosa, AL: Institute of Higher Education Research and Services, University of Alabama.

Stanford, G., and A. Roark. 1974. *Human Interaction in Education*. Boston: Allyn and Bacon.

APPENDIX 8–A

Student Drinking at the University of North Carolina, Chapel Hill

To assess the extent of student drinking and alcohol-related problems at the University of North Carolina; Chapel Hill, a Student Alcohol Survey was mailed to a sample of 658 full-time undergraduates; 465 students responded to the survey.

METHODS

Data on alcohol use were examined to identify the distribution of drinkers and nondrinkers. Students who drank were classified as light, moderate, or heavy drinkers. Each type of beverage (beer, wine, and liquor), received attention as a source for group differences in consumption.

Respondents were asked to indicate, for the four-week period prior to the survey: 1) the frequency with which they drank beer, wine, and liquor; 2) the amount of each beverage usually consumed at one time; 3) the maximum amount of each beverage consumed at one time; and 4) the frequency with which they drank the maximum amounts reported. One beer was defined as containing 12 ounces, one glass of wine as 4 ounces, and one drink of liquor as 1.5 ounces of distilled spirits.

Students were classified as nondrinkers if they indicated that they did not consume alcohol during the month prior to the survey. Fourteen percent of the sample were not drinkers and 86 percent consumed alcohol in the month before the survey. Light drinkers represented 21.4 percent of the sample and drank between one and ten alcoholic drinks per month. Almost 38 percent of the students were classed as moderate drinkers. They drank between eleven and fifty-five drinks per month. Students who consumed more than fifty-six drinks in the month before the survey were considered heavy drinkers (26.8 percent of the sample).

RESULTS

The results indicate that students within different subgroups exhibit different drinking patterns. For example, members of fraternities and sororities are

Source: McCarty, D. 1980. *Student Alcohol Survey*. Chapel Hill: University of North Carolina Center for Alcohol Studies.

unlikely to be nondrinkers or light drinkers. Instead, almost half of the Greek affiliates are heavy drinkers. Similarly, males are more likely than females to be heavy drinkers. As class standing increases, the proportion of abstainers declines, and the proportion of the respondents categorized as heavy drinkers increases.

The consumption data also indicate that UNC men and women differed considerabley in alcohol consumption patterns. While only 27 percent of the men were nondrinkers or light drinkers, 42 percent of the women fell into this category. More alcohol-related problems were found among men even after differences in consumption were controlled. Men were especially likely to drink and drive.

The Student Alcohol Survey also asked students to indicate how frequently students drank in various social contexts, for example, a bar in town, a residence hall party, in a restaurant, in a fraternity house, and in their parents' home. Males reported drinking more frequently than females in all of the social contexts except restaurants. Class standing had a significant effect on the frequency with which drinking occurred in two social contexts; a residence hall party and an off-campus apartment. Freshmen drank more frequently at residence hall parties while upperclassmen drank more frequently at off-campus apartments. The finding reflects the fact that freshmen are required to live in residence halls while many upperclassmen live off-campus.

Analyses suggested that students who drink heavily drink in more places. The two contexts that seem to be most frequently associated with alcohol use and problems are bars and driving.

ALCOHOL-RELATED PROBLEMS EXPERIENCED BY UNC STUDENTS

In the Student Alcohol Survey, respondents were asked to indicate the number of times during the four weeks prior to the administration of the survey they had experienced each of the following ten alcohol-related problems: 1) hangover; 2) feeling nauseous or vomiting from drinking; 3) driving after several drinks; 4) drinking while driving; 5) missing classes because of a hangover; 6) passing out from drinking too much; 7) being criticized for drinking too much; 8) getting into a fight after drinking; 9) injuring self or others while drinking; and 10) not remembering what happened while drinking.

Analyses determined first whether the number of problems experienced varied by sex, fraternal affiliation, class standing, or place of residence. Importantly, males experienced more alcohol-related problems than females, and members of Greek organizations had problems more frequently than nonmembers. Respondents who lived off-campus experienced more alcohol-related problems than North Campus or South Campus residents, and seniors had a significantly higher frequency of problem occurrences than sophomores.

The Student Alcohol Survey also contained two items on the extent to which respondents have observed others experiencing alcohol-related problems. The first item asked students to indicate the number of times in the last four weeks they helped a friend who became sick from drinking. A higher proportion of fraternity or sorority members (40 percent) than nonmembers (26 percent) reported the experience. No significant differences were found by sex, class standing, or place of residence. The second item asked respondents to indicate the number of items in the four weeks prior to the survey that they observed drunk students damage property. Forty-seven percent (47 percent) of the respondents who lived in residence halls and half of the fraternity or sorority members had observed intoxicated students damage property.

APPENDIX 8–B

Summary of Problems Related to Alcohol Observed by Residence Advisers

General
—Roommate conflicts, fights
—Noise
—Litter
—Vandalism, property damage

Individual:
—Depression
—Decreased ability to function academically and socially
—Decreased self-esteem
—Inferior, unhealthy diet
—Mental health problems
—Weight problems
—Unplanned intercourse or pregnancies
—Vomiting due to excess alcohol consumption
—Use of alcohol to "solve" personal problems

Contributing Factors:
—Lack of social alternatives to drinking.
—Party atmosphere during orientation induces new students to believe they can play hard and study hard without negative consequences.
—Professors who drink heavily serve as poor role models.
—Fraternities sponsoring alcohol-centered parties and thereby promoting the belief that alcohol is a prerequisite for having fun.
—Lack of knowledge about referral and treatment services available for students with severe problems.

APPENDIX 8–C

Some Basic Facts and Laws About Alcohol Use in North Carolina

The purchase, transportation, possession, and consumption of liquor is regulated by state statutes and local ordinances. To understand North Carolina's laws it is essential to keep these definitions in mind:

Malt beverage—beer, ale, malt liquor and other brewed beverages with no more than 5 percent alcohol by weight (which is just over 6 percent by volume).

Unfortified wine—wine produced by natural fermentation, which means that its alcoholic content will not exceed 14 percent.

Fortified wine—wine that has had its natural alcoholic content supplemented by the addition of liquor. Fortified wine has an alcoholic content of 14 to 21 percent. Sherry is a fortified wine (champagne is unfortified); so are brands such as Thunderbird and Twenty-Twenty, most of which are 19 or 20 percent alcohol.

Spirituous liquor—distilled spirits, containing over 21 percent alcohol. This includes whiskey, rum, vodka, gin, and all the other "hard liquors." The alcoholic content can be figured by taking half the "proof"; a bottle that says 80 proof means that the product is 40 percent alcohol.

North Carolina's statutes are written so that the term "alcoholic beverage" applies only to liquors containing more than 14 percent alcohol; in other words, the only alcoholic beverages are fortified wine and spirituous liquor. Beer and unfortfied wine are not classified as alcoholic beverages and laws that apply to alcoholic beverages—such as the statute prohibiting display of alcoholic beverages at athletic contests—do not apply to beer and unfortified wine. Generally the rules on purchase, possession, consumption, and transportation of alcoholic beverages are much stricter than those for beer and unfortified wine. Some of the most important provisions of North Carolina law are:

Source: *Alcohol Use Guidelines in the University Community.* Campus Alcohol Education Service, University of North Carolina at Chapel Hill, November, 1980.

1. No liquor of any kind may be sold without a permit from the State Alcohol Beverage Control Board. Charging an admission fee to an event and then "giving away" liquor is obviously a form of selling liquor.

2. Only people eighteen years and older may buy or possess beer and unfortified wine.

3. Only people twenty-one years and older may buy or possess alcoholic beverages; that is, fortified wine and spirituous liquor. The same age limit applies for mixed drinks.

4. It is unlawful to assist someone underage in buying liquor. It is also unlawful to give liquor to someone underage. Allowing someone else to use an ID card is obviously a form of assisting.

Alcoholic beverages—fortified wine and spirituous liquor—may only be possessed in certain places and then only in limited amounts. Possession or consumption anywhere else is unlawful. Generally, a person twenty-one or older may possess alcoholic beverages in 1) his or her home (which would include a residence hall room) or secondary residence (such as a rented motel room); 2) a private club with a "social establishment" permit; and 3) a restaurant with a brown-bagging permit. In each of those places the amount that may be legally possessed is limited to four liters (just over a gallon). The four-liter limit does not apply, though, to "special occasions," which would include a party. For the student, usually the only place where he or she can legally possess alcoholic beverages will be his or her residence hall room, apartment, or other residence. With the permission of the owner, a student might also have alcoholic beverages at some other noncommercial establishment, such as a fraternity having a party. Any drinking of alcoholic beverages at football games or on sidewalks or other public places is clearly against the law.

The laws on beer and unfortified wine are much less strict. State law generally allows the possession and consumption of beer and unfortified wine anyplace. However, the town of Chapel Hill has a local ordinance restricting drinking beer and unfortified wine on town-owned property. That ordinance does not apply to university property since it is not owned by the town, but it does apply at city parks and on most city streets and sidewalks. The ordinance prohibits drinking beer; simple possession is not against the law. As long as the beer is for one's own use and not for sale, the amount that can be possessed is unrestricted.

Only four liters of alcoholic beverage may be transported in a car at one time without a special permit. If the bottle has been opened, the alcoholic beverage must be put in the trunk of the car. The four-liter limit applies to the car; it is four liters per car, not per passenger.

There are some limits on how much wine can be transported but they are not very strict (five gallons without a permit). A person can transport as much beer as he or she wants, but if it is over eighty liters—more than nine cases and nine 12-ounce cans, or more than seven cases and one 16-ounce can—there is a presumption in the law that he or she has it for purposes of resale, which is against the law without a permit. If indeed the beer is possessed for the person's own use, the person can have as much as he or she wants. The presumption about sale does not apply if the beer is draft beer in kegs. Although a person can transport more than eighty liters of beer, that is all a store can sell to one person at one time, unless it is draft beer in kegs.

This summary only tells what the law says. People who own or control property can add their own restrictions on the use of liquor. Thus, for example, the university might adopt rules to prohibit possession of liquor in certain places, such as a prohibition against having beer in the gymnasium. A student who breaks one of these rules is not committing a crime, but is subject to university disciplinary procedures.

Use of liquor can, of course, also result in other behavior that is against the law. In North Carolina it is a misdemeanor to be drunk and disruptive in a public place. For that statute, "public place" is broadly defined to include any place that is open to the public, even if it is privately owned. Thus it is a violation of that law to be drunk and disruptive in a residence hall, bar, parking lot, or similar place.

Another common offense associated with drinking is driving under the influence (DUI). North Carolina makes that offense a misdemeanor and provides that drivers lose their licenses if convicted or if they refuse to take the breathalyzer test after being arrested. Another similar crime is driving with a blood alcohol level of .10 or more. For that crime, also a misdemeanor, it is not necessary to show that the driver was under the influence, only that he or she had a high blood alcohol level.

North Carolina's liquor law is sometimes complicated and hard to remember. The student should remember more than anything else that alcoholic beverages—fortified wine and spirituous liquor—are tightly regulated and that they may be possessed and consumed only at places named in the law. The rules are more liberal for beer and unfortified wine.

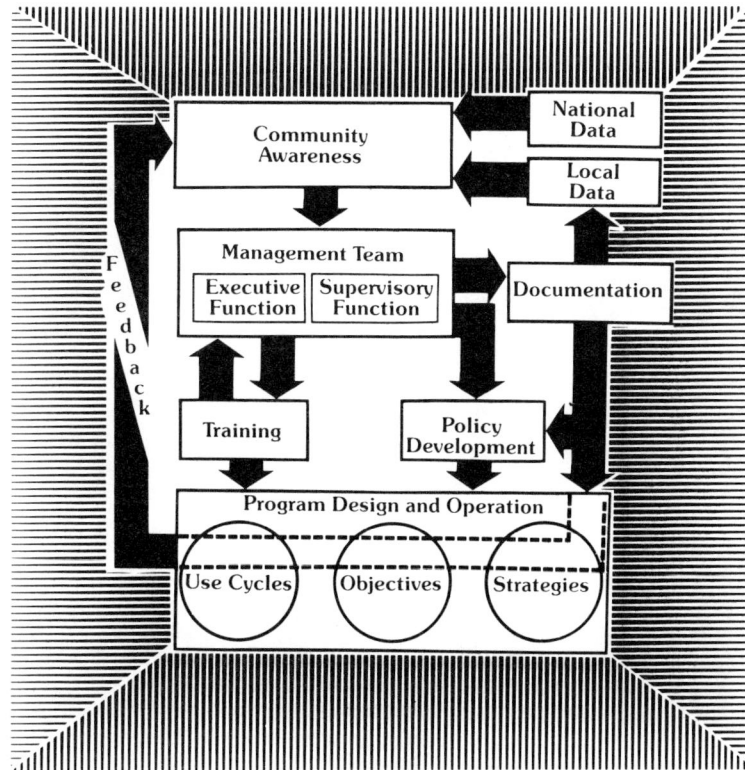

Chapter 9

ASSUMPTIONS OF THE PROBLEM-SPECIFIC APPROACH

When you have finished this chapter, you should be able to:

1. List the six assumptions of the problem-specific approach to alcohol education; and
2. Describe the implications of each assumption for alcohol program planners.

Assumptions are operative beliefs about how things work. Scientists' assumptions are first stated as theories ("the theory of relativity"), and if the assumptions are proven to occur with predictable regularity, they are stated as law ("the law of gravity"). In everyday life our behavior is based on assumptions we make about social relations and the expected behavior of others. We assume that if we treat our friends and associates fairly, they will treat us fairly. We assume that people will ordinarily not behave in a bizarre or uncharacteristic fashion. Alcohol educators cannot state their assumptions as scientific laws, because the social and psychological sciences are not that advanced. However, alcohol educators can operate their programs on the basis of logical assumptions about patterns of human interaction, behavior, and learning.

Six assumptions of the problem-specific approach to alcohol education are outlined in this chapter. An explanation follows each assumption statement, including implications for designing alcohol programs. Assumptions are made regarding:

1. The origins of community alcohol problems;
2. Problem-reduction as a function of decreased consumption;
3. The consensual nature of the process of solution seeking;
4. The function of the minor consequences of alcohol use in attitude formation;
5. The accumulation of risk following repeated patterns of intoxication; and
6. The context-related nature of alcohol problems.

ASSUMPTION 1: *Community alcohol problems are the product of the norms, values, and traditions of the community and the drinking environment in which these elements operate.*

Alcohol programs have traditionally centered on problems associated with individual "abuse" and have tried to solve those problems by promoting "responsible use." Community alcohol problems are not the product of deviant behavior by a few individuals, they are the result of collective behavior and therefore must be solved collectively.

A community approach to alcohol problem management assumes that all the citizens of a community are responsible for the problems and for their solution. Program goals targeted on individual behavior are often not related to the problems experienced by the community as a whole and are not likely to reduce communitywide problems. Rather than beginning with individual problems as a basis for treating

135

community problems, alcohol program planners should carefully document community problems and help the community's citizens develop their own solutions.

Individual problems are a legitimate concern for alcohol educators, and most alcohol programs contain some provision for dealing with them (referral and treatment services), but these problems should not be the primary concern of a *community* alcohol program. Program planners should think in terms of "we" statements instead of "you" statements: "*We* have a problem with drinking drivers," not "*You* are a problem because you drink and drive."

ASSUMPTION 2: *Problem levels within a community increase directly with increased consumption levels, therefore reducing consumption should replace problems.*

Social research studies have demonstrated that groups of heavy drinkers experience more problems than groups of moderate drinkers, and moderate drinkers have more problems than groups of light drinkers or abstainers. The direct relationship between increased drinking and increased problems is a statistical fact when measured over groups: for a given individual within a drinking group, however, this relationship may not apply. A group may be collectively aware of problems shared by the group, but an individual member may not feel that these problems are relevant to his or her own life.

Two implications for program planners can be derived from this assumption. First, program messages must be directed at groups, addressing their collective awareness of alcohol-related problems; program activities must involve the groups that are experiencing problems in order to stimulate group solutions. Second, alcohol program planners should attempt to shift the group drinking norm down the scale, from heavy to moderate, from moderate to light, in order to reduce problem levels. These two principles are illustrated graphically in Figure 9–1.

ASSUMPTION 3: *Community solutions to alcohol-related problems can only be derived consensually, which means that all interest groups must be involved in the solution-seeking process.*

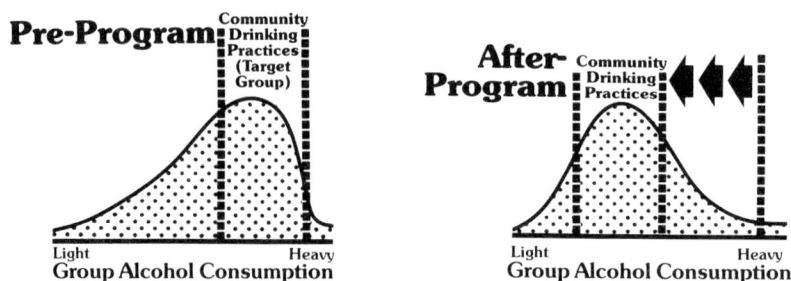

Figure 9–1. The goal of a program.

Community change is only possible if all levels of the community participate and reach agreement on the change. If any group is left out of the decisionmaking process, the result may be conflict, polarization of the community, and ultimately the failure of the proposed change. For an alcohol program to be successful, all levels of authority and all interest groups in the community must be represented in the program. Failure to involve the university administration in a campus program will mean loss of indispensable support and will ultimately limit both the effectiveness and life span of the program. Failure to include social and fraternal organizations implies an "us-versus-them" attitude that poisons the atmosphere and makes cooperation difficult or impossible.

ASSUMPTION 4: *Minor consequences resulting from moderate drinking usually shape one's beliefs and attitudes toward alcohol, even after consumption is no longer moderate.*

Our beliefs about the consequences of consuming five or six drinks may be based on our experience with one or two drinks, but the consequences are different. In this situation the drinker may behave like the patient who, upon taking the prescribed dose of medicine for an ailment, feels so much better that he decides to take three times the prescribed dose next time. In both cases, the results are unpredictable.

The assumption provides two objectives for the educator: 1) to raise the awareness of the target population to the more subtle influences of drinking on behavior (the minor consequences); and 2) to use the "minor consequences" principle to explain the formation of beliefs and attitudes toward alcohol. These goals could be achieved by an analysis of the situations or contexts in which we drink, a discussion of the positive and negative consequences of drinking, and explanation of the reasons alcohol use seems to create strongly held beliefs.

Assumption 4 shifts the educational emphasis away from the severe and chronic drinking problems shared by a small proportion of the population. These problems may be of little interest or importance to college students since most of them do not have problems of this magnitude themselves. Moreover, scientific studies indicate that minor consequences may not inevitably lead to major problems with alcohol. Minor problems are in themselves appropriate points around which a meaningful discussion about drinking can center.

ASSUMPTION 5: *The biological, behavioral, and social consequences that follow repeated patterns of intoxication accumulate gradually, and drinkers are usually unaware of the mounting risk.*

Intoxication is the drug effect produced by consuming alcohol and has biological, behavioral, and social consequences. Though intoxication may not be the original goal of the drinker, it is an immediate consequence of drinking. The consequences of intoxication in turn are governed by a variety of forces that are not readily apparent to the drinker. An understanding of alcohol use depends on an understanding of the continual and repetitive interaction between the effects of alcohol and patterns of drinking behavior. Community alcohol education programs attempt to increase awareness of the unanticipated consequences of alcohol use. Discussion groups, workshops, media campaigns, pamphlets, and so forth, can supply information about the subtle and cumulative effects of patterns of drinking.

ASSUMPTION 6: *The risk of alcohol-related problems increases with the number of situations (contexts) in which alcohol is consumed.*

Problems that result from alcohol use can occur in any number of commonplace settings: driving a car, riding a commuter train, cooking, walking up or down stairs, or even in the bath. Multiplying alcohol's drug effect (intoxication) by the number of settings increases the risk. The risk is even greater when drinkers combine physical activity and drinking.

By describing "high risk" and "low risk" situations, the peer educator can help students understand the degree to which the use of alcohol is context related. For example, a group discussion of the situations in which drinking usually occurs can lead to group suggestions about alternatives to alcohol in those situations. These group-generated alternatives can help avoid context-related consumption and thereby decrease the risk of problems.

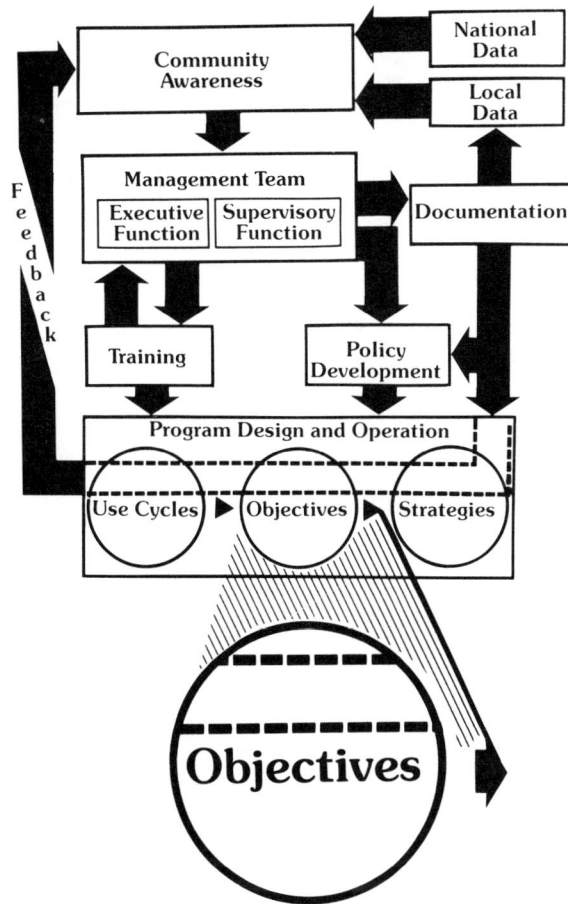

Chapter 10

GOALS AND OBJECTIVES

Most people think of learning purely in terms of mastery of factual information through memorization, translation, extrapolation, and similar *cognitive* processes. However, learning also includes the development of new values, attitudes, and beliefs through individual and group experiences. It is on this *affective* side of learning that alcohol educators must concentrate. This chapter outlines principles to help develop affective and cognitive objectives for alcohol programs.

There are a number of important reasons for writing goals and objectives before embarking on program activities. First, by specifying exactly what you wish to accomplish, you can choose strategies more intelligently. Second, written aims can be discussed and critiqued by the peers responsible for implementing them, thereby providing a double check on both the validity of the objectives and the appropriateness of the proposed strategies. Third, the achievement of specific aims can be measured with accuracy, which is an important basis for decisions about whether to continue or to discontinue the strategies. If program goals and objectives are unwritten or stated imprecisely, measurement is often impossible. There are a number of books that describe the methods for writing behavioral objectives, and if you are interested in more detailed information, see the books listed at the end of the chapter.

In everyday language the terms "goals" and "objectives" are used interchangeably, but in education these words have fairly specific and exclusive meanings. A goal is an overall target: "learning anatomy" and "mastering conversational French" are *goals*. Objectives are more precise and are normally in terms of behavioral performance: "correctly naming the bones in the wrist" and "using twenty idiomatic expressions correctly in French conversation" are *objectives*. Notice that these objectives can be measured through testing or observation of behavior. Goals are more difficult to evaluate because of their more general nature, and their measurement usually requires broad instrumentation. If the specific objectives under each goal are achieved, it is likely that the goal has also been reached.

In alcohol education, a typical program could have several goals derived from documented problems—"reducing drinking and driving by students," "reducing the number of campus parties devoted exclusively to drinking," and "reducing confusion about laws and regulations affecting student drinking" are examples of alcohol program goals. In order to reach those goals program planners must first develop specific, measurable objectives for each one. For example, the goal "reducing the number of campus parties devoted exclusively to drinking" (derived from documented incidents of property damage and medical emergencies associated with these parties) may be achieved through several program objectives: 1) increase the number and variety of beverages served at campus parties; 2) increase nonalcoholic alternatives for parties; and 3) promote the practice of serving food with alcoholic beverages.

Several strategies can be designed for each objective. The objective "increasing the number and variety of beverages served at campus parties" could involve 1) distributing an information booklet on party planning using alternative beverages; 2) training social chairpersons in residence halls, fraternities, and sororities in alternative party planning; and 3) developing a consensual campus policy about party guidelines. The next chapter deals specifically with strategy selection, but as a general rule strategies should conform to local needs, politics, and traditions (and therefore must be generated locally in order to take these elements into account).

One of the primary aims of an alcohol program is to change community values, norms, and traditions and individual beliefs and attitudes regarding drinking. Although there are many ways to accomplish these affective goals, the most effective methods are *experiential* (group activities, individual experiences, in-service training, etc.) and emphasize *positive, motivational* methods (working within the social group or organization, not labeling individuals or groups as "abusers" or using other pejorative terms, developing consensual solutions with tangible rewards, etc.).

Although alcohol programs must also provide factual information about alcohol (information relevant to local needs), the simple acquisition of knowledge about alcohol will not alter drinking behavior. If information alone were sufficient to change behavior, few people today would smoke, take drugs, overeat, or engage in any number of other health-imperiling behaviors.

The alcohol use cycle, which was introduced in Chapter 7, provides a convenient framework through which one may analyze and interpret documented problems and develop objectives to reduce problem levels. Figures 7–1 and 7–2 will help you review the components of the cycle and its application in the development of program objectives and strategies. Some specific examples of the process will help clarify its application to real problems.

Problem.   On a survey, 50 percent of fraternity members reported driving regularly while intoxicated. Local police records showed that the incidence of alcohol-related accidents among students had doubled over the last three years. With reference to the alcohol use cycle, this problem can be explained by 1) community values and norms that sanction the behavior (no one will try to prevent an individual from driving drunk), and 2) individual beliefs and attitudes developed through experience and through the acceptance of community norms (if a person has driven repeatedly "successfully" while intoxicated, he or she will continue to do it, particularly if it is an acceptable behavior in one's social group).

Goal.   Reduce the incidence of drinking and driving among fraternity members. (Since the survey provided a baseline figure of 50 percent, a second survey given after program activities should show a reduction in that figure.)

Objectives.   By the end of the project, fraternity members should be able to:
1. Describe the nature and extent of the problem to the fraternity leadership. (Possible strategies could include giving formal presentations of survey data to the interfraternity council or mailing letters to the officers of each fraternity with individual follow-up visits.)

2. Provide peer-group support for preventing intoxicated fraternity brothers from driving. (Strategies: Offering participatory workshops at each fraternity (sanctioned by officers) to discuss the problem and to demonstrate practical ways to prevent drunken friends from driving. Conducting workshops at sorority houses on the same subjects, since fraternity dates must also support the idea.)

3. Explain the financial, legal, and personal implications of driving while drunk. (Strategies: Distributing information leaflets, posters, and broadcasting public service announcements on local radio stations. Providing participatory workshops using special films to trigger discussion.)

Evaluation.   Each of the objectives could be evaluated by means of a survey questionnaire. The achievement of the goal would ultimately be reflected in local arrest and accident statistics.

Notice that these objectives used active, behavioral verbs: *describe, provide, explain.* These words clearly suggest certain kinds of activities and just as clearly eliminate others: to "provide support" for something among members of a group, group activities must be employed. In this example, as in most programs, a combination of affective and cognitive objectives was necessary to accomplish the goal ("describe" and "explain" are cognitive; "provide support" is affective), but they were used in conjunction to support and strengthen each other. When fraternity leaders can describe the nature and extent of the problem, one has raised their awareness of the problem and its effect on their membership and the campus community, which in turn makes them willing to support the other activities in the project.

Problem.   After every football or basketball game the emergency room of the student health service has twenty to thirty patients suffering from traumatic injuries (sprained ankles, broken limbs, concussions, cuts, scrapes, and burns) resulting from intoxication. Referring to the alcohol use cycle, these unanticipated consequences of drinking can be traced to the college's tradition of drinking at sporting events (although the practice is illegal) and to celebrate victories or defeats. Often, students do not intend to drink as much as they do, but the community traditions and drinking practices seem to dictate overindulgence.

Goal.   Reduce the number of student injuries resulting from drinking during and after weekend sporting events.

Objectives.   Through the leadership of peer educators, students will:
1. Develop "new traditions" to celebrate sports victories and exorcise defeats. (Possible strategies: Sponsoring celebrations such as bonfires, rallies, and parades that do not center on alcohol. Interviewing sports heroes on campus radio to promote the "new traditions." Using media to promote a new campus image different from the old alcohol-centered image.)

2. Develop a consensual campus policy in support of the ban on drinking at sporting events. (Strategies: Holding discussions with all concerned groups, coordinating their decisions and publishing the result. Alerting students to the new policy through the campus media.)

3. Promote security measures to enforce the ban on drinking at sporting events. (Strategies: Training campus security officers in nonconfrontational techniques for

preventing students with alcohol from entering the stadium. Informing students and alumni about the new security measures; sponsoring meetings in residence halls to discuss the implications for students.)

4. Develop party guidelines with social committees/chairpersons to reduce the number of alcohol-centered parties. (Strategies: Informing social chairpersons about the nature and extent of the problem and soliciting their ideas about party guidelines through group meetings. Providing examples of party guidelines from other campuses. Sponsoring parties that demonstrate positive alternatives to the alcohol-centered party.)

Evaluation.   Attendance at the events in Objective 1 would provide an immediate measure of impact, but a more significant indicator of success would be the repetition of these events over the years (and the willingness of other campus groups to sponsor them). Objective 2 should result in a published policy based on input from all concerned groups. Objective 3 should ultimately result in a reduction of the number of students stopped at the stadium gates carrying alcohol. The party guidelines in Objective 4 could be considered successful if the number of alcohol-centered parties on campus decreased (as measured by survey instruments).

By way of a summary, the important points to remember about program goals and objectives are:

1. A *goal* is an overall target; an *objective* is a very specific aim, usually stated in behavioral terms (observable performance).
2. Writing out program goals and objectives is a prerequisite for designing effective strategies.
3. The achievement of specific performance objectives can easily be measured. Vague, general objectives cannot be evaluated easily, and often cannot be evaluated at all.
4. Alcohol education is primarily concerned with *affective* objectives (changing values, norms, traditions, beliefs, and attitudes), and only secondarily concerned with *cognitive* objectives (learning facts, principles, definitions, and theories).

The appendixes to this chapter are examples of alcohol program literature that promote the use of goals and objectives to focus program strategies. You are encouraged to analyze these materials (using the principles set forth in this chapter) and adapt and strengthen them for your own use.

Thought Questions

1. This book is written on the basis of goals and objectives. Can you identify the goals? Where are the objectives found?
2. Is traditional college education concerned primarily with cognitive or affective objectives?
3. Why should alcohol education be concerned with affective objectives?

References

Gagne, R.M. 1977. *The Conditions of Learning,* 3rd ed. New York: Holt, Rinehart and Winston.

Kibler, R.J.; D.J. Cegala; D.T. Miles; and L.L. Barker. 1974. *Objectives for Instruction and Evaluation.* Boston: Allyn and Bacon, Inc.

Krathwohl, D.R.: B.S. Bloom; and B.B. Masia. 1964. *Taxonomy of Educational Objectives. Handbook II: Affective Domain.* New York: McKay.

Mager, R.F. 1975. *Preparing Objectives for Instruction,* 2nd ed. Belmont, CA: Fearon.

Appendix 10–A

Prevention Strategies for Specific Problems

GOAL OF PREVENTION ACTIVITIES

Decrease driving while intoxicated	Increase parties not focused on drinking

Objectives:

1. Decrease number of students at risk.

1. Increase parties where socialization is enhanced without excessive drinking.

2. Decrease number of accidents.

2. Devise consistent, reasonable, and enforceable set of university rules and regulations governing parties.

3. Increase peer support for persons not driving while drunk.

3. Support norms that allow comfortable nondrinking.

Key Concepts:

1. Driving drunk is dangerous to others as well as to self.

1. Parties can be more fun without too much alcohol.

2. Friends help prevent drunken friends from driving.

2. Drinking can be spaced out, not constant.

3. Host, hostess, or bartender have responsibility to prevent drunken guests from driving home.

3. Men and women lack assertiveness to say "no" if they do not want to drink.

Need:

1. About 25% of students each year at risk.

1. Many parties occur each week where only planning involves purchase of alcohol.

2. Police statistics much lower (0.02 percent arrested per year).

2. Many students report not knowing if nonalcoholic beverages are available.

3. Off-campus students at potentially greater risk.

3. Lack of creative, popular, and affordable ideas.

4. Lack of peer and social norms.

Prevention Approach

a. Change drinking behavior

—*Alcohol specific*

1. Driver educated to limit drinking. Provide sufficient "sober-up" time.

1. Provide punches at all parties, both alcohol and nonalcohol based, which are both appealing and tasty.

2. Peers help driver keep from drinking. Regulate amount of alcohol available at parties where guests must drive home.

2. Educate peers to promote comfortable nondrinking as an option. Regulations encourage parties that limit alcohol consumption.

—*Alcohol nonspecific*

1. Provide activities or focus to event that reduces drinking and, it is hoped, reduces number of drivers leaving drunk.

1. Parties focused on games, activities, or entertainment that encourage socialization.

b. Change reaction

1. Train campus police to enforce rules that arrest drunken drivers (initially will increase arrest rate, later should deter).

1. Educate students to attend parties that focus on socialization, and minimize importance of presence or absence of alcohol.

2. Party hosts/hostesses and peers refuse to let drunken person drive home.

2. Increase reluctance of staff and key student leaders to approve parties where drinking is primary activity.

c. Insulate behavior

1. Provide overnight lodging for drunken party guests.

1. Allow only limited number of alcohol-focused events, in places that are separate from populated campus locations.

Educational Method

a. Media and materials

1. *Driver oriented:* Information about drinking and driving. Awareness of alternative transportation available.

1. *Party Attendees:* Theme on assertiveness, that one needs to learn to ask for nonalcoholic beverages. Focus on need for social contacts, not alcohol.

2. *Peer group oriented:* Emphasis on friends helping friends.

2. *Hosts/Hostesses:* Party planning ideas and ways to focus on activities besides alcohol consumption.

3. *Hosts/Hostesses oriented:* Emphasis on sober-up time or having drunken guests sleep over or get home without driving.

b. Special displays

1. Breathalyzer display outside campus pub, helping students learn relationship between blood alcohol concentration (BAC) and legal definition of drunken driving.

1. Provide information on party planning, with ideas for events without alcohol consumption as main focus.

c. Speeches, lectures, panel presentations

1. Police demonstrate breathalyzer and discuss dangers of driving after drinking.

1. Discussion of ways people can have fun without drinking.

2. Focus on party ideas and activities, how to plan, and how to get people there.

d. Discussion groups

1. *Driver:* Discuss safety and legal risks.

1. *Party attendees:* Discuss ways to say "no" to alcohol and focus on desired socialization.

2. *Peer group:* Discuss ways to prevent drunken person from driving.

2. *Hosts/hostesses:* Discuss ways to plan parties not focused on drinking.

3. *Hosts/hostesses:* Discuss ways to prevent excessive drinking.

e. Community development

1. *Police:* Help educate regarding law and proper enforcement.

1. *Hosts/hostesses:* Educate regarding sensible parties and their planning.

1. *Off-campus students:* Develop ways to educate and get home safely.

2. *Enforcers:* Assist to develop and enforce reasonable guidelines.

Source: Kraft, D.P. 1978. *Alcohol Education and Prevention: Implications for Programming at the University Level.* Unpublished manuscript presented at symposium on drinking among college students, Boston. Pages 15–16, chart A.

Appendix 10–B

Capsule Communications Plans for Selected Target Audiences
Problem: The Drinking Driver

Target Group: Adults involved in alcohol-related situations (Part of General Audience)

Importance: Persons most likely to interact with potential drunk drivers. Most opportunity to intervene to prevent occurrence of drunk driving.

Major Issues: Acceptance of responsibility for alcohol/driving behavior of self and other persons in situations where alcohol is served.

Objectives	Strategies	Communications Outlet	Assessment of Impact
1. Increase knowledge and awareness of the extent, causes, and consequences of excessive drinking in combination with driving.	1. Provide facts about alcohol effects on mind, body, and driving skills.	1. TV.	1. Community surveys before and after overall or selected education efforts.
2. Stimulate acceptance of personal responsibility for preventing the occurrence of drunk driving.	2. Suggest alternatives to heavy drinking at social or business occasions.	2. Radio.	2. Control/experimental groups.
3. Persuade individuals to adopt policy of responsible alcohol use in and outside their own home, alone and with others.	3. Develop concept of role model. Show how to act to prevent drunk driving.	3. Print ads.	3. Pre/post-tests.
4. Increase number of people willing to take action to prevent drunk driving.	4. Demonstrate specific intervention behavior in socially acceptable manner.	4. Direct mail.	4. Changes in numbers of alcohol-related crashes.
		5. Collateral materials.	
		6. Organizational meetings (clubs, employers, etc.).	

Target Group: Youth (Part of General Audience)

Importance: Overinvolvement in alcohol-related crashes in relation to their proportion of licensed drivers. Beginning to establish behavior related to drinking/driving.

Major Issues: Willingness to ignore peer group pressure to drink excessively and drive, willingness to give and accept help if intoxicated.

Objectives	Strategies	Communications Outlet	Assessment of Impact
1. Increase knowledge of the extent, causes, and consequences of excessive drinking in combination with driving.	1. Provide factual, non-moralistic information.	1. Youth-oriented radio.	1. Surveys before and after public education efforts.
2. Increase perception of risk of accident or arrest if driving under influence of alcohol.	2. Emphasize peer interaction.	2. School classrooms.	2. Pre/post-testing.
3. Foster willingness to accept help when intoxicated and to give help to prevent a drunk friend from driving.	3. Offer specific intervention behavior that can be used to prevent drunk driving.	3. Special assemblies.	3. Control/experimental groups.
4. Begin to build new social norm of responsible drinking/driving behavior.	4. Use multi-media approach.	4. Clubs	
5. Help examine personal values associated with drinking and driving.	5. Actively involve young people in design and implementation of campaigns.	5. Family settings.	
6. Help develop personal skills for making decisions on alcohol issues.	6. Use speakers who can gain and hold respect of the audience.		
	7. Educate parents on how to approach young people.		

Target Group: Parents

Importance: Role models, conveyors of social values related to alcohol and driving.

Major Issues: Personal responsibility for teaching and setting example of responsible drinking/driving behavior.

Objectives	Strategies	Communications Outlet	Assessment of Impact
1. Persuade parents to raise issue of drinking/driving with children. 2. Persuade parents to adopt responsible drinking/driving behavior as role model to children.	1. Appeal to instincts as role model, conveyor of social values. 2. Appeal to concern for safety and well-being of children. 3. Provide information on how to talk with children.	1. PTA, other parent groups. 2. Literature from schools. 3. TV. 4. Radio. 5. Print ads.	1. Pre/post-surveys of parents. 2. Pre/post-surveys of children.

Target Group: Hosts and Hostesses

Importance: Opportunity to encourage responsible drinking/driving behavior among guests.

Major Issues: Responsibility for drinking/driving behavior of guests.

Objectives	Strategies	Communications Outlet	Assessment of Impact
1. Increase knowledge and awareness of the extent, causes, and consequences of excessive drinking combined with driving. 2. Persuade to adopt measures to discourage intoxication among guests. 3. Convince to intervene with intoxicated guests to prevent them from driving. 4. Stimulate acceptance of personal responsibility for guests' behavior.	1. Provide information about alcohol effects on mind, body, driving skill. 2. Provide specific information about measures to discourage intoxication and methods of intervening with intoxicated guests. Present as acceptable social behavior. 3. Provide information about BAC equivalency of various drinks and recognition of impairment. 4. Suggest alternatives to alcohol as focus for social activities.	1. Hostess packets containing information and protein-rich recipes for distribution in supermarkets and liquor stores. 2. Print ads. 3. TV commercials. 4. Radio.	1. Community surveys before and after overall or specific education efforts.

Target Group: News Media

Importance: News media are the single most pervasive source of information about the social norms and sanctions related to alcohol.

Major Issues: Coverage or treatment of alcohol use and misuse.

Objectives	Strategies	Communications Outlet	Assessment of Impact

1. Provide facts about alcohol effects on body, mind, and driving skills, and consequences of misuse or abuse.	1. Collect data from news coverage and entertainment programs on the manner in which alcohol and alcohol-related problems are presented. Present information to media.	1. Media workshops with
		  a. management,
		  b. news staff,
		  c. program directors, producers, and writers.
			1. Pre/post-interviews.
			
			2. Analysis of coverage before and after education efforts.

2. Obtain media participation in drafting and adhering to programing code for coverage of alcohol use and misuse.	2. Persuade key media managers to serve on advisory board.	2. Meetings of local press club, unions.	
3. Encourage media to take initiative in helping redefine social norms about alcohol use.			
4. Obtain media cooperation in airing or printing public education materials.			

Target Group: Police

Importance: Authority to arrest or discretion to ignore drunk drivers, thus determining public perception of the chances of arrest for drunk driving.

Major Issues: Recognition of drunkenness, professional and social responsibility to respond to drunk driving as a serious problem by enforcing pertinent community laws.

Objectives	Strategies	Communications Outlet	Assessment of Impact
1. Convince police of severity of drunk-driving problem.	1. Convince police of their role as model.	1. Police training classes.	1. Pre/post-surveys.
2. Provide information on the symptoms of drunk driving, predisposing factors, court procedures, treatment resources, appropriate manner for handling drunk drivers.	2. Ask police chief or other policymakers to take active role on advisory board.	2. Roll call.	2. Analysis of arrest records for volume and characteristics of arrested drunk drivers.
	3. Recruit police to talk to groups of young people.	3. Professional organization meetings.	3. Interviews with police chief and individual officers.
3. Encourage active role in stopping and arresting drunk drivers instead of letting them off with a warning. Seek departmental policy on handling of drunk drivers.	4. Show police how they are major link in system to rehabilitate people who drink excessively.	4. Face-to-face meetings with supervisors.	
		5. Direct mail.	
4. Persuade police that their response to drunk drivers establishes the public's perception of the risk of arrest.		6. Newspaper and TV features.	
		7. Printed materials.	
5. Convince police to treat drunk-driving teenagers the same as adults.			

Target Group: Lawyers

Importance: Key contact point for persons involved in legal proceedings connected with alcohol-related traffic accidents, prosecution of drunk-driving or public-intoxication offenders, potential elected officials and policymakers.

Major Issues: 1. Treatment of alcohol-related offenses as serious problems affecting not only the offender but also people around him/her and other innocent individuals.

Objectives	Strategies	Communications Outlet	Assessment of Impact

1. Persuade local lawyers to adopt code of practice that treats drunk drivers as serious offenders who endanger themselves and other persons.	1. Appeal to them as models for community behavior.
	
	2. Follow their drunk-driving cases to build list of observed behavior.
		1. Organized meetings:
		  a. district attorney's office,
		  b. public defender's office,
		  c. state and local bar association.
			1. Pre/post-surveys.
			
			2. Control/experimental groups.
			
			3. Comparisons of lawyers' actions in court before and after public education campaigns.

2. Provide with accurate information about severity of drunk-driving accident problem and responsibility of legal profession to seek reduction of problem through its work.		2. Direct mail to lawyers' offices. 3. Articles in professional journals. 4. Manned exhibit in courtyard area trafficed by lawyers.	
3. Provide with information about arrest procedures, court procedures, methods of diagnosing drunk driving, treatment possibilities.			
4. Enlist active involvement of prosecuting and defense attorneys in recommending treatment for offenders with alcohol-related problems.			

Target Group: Judges

Importance: Professional group that, by their disposition of drunk-driving cases, have the authority to affirm irresponsible decisions about alcohol and driving or to contribute significantly to a redirection of public behavior toward responsible action. Precedent-setters and policymakers.

Major Issues: Reluctance to treat drunk driving as a serious offense requiring rehabilitation of the offender, or to impose a fine or other punitive action.

Objectives	Strategies	Communications Outlet	Assessment of Impact
1. Convince judges that drunk driving is a serious offense.	1. Appeal to status as precedent-setter and policymaker.	1. Workshops.	1. Comparison of disposition of drunk-driving cases before and after public education campaign.
2. Provide them with information about treatment possibilities.	2. Record outcomes of drunk-driving arrests over month period to show to judges.	2. One-to-one information sessions.	2. Interviews with judges before and after public education efforts.
3. Persuade them to refer drunk drivers to treatment.	3. Ask traffic court judge to serve on advisory board.	3. Journal and newspaper articles.	
4. Obtain cooperation of judges in drawing up and adhering to responsible policies for the disposition of drunk-driving cases.	4. Enlist judges to talk before youth and civic groups about the outcome of drunk-driving cases.		
5.			
6. Enlist bar association in drawing up and promoting standard policy about responsible use of alcohol among its own members.			

Target Group: Physicians

Importance: Physicians frequently attend to physical disorders of persons with drinking problems. As respected and often revered professionals in their community, they can be influential in persuading persons with alcohol-related problems to seek treatment.

Major Issues: Social and professional responsibility to identify persons with drinking problems and urge them to undertake treatment.

Objectives	Strategies	Communications Outlet	Assessment of Impact
1. Establish high level of awareness about magnitude of alcohol problems and their relationship to highway safety. 2. Gain acceptance, on individual physician basis, of professional and social responsibility to treat or seek treatment for persons with drinking problems. 3. Obtain cooperation of organizations of doctors and hospital boards in establishing and following a code of conduct related to the identification and treatment of alcoholism and alcohol-related problems. 4. Persuade doctors' groups to adhere to policy of responsible drinking and driving in their own personal lives.	1. Appeal to doctor's self-image as responsible professional who can provide an invaluable contribution to society. 2. Provide specific information about alcohol-related crashes. 3. Provide professional materials about the treatment of drinking problems and community treatment centers. 4. Ask influential physician to serve on advisory board. 5. Enlist the active participation of doctors in addressing community groups on the alcohol/driving problem.	1. Organized meetings: a. hospital staff, b. local chapter AMA or other professional society, c. medical school classes, d. continuing education courses. 2. Direct mail to physicians' offices. 3. Professional journals, newspapers.	1. Pre/post-survey of random sample of physicians. 2. Comparison of number of monthly referrals to treatment before and after public education efforts.

Target Group: Pharmacists

Importance: Authoritative source of information about the effects of alcohol and other drugs and their synergistic effects when mixed together. Important communications channel about these problems for people purchasing prescription and nonprescription drugs.

Major Issues: Alcohol mixed with other drugs can be extremely harmful physically and produces intoxication quicker than when consumed by itself.

Objectives	Strategies	Communications Outlet	Assessment of Impact
1. Inform about purpose of community education program, update their information about effects of mixing alcohol with other drugs.	1. Persuade of position that provides capability to have people listen to advice about drugs.	1. Professional Association 2. Direct mail. 3. Personal visits.	1. Before-and-after comparison of quantity of materials displayed and distributed.
2. Persuade to label prescription drugs with warnings not to mix with alcohol.	2. Convince of social responsibility and minimal effort required to fulfill it.		
3. Encourage to warn patrons orally of dangers of mixing alcohol with other drugs.	3. Provide information and support for their intervention actions.		
4. Recruit to display community education materials in stores.	4. Recruit for speakers' bureau presentations.		
	5. Provide materials for distribution and display.		

Target Group: Employers and Businessmen

Importance: May be helpful in reaching large audiences. Are aware that much absenteeism from work results from alcohol abuse or misuse. Usually respected in community and serve as models for behavior.

Major Issues: Alcohol abuse or misuse has negative effect on business productivity.

Objectives	Strategies	Communications Outlet	Assessment of Impact
1. Inform about severity of problem, give facts about effects of alcohol on body and mind.	1. Reduce absenteeism, increase productivity by educating employees and obtaining treatment for those with alcohol problems.	1. Employee staff meetings.	1. Pre/post-surveys.
2. Obtain support for office and factory educational programs.	2. Convince employers of their role as leadership models, norm setters.	2. Pay envelope inserts, posters.	2. Increases in numbers of involved employers and businessmen organizations.
3. Persuade to intervene personally with employees who have alcohol-related problems, helping them obtain treatment.	3. Enlist active involvement of key businessmen on advisory board.	3. Meetings of groups of businessmen, e.g., Jaycees, Kiwanis, etc.	
4. Undertake personal responsibility to control drinking at business functions.		4. Letters from employer.	
5. Obtain active involvement of groups of businessmen in educating public.		5. Meetings of employee organizations, e.g., unions.	
6. Persuade to establish policies about responsible drinking behavior at professional meetings and functions.		6. Company publications.	
		7. Company bulletin and exhibit areas.	

Target Group: School Teachers and Administrators

Importance: Half of youths 14 to 18 report being in alcohol-related situations once a month or more. Schools and school teachers are dominant influences on the formation of alcohol-related values. Schools have a captive audience in this age and younger age groups.

Major Issues: About half of all youths say they drink. Many drive drunk or ride with a drunk driver. Teenagers are overrepresented in alcohol-related crashes. Schools, as value-instilling environments, have a social responsibility to help students make responsible decisions about alcohol use.

Objectives	Strategies	Communications Outlet	Assessment of Impact
1. Get schools to undertake alcohol/driving education program as a regular part of curriculum. 2. Obtain school cooperation in encouraging peer influence in favor of responsible drinking/driving behavior. 3. Provide with information about alcohol's impact on body, mind, and driving skills, symptoms and consequences of alcohol problems, and availability of treatment. 4. Convince teachers and school personnel to suggest alternatives to drunk driving. 5. Persuade schools to treat drinking by teenagers, on or off school premises, as a serious problem.	1. Ask school administrator to participate on advisory board. 2. Persuade school management that you can help them fulfill social responsibility to inform students about alcohol abuse. 3. Offer curriculum materials and/or speakers to discuss alcohol/driving in classes. 4. Convince school teachers of the importance of their role as models.	1. One-to-one meetings with school management. 2. Teacher staff meetings. 3. Printed and audiovisual teaching aids. 4. Union meetings. 5. Direct mail to school personnel.	1. Pre/post-survey of school personnel. 2. Pre/post-inventory of alcohol-driving curriculum offered in schools. 3. Survey of students.

Target Group: Tavern Owners and Bartenders

Importance: Daily interaction with drinker/drivers. Power to shut off a patron's alcohol or arrange alternate transportation.

Major Issues: Awareness of risks associated with drunk driving. Responsibility for keeping patrons who must drive from getting drunk. Recognition of impairment.

Objectives	Strategies	Communications Outlet	Assessment of Impact
1. Increase levels of knowledge about and awareness of causes and consequences of getting drunk.	1. Provide factual information about alcohol/driving including BAC equivalency between different kinds of drinks; quantity needed to get drunk; how to determine impairment; alternatives to driving drunk.	1. Personal visits.	1. Personal interviews before and after education effort.
2. Obtain agreement of tavern owners and bartenders to intervene to prevent drivers from getting drunk or drunk patrons from driving.	2. Persuade them of their role in fostering new social norms.	2. Meetings with group of tavern owners, informally or in cooperation with state liquor authority.	2. Observing behavior in bars before and after education efforts.
3. Persuade tavern owners to display anti-drunk-driving information and to pass along information to patrons.	3. Convince them that a loss in sales will not significantly hurt them.	3. Direct mail.	3. Informal survey of bar patrons before and after education efforts.
	4. Urge them to suggest to patron that he or she stop drinking or switch to nonalcoholic beverages when intoxication seems likely.	4. Print ads in newspapers.	

Target Group: Liquor Store Operators

Importance: Primary contact point for persons who purchase alcoholic beverages.

Major Issues: Acceptance of some responsibility to provide information about responsible drinking/driving to customers who are potential candidates for arrest.

Objectives	Strategies	Communications Outlet	Assessment of Impact
1. Increase knowledge and awareness of the extent, causes, and consequences of alcohol-related accidents.	1. Offer bottle bags or other useful product to store owner for distribution with alcohol purchases.	1. Personal visits.	1. Surveys before and after education effort.
2. Persuade to accept some responsibility for encouraging customers to drink and drive responsibly.	2. Convince owner/operators of their contribution to a responsible drinking/driving society.	2. Informal meetings.	2. Random check of behavior when anonymously purchasing alcohol.
3. Persuade to adopt policy of refusing to sell to intoxicated customers and to obtain assistance in finding drunk patrons alternate means of transportation.	3. Convince owner/operator that his participation will not drastically harm sales.	3. Meetings cosponsored by state liquor authority or alcohol distributors.	3. Personal interview.
4. Recruit to distribute information about responsible drinking/driving to customers.	4. Invite owners to speak before civic groups or otherwise stimulate their active participation in education effort.	4. Direct mail.	4. Random interviews of store customers.
		5. Bottle bags, swizzel sticks, hostess packets, and other collateral materials.	

Target Group: Social Workers, Clergy, etc.

Importance: Interaction with persons who have alcohol-related problems.

Major Issues: Knowledge about the extent, causes, and consequences of excessive drinking. Willingness to seek treatment for persons with alcohol-related problems and to encourage constituency to drink and drive responsibly.

Objectives	Strategies	Communications Outlet	Assessment of Impact
1. Increase knowledge and awareness of the extent, causes, and consequences of excessive drinking, especially in combination with driving.	1. Convince hierarchy of church or social action agency of importance of their involvement. Ask them to cosponsor some education efforts.	1. Personal meetings with church or agency management.	1. Surveys before and after education effort.
2. Inform about appropriate way of relating to problem drinkers.	2. Emphasize role as initiator and conveyor of social norms. Also modeling role.	2. Staff meetings.	
3. Increase awareness and willingness to refer persons to alcohol treatment facilities.		3. Printed materials.	
4. Obtain active involvement in continuing education effort among constituency.			

Target Group: Volunteer Organizations (civic, women's, church, social action groups)

Importance: Extensive membership, many of whom host or participate in alcohol-related situations. Sponsorship of many educational activities.

Major Issues: Willingness to undertake activities to inform themselves and persons with whom they interact about responsible drinking/driving behavior.

Objectives	Strategies	Communications Outlet	Assessment of Impact
1. Increase level of knowledge about the extent, causes, and consequences of excessive drinking.	1. Appeal to role as model citizens.	1. Organization meetings.	1. Pre/post-surveys.
	2. Persuade of contribution to society.	2. Print ads.	2. Follow-up interviews with organization officers.
2. Increase acceptance of personal responsibility to prevent drunk driving by themselves and those with whom they drink.	3. Provide facts, information about alcohol effects and related responsible decision making.	3. Direct mail.	
3. Gain willingness to act as change agent regarding drinking/driving social norms by setting example for responsible behavior and adopting policy of responsible alcohol use.	4. Ask members to speak before other groups.		
4. Persuade to undertake educational efforts on behalf of responsible drinking/driving. Provide time and/or money.			

Target Group: Problem Drinkers, Alcoholics, Families of Each.

Major Issues: Willingness to seek treatment.

Importance: Most likely groups to be involved in alcohol-related accidents. People who are closest to the problem.

Objectives	Strategies	Communications Outlet	Assessment of Impact
1. Increase levels of knowledge and awareness about extent, causes, and consequences of drunk driving.	1. Provide facts about alcohol's effects on body, mind, driving skill.	1. AA, other alcoholic groups.	1. Before-and-after comparison of records of treatment facilities and police records.
2. Encourage acceptance of fact that problem exists and to seek treatment.	2. Provide information about treatment facilities.	2. Physicians, social workers, clergy, other counseling groups, employers, bartenders, liquor store operators.	2. Pre/post-community-surveys.
3. Decrease drunk-driving episodes.	3. Provide support for intervention to treat problem.		
4. Increase, among those associated with problem drinkers and alcoholics, willingness to intervene to help them obtain treatment.	4. Provide information about specific intervention behaviors to prevent a drunk from driving.		

Source: *A Manual for Managing Community Alcohol Safety Education Programs.* U.S. Department of Transportation, National Highway Traffic Safety Administration, DOT HS 802 515, January 1978.

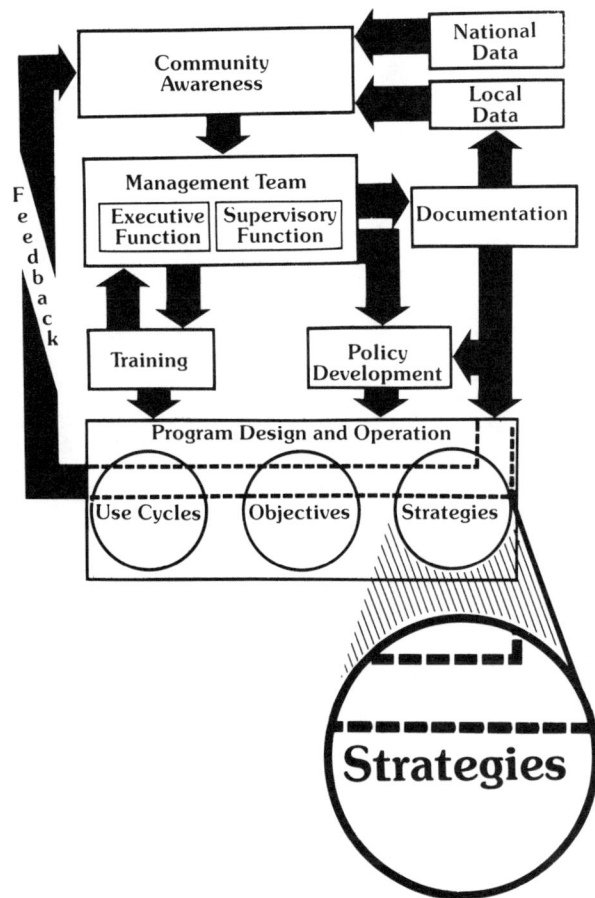

Community Awareness

National Data

Local Data

Management Team
Executive Function | Supervisory Function

Documentation

Feedback

Training

Policy Development

Program Design and Operation

Use Cycles | Objectives | Strategies

Strategies

Chapter 11

STRATEGIES

OBJECTIVES

When you have finished this chapter, you should be able to:

1. List the four categories of strategies;
2. Give examples from each category; and
3. Describe appropriate and inappropriate uses of each strategy.

The purpose of a problem-specific alcohol program is to reduce problem levels through community action. Participation in activities that promote new norms and values about alcohol is the primary means by which programs achieve this aim. The previous chapter pointed out that these *affective* changes can best be accomplished through structured group experiences rather than formal instruction. Of course, providing a certain amount of factual information is necessary 1) to raise community awareness of the nature and extent of alcohol problems. 2) to counter popular myths and misinformation about alcohol use, and 3) to create a factual foundation for new beliefs and attitudes.

Program strategies can therefore include conducting group experiences (workshops, discussions, and demonstrations), providing informational products (newsletters, advertisements, posters, leaflets, and radio announcements), promoting organizational development (creation of policies, committees, and task forces), and even making environmental changes (such as providing transportation to and from off-campus parties to reduce the opportunity for driving while drunk). In spite of this diversity, these strategies should have one common element—they must all be based on specific objectives that are derived from documented problems.

Chapter 7 suggested that a variety of strategies for each objective would be more effective than a single-strategy plan. Changing beliefs and attitudes is a very complicated process, made even more complex by individual variations in personality, character, and learning styles. Therefore, if one uses more strategies, and chooses diverse strategies for each objective, program impact will be much greater.

Strategies can be grouped into the four broad categories listed above and are illustrated in Figure 11–1; group experiences, informational products, organizational development, and environmental changes. This chapter covers each of these categories in turn, and its appendixes contains supplementary materials and examples from alcohol programs at colleges and universities across the United States.

Group Experiences

Research studies on attitude formation indicate that the most powerful factor associated with attitude change is "human modeling" (Bandura and McDonald 1963; Bandura 1965; and Thornburg 1975). For young children, teachers and parents are the primary models, but in adolescence the old models are usually rejected and peer models become predominant. New beliefs and attitudes are required from college roommates, fraternity brothers, and other students. Group social activities frequently provide the

167

Figure 11–1.   The four types of strategies.

setting for learning new beliefs and attitudes in college, so if one wishes to change prevailing beliefs, peer group experiences seem logically to be the most effective means. Peer educators who have been trained (Chapter 8) to model the new attitudes and to conduct group activities that promote new attitudes are a powerful force for change.

Sponsoring discussion groups is one of the most popular strategies used in campus alcohol programs. In a discussion group, peer educators use participatory techniques such as values clarification exercises to stimulate student interaction. Discussions can help raise student awareness of problems, serve as a forum for examining current beliefs, stimulate sharing of perceptions about alcohol use on campus, and develop a consensus about a problem or its proposed solution. (Their use in the documentation process was covered in Chapter 5.)

In order to insure good attendance, discussions must be centered on topics highly relevant to the participants and must be heavily promoted among members of the target audience. In some programs, peer educators have persuaded faculty members to devote one or two regular class periods to the discussion of alcohol issues. Professors teaching courses in sociology, psychology, public health, and related fields are often receptive to this idea, particularly if their courses already contain specific components dealing with alcohol programs.

A higher level of involvement and interest can be achieved through a more elaborate type of group meeting (often called a "workshop") in which students are given the opportunity to participate in games, role playing, demonstrations, and other active exercises. Appendix 11–A is a sample workshop plan used by the Lambda Chi Alpha fraternity. Since it is such a popular format, Chapter 12 is devoted to a detailed examination of the group meeting/workshop strategy.

A more unconventional type of group educational experience is the non-alcohol-centered party. By giving "sample" parties that are fun, promote socializing, and incorporate alternative beverages, peer educators provide models for other students to emulate. A well-planned party will demonstrate that alcohol is not a prerequisite for having a good time or for socializing with the opposite sex. In a related technique, breathalyzer demonstrations can be set up at regular parties as an "educational diversion."

Informational Products

Posters, advertisements, leaflets, radio announcements, and similar items are widely used in campus alcohol programs, but studies of the effects of communication indicate that these techniques have varying influence on attitude change. However, media can be used very effectively to inform people about the alcohol program, to train peer educators, and teach factual information about alcohol.

"Awareness events" combine informational techniques in intensive one- or two-day public information campaigns. Health fairs are an example of this kind of event. These campaigns are useful for raising awareness of campus problems and for informing students about health services available on campus.

Special displays are another popular media-related technique for raising awareness, stimulating interest in program activities, and for providing factual information. Displays are usually set up in the student union or a similar location frequented by large numbers of students and volunteers stand by to answer questions. One of the most effective exhibits is a display of the breathalyzer apparatus showing how it is used to gather evidence on the drinking driver. Often, local attorneys or police officers stand by to answer questions about drinking and driving arrests. Similar displays can be used to educate students about the alcohol program or to illustrate interesting and relevant information about alcohol and its use (e.g., "Hangover Prevention," and "Local Laws Affecting Students").

Appendix 11–B at the end of this chapter lists the advantages and disadvantages of various forms of media that might be used in an alcohol program. Appendix 11–C is a collection of posters and signs that have been used with positive results in programs at several colleges and universities.

Organizational Development

This strategy requires a high degree of structure and formal organization for task-related purposes. Formal organization implies responsibility for accomplishing specific tasks—committees and "task forces" are created ostensibly to *do* something—and therefore the alcohol educator must carefully specify the tasks these groups are to perform. For example, if program goals require the organization of a residence hall committee to seek solutions for alcohol problems in the hall, committee members must be educated in the purpose and nature of the campus program and be shown exactly how their task fits into the overall plan. They must be guided to use consensual techniques in their activities and to avoid the pitfalls of confrontational tactics and over-regulation.

As a strategy, organizational development is valuable for promoting project continuity and for insuring that the solutions to the local problems are handled by the groups most directly concerned. The problem-specific approach, as outlined in this book, is an example of an overall strategy of organizational development.

Environmental Changes

In order to reduce problem levels, alcohol education programs must concentrate on changing attitudes and beliefs, but in the short run it is possible to alleviate some problems by reducing the opportunities for their occurrence. At the same time, these "environmental" strategies may also serve as an impetus for the formation of new beliefs. Examples of environmental changes are: limiting large parties to off-campus facilities where noise will not bother town residents, providing buses for weekend ski trips where the risk of drinking and driving is high, setting up a short obstacle course with rubber pylons at a parking lot exit to detect drunk drivers before they reach the highway.

The most popular environmental strategy is the on-campus pub. In states where alcohol can be sold on campus, many student centers have opened pubs for profit. The pubs are managed by peer educators who integrate problem-reduction techniques into their operating procedures. The National Clearinghouse for Alcohol Information has prepared a handbook for colleges and universities called the *Pub Module* (Kassebaum, Hewitt, and Schlegel 1981); it is available from:

NCALI
P.O. Box 2345
1776 Plaza
Rockville, Md. 20852

At one university, a campus pub was created to serve a residence area that had a number of problems related to parties and other social gatherings: damage to furniture and walls, litter, students throwing up, excessive noise, and broken windows. These problems had not reached epidemic proportions, but the alcohol program documentation identified the area as one of "high risk." In addition to media promotions, special displays, demonstrations, and other awareness strategies, the peer educators decided to install a pub in the residence area to change the environment in which social events were conducted.

The pub was housed in two large, old, storage rooms in the basement of one of the large residence halls. The rooms were cleared and a bar was purchased from a local hotel with social funds. (The bar was sold cheaply as an educational contribution.) Construction and decoration teams installed the bar, hung pleasant pictures and plants around the rooms, provided a dance floor, and even scavenged furniture from various sources on campus.

The pub was then opened to the students living in the residence area. An open house was sponsored for residence advisers, floor officers, and staff. The members of an all-male dorm were invited to hold their traditional fall football season bash in the pub. In previous years, the party was planned by buying as many kegs that funds could provide, which usually resulted in extensive intoxication and property damage. Reaction to the party was very positive—people enjoyed the alternative beverages, the party was planned around an entertaining theme, and disruptive events decreased.

Over the next semester the pub was the site for almost a hundred special events. There were weekly workshops and films on drinking and driving. A weekly nonalcohol happy hour became a popular Thursday afternoon break. Students began to experiment with recipes for appealing low-alcohol, low-cost beverages, which became standard fare at all parties in the pub, whether or not the alcohol project peers and staff attended. Over the semester, the pub provided a realistic and entertaining setting in which the students could practice new behaviors and beliefs about alcohol use. A variation on the pub idea is the TGIF Program at Hanover College. Appendix 11–D is a description of that program and its origins.

Thought Question

From your knowledge of campus alcohol problems and the local conditions, does any particular strategy or group of strategies seem particularly appropriate for your own community?

References

Bandura, A. 1965. "Influence of Model's Reinforcement Contingencies on the Acquisition of Imitative Responses." *Journal of Personality and Social Psychology* 1: 589–595.

Bandura, A., and F.J. McDonald. 1963. "The Influence of Social Reinforcement and the Behavior of Models in Shaping Children's Moral Judgments." *Journal of Abnormal and Social Psychology* 67: 274–281.

Hovland, C.I.; I.L. Janis; and H.H. Kelley. 1953. *Communication and Persuasion.* New Haven, Ct: Yale University Press.

Kassebaum, P.; K. Hewitt; and M. Schlegel. 1981. *Prevention On Tap: An Environmental Alcohol Abuse Prevention Approach for Campus Pubs.* National Clearinghouse for Alcohol Information of the NIAAA. Draft.

Thornburg, H.D. 1975. *Development in Adolescence.* Monterey, CA: Brooks/Cole.

Appendix 11–A

Alcohol Awareness: Case Studies, Role Playing, and Exercises (Lambda Chi Alpha Fraternity)

CASE STUDY

Tom Schulte, a usually responsible and hard-working brother, has had a rough week and decides that at the party scheduled for Saturday evening he is going to "get blasted" and drown his miseries. The brothers in the chapter joke about it and think it is funny because Tom is usually quite a sight to watch when he is under the influence.

On Saturday night Tom drinks enough to lose many of his usual inhibitions and becomes loud and obnoxious, and in the process insults and spills drinks on the other brothers' dates. Eventually Tom becomes so intoxicated that he begins to damage chapter property when girls won't dance with him and things don't go his way. To top it all off, Tom insists that he is going to drive home no matter what anyone says, and starts out of the house toward his car with keys in hand.

1. Is it Tom's "right" to get this drunk?
2. What is your responsibility once the insults and property destruction begin?
3. What action, if any, should be taken against Tom as a result of his actions?
4. What may be done to prevent this type of occurrence in the future?

ROLE PLAYING EXERCISES

1. Lately the chapter has been getting a reputation for the contents of its garbage cans. If the number of bottles is any indication of the use of alcohol for medicinal purposes, this must be the healthiest fraternity on campus. If it were quiet you wouldn't make an issue of it, but a few of the men are openly displaying bottles on their window sills, seemingly getting a thrill out of violating fraternity ideals and campus rules. You're not trying to play temperance league, but things are getting a little ridiculous and this isn't the image you want for your fraternity. You raise the issue with the social chairman, quite informally.

2. Part of a fraternity's task is to develop the social graces. In contemporary America, alcohol is a constant fixture at social gatherings. Besides, it's not knowing how to use it that leads a man to make a fool of himself. You aren't responsible for its use in the house, but you wouldn't see any point in curtailing it. This is one area that should be revised in the laws of the fraternity since the era of prohibition is long past. Legislation, to your way of thinking, has to keep up with the customs and the norms of society. A chapter is not a gathering of idealists resisting the world around them, is it? You are just not tuned in to concern over this thing.

3. You drink almost every day, usually ending up fairly drunk and obnoxious. The other day you came to a party and were very drunk. You did two things that alienated everyone there. First of all you went over to a sorority house and persuaded the father of a fraternity brother who was visiting his daughter there to come over to the house for a beer. When you and he walked in, the situation was obvious and everyone was embarrassed. Then about an hour later you became ill publicly. You really impressed the brothers this time.

4. You are really in a bind. You know that the active chapter is very angry with the drunk brother. Certain key brothers feel that this is the "last straw" for this brother, since he had been warned several times to behave himself. Yet you realize the guy has emotional and psychological problems that could really blow up if things aren't handled delicately. On the other hand, you have to protect the rights and feelings of the brothers and the fraternity also. You are undecided on how to handle this serious situation.

5. You are a senior and are leading the brothers who are demanding that the drunk brother be thrown out of the fraternity for his continued drunkenness and obnoxious behavior. You contend that he has been warned several times and that each time he promises to behave, and then in a month or so he is always back to his old tricks again. You and many of the brothers are fed up with his childish and inconsiderate behavior and are demanding that he be expelled from the fraternity forever.

172

Exercise 1. In America we do not have a consensus as to what constitutes responsible drinking behavior. This then leads to controversy and confusion regarding the definition of problem drinking and when sanctions against irresponsible drinking are discussed.

Please rank the following examples from 1 (least responsible drinking behavior) to 5 (most responsible drinking behavior). Then within your group please discuss your ranking and arrive at a consensus ranking.

A. _____ Randy has just left the chapter date party and is taking his date home. His blood alcohol concentration of .10 is the legal definition of alcohol intoxication in most states. He is weaving erratically down the street and almost crashes into an oncoming car.

B. _____ Sam really likes mixed drinks and about twice a week in his chapter house room will make himself several drinks using his favorite 80 proor liquor (40 percent alcohol). Sometimes he has more than several and completely misses dinner at the chapter house.

C. _____ Frank, having been frustrated all day, went to the local bar that evening and drank six beers in one hour. Frank weighs about 150 pounds (his blood alcohol concentration is about .09), but he gets angry and starts a fight by breaking a bottle over the head of a much larger man sitting next to him.

D. _____ Already feeling high, a group of brothers on their way to a party decided to chug that most consumed alcoholic libation in America, a can of beer. Before leaving one of the brothers pulls an overhead light from its fixture. Laughing, the others start to wrestle and in falling against a trophy case cabinet they break the glass.

E. _____ Sandy, a graduate student who is divorced and living with her small child, is becoming an alcoholic (one of 15 percent of all Americans who drink very irresponsibly). She drinks beer throughout most of the day, which has caused her to gain excessive weight. One afternoon a friend stops by to visit and finds her asleep amidst an unkempt living room and the child crying and hungry in her crib.

Exercise 2 Lambda Chi Alpha does not have a consensus as to what constitutes responsible drinking behavior. This leads to confusion regarding the definition of problem drinking and standards of responsible drinking in the chapter.

Please rank the following examples from 1 (most responsible drinking behavior) to 8 (least responsible drinking behavior). Then, within your group, please discuss your ranking and arrive at a consensus ranking.

A. _____ George is in charge of the Fraternity Education Program. He always talks seriously to all the associate members about their drinking habits and the problems of drinking too much.

B. _____ Don and the rest of the associate members have just completed initiation. Though tired and emotionally drained, they decide to go drinking to celebrate the occasion.

C. _____ Jim has never enjoyed drinking. He always chose not to drink until he joined the fraternity. Jim began drinking because he was tired of being left out or teased for not drinking.

D. _____ Mark is recruitment chairman for his chapter. When Mark plans a recruitment function, alcohol is the main ingredient. Each brother is given a few drinks to loosen him up and each rushee is quickly ushered to the beer for a few ice-breakers.

E. _____ Rich and Mike do not drink, but they still enjoy the parties. After each party, they always offer to drive home people who have had too much to drink.

F. _____ Scott is the social chairman for his chapter. When Scott plans a party he goes all out; there is always good food and plenty of beer and wine. He also makes sure that there is a nonalcoholic beverage available for those who choose not to drink.

G. _____ Jack has a strong sense of brotherhood. When he noticed one of his brothers was drinking heavily, missing classes, and withdrawing from other people, Jack confronted his brother about his drinking

H. ____ After a hard days work, Steve usually comes back to the chapter house and has a few beers in order to relax.

Exercise 3.   A.   The following are some reasons why you may or may not drink.

1. If you drink place an "X" next to those reasons why you have and/or why you currently do so.
2. If you do not drink place an "O" next to those reasons explaining why you haven't or currently do not.

____ promotes social interaction
____ against religious principles
____ like the taste
____ nothing else to do
____ habit at mealtimes
____ parental restrictions
____ to relax after a hard day
____ compounds problems
____ to have fun
____ to reduce inhibitions
____ produces depression
____ everyone else does
____ do not have to be responsible for actions
____ thirst
____ excuse to become rowdy
____ helps relieve pressure from problems
____ to get high
____ medical reasons
____ just need a drink
____ family tradition on holidays
____ against moral standards
____ when feeling lonely or depressed
____ hangovers result
____ signifies maturity with adult status
____ do not like the taste
____ gain self confidence
____ to beat the system when under 21 years old
____ afraid of consequences due to drinking

B. Are there other reasons why you drink or do not drink that are not on this list? Please write them down.
C. Share your responses with the group.

ALCOHOL AWARENESS PROGRAM: RECOMMENDED GUIDELINES FOR CHAPTER SOCIAL FUNCTIONS

The following guidelines for chapter social functions and chapter programming alternatives are de-signed to provide some minimal awareness of the role alcohol plays in chapter planning. In addition, they are intended to provide certain facts about alcohol's relationship to social programming, some alternative programs that are available, and some conceptual comment about alcohol in order to provide the members of Lambda Chi Alpha with information that can be used to evaluate the role alcohol plays in their individual lives and the life of their chapter as well.

The following comments are presented to meet these objectives, in part:

1. The primary purpose of any organized social gathering is to bring people together—not just to drink. Alcohol traditionally has been used to assist in the socialization of groups and not as an end in itself.

2. Chapter social functions don't have to be planned around alcohol consumption. Alcohol could be used, at times, to support other planned activities.

3. When serving alcohol, it is wise to always provide an alternative nonalcoholic beverage for members and guests who do not wish to drink. Note: The alternative beverage should be compatible with alcoholic beverages being served for those who may wish to switch from alcoholic to nonalcoholic beverages, or vice versa, during the function.

4. As a matter of practice, food should always be served when alcohol is being served. High-protein snack foods such as cheeses, nuts, and meat are the most suitable since they slow down absorption of alcohol into the bloodstream. (This should be included in the budgeting of each social function.)

5. Publicize the starting and *ending* time for each function, and stick to them. This will allow members and guests to plan the consumption of alcohol at their own rate and will allow the social chairman to plan the purchase of adequate food and refreshments. A function with a reasonable ending time (depending on the nature of the social gathering) could also lessen the "overindulgence" of some members and/or guests.

6. Plan the purchase of alcoholic beverages, if the chapter is providing them, so there is just enough for the function. It is better to run out a little earlier than expected than to have too much alcohol that may extend the hours of the function, the amount of alcohol consumed, and the potential for abuse.

7. As a matter of practice, the chapter should stop serving alcohol an hour or an hour and a half before the scheduled end of the party (or the scheduled end of the party should anticipate guests remain-

ing another hour or so). At that time provide *substantial* snacks with coffee, tea, fruit juices (avoid carbonated beverages). This will not sober up the members and guests, but it will give added time for their body to absorb and dispose of the alcoholic intake. Again, remember to plan the additional budgetary impact.

8. When serving alcohol at a social function, it is often best to serve it in the form of a punch rather than mixed drinks (always provide two punch bowls—one with alcohol and one without).

9. When planning the annual social calendar, a special effort should be made to provide the chapter with a good mix of functions. It is not necessary to provide alcohol for every social gathering. For those functions that do include the use of alcohol, use imagination to vary the type of function. Kegs of beer, although relatively inexpensive and the most convenient to arrange for, are not always the solution for a "successful" party.

10. If mixed drinks are served at a party chapter function, *always,* as a matter of chapter policy, provide a bartender to pour properly proportioned drinks—never "doubles" or more. It is unwise to provide an open bar where guests mix their own drinks. This is too expensive and too many people can get too drunk too fast.

11. If a member or guest gets drunk, stop serving that person. You will be doing him or her a favor, especially if there is some chance that he or she will be driving. Everyone is aware that most drunk people don't want to stop drinking, are sure that they are "OK," and don't want someone else interfering in their enjoyment. The situation is difficult, at best. A respected chapter leader or one of the person's closest friends stands the best chance of influencing the individual who has overindulged. Start by taking the person away from the main part of the party and providing him or her with food.

It is best not to attempt to deal with the person's drunkenness on a personal basis until he or she has sobered up. Discussion the following day could be helpful in assisting the individual to understand his or her behavior of the previous day and how alcohol influenced that behavior. Although a discussion of this type is often difficult, it should not be delayed beyond the following day if it is to have any impact in helping the individual involved.

12. Don't allow any intoxicated member or guest to drive. Provide an alternative method of getting them home via someone who is not intoxicated. If necessary, take the person's car keys away (over one half of all auto accidents involve someone who has been drinking!).

There is no fast way to sober up a drunk. It takes about one hour for the human body to absorb and dispose of the alcohol in each average cocktail or can of beer.

If alternate transportation is not available, put the intoxicated person to bed to "sleep it off."

13. Use chapter funds to invest in a couple of good punch cookbooks (your cook or mothers' club can help). Interesting and good-tasting nonalcoholic punch drinks will add to any party and will not force individuals who prefer not to drink the alcoholic drinks. Remember, people attending a party want to participate. When planning functions, always spend an equal amount of energy in planning for those who do not drink.

14. Discourage the member or guest who insists that everyone must always have a full drink in their hand. Don't force people to drink! Give chapter members and guests the freedom to determine their own rate of consumption.

15. Become aware of the laws concerning alcohol in your particular state. Remember, the chapter can be held liable in case of accident, injury, or death, if the alcohol was provided by the chapter or was consumed by an underage individual on chapter property or at a chapter sponsored event. In some states the chapter may also be liable if a person of legal drinking age consumed alcohol at the chapter house or at a chapter-sponsored event. Similarly, parents who provide their home for chapter social functions can be held liable for the actions of the chapter, its members, and guests.

The following are some possible alternative social functions at which alcohol could be served (if allowed by campus policies):

—Cocktails and dinner exchange (cocktails for no more than one hour before dinner).
—Dinner exchange with the menu consisting of spaghetti and a *good* hearty burgundy. Figure about one bottle for every four to five people. The chapter should invest in wine glasses—don't serve wine in a water glass (plastic wine glasses, as a last resort, are available in most locations).
—Sunday champagne brunch at the chapter house for faculty, guests, and/or parents.
—Wine tasting party with faculty, dates, and/or parents. Find an expert in fine wines to assist in understanding the differences between the variety of

wines being tasted. Most campuses and their communities have such an expert.

—Wine and cheese reception for faculty. Have a sorority assist in the planning.

—Homecoming or any home game: Schedule a chapter reunion for alumni and members and their guests for a limited time before the game. Food (the amount determined by the time of the game) and alcoholic beverages, in limited quantities, could be provided.

—BYOB parties, as opposed to parties at which free refreshments are provided, tend to limit the amount of alcohol consumed by members and guests (it also helps the chapter social budget). The chapter should provide nonalcoholic refreshments and food.

—Theater parties can be planned with all members and guests meeting at the chapter house for a *brief* cocktail hour prior to curtain time. An alternative would be to meet at the chapter house after the play for an hour or so to discuss the presentation over wine and cheese.

—Beach or river parties with full picnic lunch and limited quantities of beer.

By now you should have noted that the overriding theme in the social functions suggested above is to provide *a pleasant social environment* in which alcohol is served in limited quantities but *is not* the primary reason for the gathering. Each chapter can think of many more entertaining and/or educationally viable programs that will meet this same objective.

The following are a list of social functions at which alcohol need not be served. These too, meet the objective of providing an opportunity for members and guests to gather together to enjoy each other's company:

—Roller or ice skating exchanges or date functions functions.

—Square dancing at the chapter house (Western theme).

—Film exchange or date function at the chapter house.

—Parents night, with guest speaker from campus, at chapter house.

—Philanthropic events.

—Theater productions (on or off campus).

—Museum tours.

—Camping, hiking, cycling.

—Local politicians for dinner at the chapter house, with discussion afterwards.

—Breakfast, brunch, or supper at the chapter house before athletic events (without alcohol).

—Ice cream socials.

—Athletic exchanges (volleyball, softball, etc.) with sorority—breakfast, lunch, or dinner before or after.

—Christmas party in July (gifts could go to local charity), egg hunt at Easter, etc.

—Develop a film series, with an educational/entertaining theme, shown at house on a biweekly basis.

The suggestions included in these guidelines are not all-inclusive. Every chapter with very little effort will be able to develop social programs that are fun and meet the interests of its members. The suggestions provided here also serve to illustrate that if the planning of all social functions is started with the assumption that alcohol must be available, the resultant functions will lack the variation and innovation that will make the chapter's annual social calendar one of interest, deserving the full support of all members. Use imagination in providing a variety of functions, and when alcohol is planned as a part of the social function, make certain that its consumption, as well as the chapter's responsibility in both human and legal terms, is not abused. Your members will receive a far greater benefit from well planned and executed chapter social functions.

Source: Lambda Chi Alpha, Office of Administration, 8741 Founders Road, Indianapolis, Indiana.

Appendix 11–B

Audiovisual Resources

The following audiovisual media are available at most colleges through campus "media centers" or similar facilities. Since audiovisuals are powerful tools for information delivery and for stimulating discussions, their effective use can be very beneficial for an alcohol program. The list below contains the major categories of instructional media and the advantages and disadvantages of each.

I. AUDIOTAPE

Advantages	Disadvantages
—Can make use of off-air taping of radio (following Fair-Use Guidelines of the Copyright Law of 1979.)	—Allows intrusion of irrelevant, uncontrolled visual stimuli, which may interfere with the audio message.
—Powerful emotive effects (good for affective change).	—Difficult to edit or revise.
—Stimulates visual imagery in listeners.	
—Sound effects, music, etc. possible to enhance narration.	
—Equipment usually available, easy to operate.	
—Relatively inexpensive.	

II. VIDEOTAPE

Advantages	Disadvantages
—Can make use of off-air taping following Fair-Use Guidelines of the Copyright Law of 1979.	—Image size too small for large group viewing (requires one TV monitor for every ten viewers).
—Excellent motivational tool.	—Cannot easily be edited or revised.
—Attributes of color, motion, and sound have high affective impact.	—Lack of standardized format (reel-to-reel, cassette, 3/4 inch, 1/2 inch, etc.) can make use difficult.
—Provides vicarious experiences for audience impossible to experience directly (automobile crashes, interviews with national figures, etc.).	—Equipment may not be available in some locations.
—A familiar (and therefore comfortable) medium for the audience.	—Expensive to produce

III. FILM

Advantages	Disadvantages
—Excellent motivational tool.	—*Very* expensive to produce; fairly expensive to rent.
—Attributes of color, motion, and sound have affective impact.	—Requires equipment for viewing that may not be readily available.
	—Often cannot be reviewed.

IV. SLIDES (2" × 2")

Advantages	Disadvantages
—Local production easy, therefore can be used to illustrate highly relevant *local* images.	—Images static (cannot show motion).
—Fairly inexpensive to produce	—Dimmed lighting required for projection inhibits discussion
—Color slides have high visual impact on audience.	
—Large image size appropriate for group viewing.	

—Easily edited (changed) for different applications, different audience.

—Equipment for production, viewing, usually available locally.

—User controls timing of images, can easily stop for discussion or back up to previous slides.

V. SLIDES/TAPE PROGRAMS

Advantages	*Disadvantages*
—Combining sound with visual image increases impact.	—Pacing of images is fixed by the preprogrammed tape.
—"Packages" the presentation and therefore insures standardization of message delivery (and also can be *shared* with other agencies, programs, colleges, etc.)	—Production equipment for synchronizing tape may not be readily available.
—Can be stopped for discussion.	
—Large image appropriate for group viewing.	
—Can be edited, revised, and updated for different applications, different audiences.	
—Equipment for viewing usually available locally.	
—Continuous-loop tape cassette makes continuous presentation possible (for a display or awareness project).	

VI. OVERHEAD TRANSPARENCIES

Advantages	*Disadvantages*
—Can be produced by user or by professionals.	—Static image.
—User controls pacing, sequencing, image development (gates and overlays).	—Professional production may be expensive, difficult to obtain.
—Large image size appropriate for group viewing.	—Color transparencies usually only available through professional production.
—Can be projected in normal room light, thereby permitting other activities to occur simultaneously (discussion, note-taking, etc.).	
—Can be written or drawn on directly.	
—Easily revised, updated, or edited.	
—Projectors available everywhere.	

VII. PRINT/POSTERS

Advantages	*Disadvantages*
—Cost-effective method for reaching large number of people.	—Generally poor method for changing attitudes.
—Can explain issues, provide information succinctly (raise awareness).	—One-way communication, therefore no opportunity for audience feedback.
—Newsletters, brochures, etc., can be sent to a selected target group.	
—Promotional items such as bookmarks, litterbags, decals, coasters, bumper stickers, and napkins provide high program visibility.	

Appendix 11–C

Successful College Posters and Signs

A few drinks can help
you unwind and relax.

Maybe.
But if you use
alcohol as a crutch,
it's time to
seek help.

Drinking Myths Series
Alcohol Education Project
Student Wellness Resource Center
Southern Illinois University at Carbondale
Carbondale, Illinois 62901
Phone (618) 536-7702

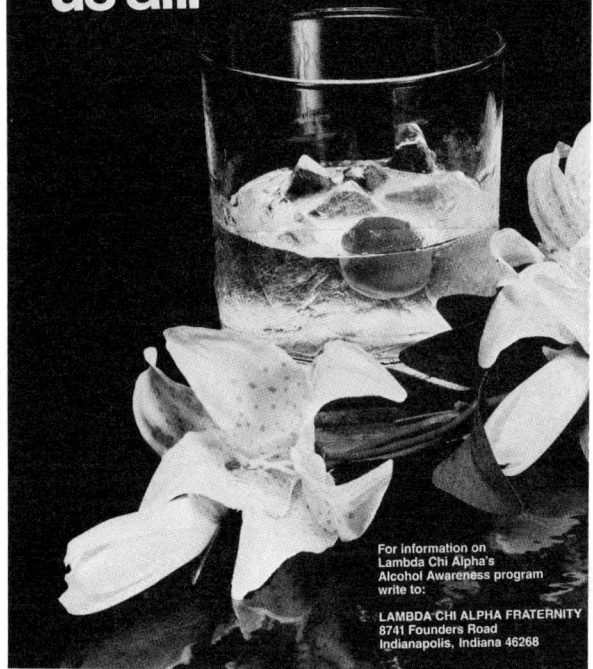

The Life of
the Party can be
the Death of
us all.

For information on
Lambda Chi Alpha's
Alcohol Awareness program
write to:

LAMBDA CHI ALPHA FRATERNITY
8741 Founders Road
Indianapolis, Indiana 46268

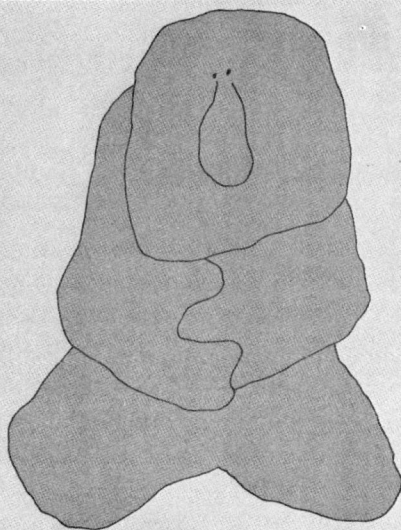

It's rude to
refuse a drink.

Nonsense.

What's rude is trying to push
a drink on someone who doesn't
want it. Or shouldn't have it.

Drinking Myths Series
Alcohol Education Project
Student Wellness Resource Center
Southern Illinois University at Carbondale
Carbondale, Illinois 62901
Phone (618) 536-7702

Give him black coffee.
That'll sober him up.

Sure...in about five hours.
Cold showers don't work either.
Only time can get the alcohol out
of the system as the liver
metabolizes the alcohol.
Slowly.
There's no way to hurry it.

Drinking Myths Series
Alcohol Education Project
Student Wellness Resource Center
Southern Illinois University at Carbondale
Carbondale, Illinois 62901
Phone (618) 536-7702

After Hours Program, Alcohol Education Office, University Center, Northern Michigan University.

Appendix 11–D

TGIF Program

As we reviewed and analyzed the use of alcohol on the Hanover College, Hanover, Indiana, campus, it was generally agreed that Friday afternoons and evenings were a heavy usage time for many of our students. Further discussion resulted in the suggestion that alternatives to drinking be found and offered to fill this time block.

A hand-picked student committee was formed immediately to do brainstorming. Atmosphere and entertainment were determined to be important aspects of the local establishments appealing to students on Fridays. If we could create a similar environment without alcohol, students would stay on campus. The questions of atmosphere, entertainment, and publicity were immediately addressed. Funds for entertainment and publicity were requested from the Student Programming Board. We were funded $2,500.00 for the remainder of the year. Each student member was assigned a Friday and a budget.

The Campus Center Director and a member of the Student Affairs staff worked to create a special Friday atmosphere in our student snack bar.

Snack Bar Changes for Atmosphere:
1. using tall room dividers to break up large open spaces and create more intimate conversation areas
2. construction of movable stage and backdrop for Friday performances
3. red tablecloths for all tables
4. closing of curtains and lowering of lights

Promotional Ideas:
1. free T-shirts advertising entertainment for the week

2. free food item—not regularly available on menu, such as bagels and cream cheese, pizza, popcorn, and pretzels
3. taped announcements in Campus Center
4. more unique posters all over campus

Programs to Date:
January 25—Folk singer who is popular favorite in local bars
February 1—Harmonica Bob (professional)
February 8—Student Talent Show
February 15—Mime (professional)
February 22—Roommate Game

Future Programs:
Crazy Charlie—Magician and Impressionist
Faculty/Staff Talent Show
Friday Frisbee Fling—Frisbee/golf, contests in accuracy, distance, tricks
Group Games—Team from every living unit
Outdoor Music Festival

Evaluation to Date:
Program has been well received. Smallest crowd has been 75 people. Largest crowd has been around 400 people. Student feedback and enthusiasm is positive. Student Programming Board is in process of establishing TGIF Committee as a permanent committee.

Source: Hanover College Alcohol Program Materials: T.G.I.F. Program. Office of Student Affairs, Hanover College, Hanover, Indiana. (no date).

181

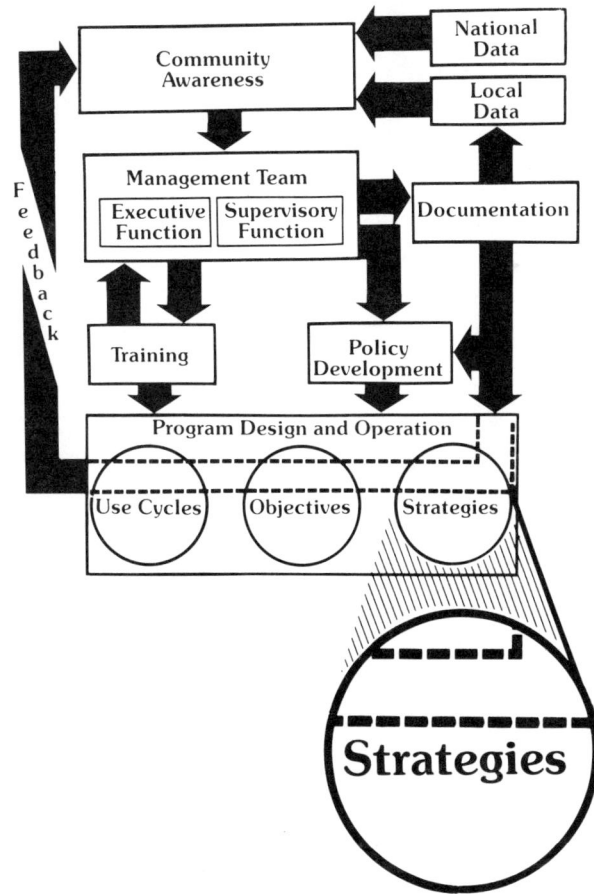

Chapter 12

THE PEER GROUP MEETING

By the end of this chapter, you should be able to:

1. List three functions the peer meeting can serve;
2. Define group learning;
3. List six techniques that help build group cohesiveness quickly; and
4. Outline the major steps in design and delivery of an alcohol education workshop.

A group meeting/workshop is structured group learning experience designed around specific objectives shared with the participants. Quite simply, instructional objectives are statements of the ways one expects the participants to be different after the group experience. The targeted changes will dictate the form and content of the workshop. Ideally, these objectives should be linked to the alcohol use cycle and should strongly emphasize participatory activities.

This strategy can provide:

1. Knowledge and information to the individual;
2. An opportunity to compare attitudes with others;
3. Opportunities to practice new behaviors; and
4. A forum for public expression of new beliefs, attitudes, and behaviors, which may create new social norms for a particular group.

Peer educators conducting group meetings should strive to create a congenial atmosphere for group learning. Group learning is active participation by every member of the group, and involves communication between members, appropriate feedback, and individual commitment to group goals. Most college courses, training seminars in industry, and high school classes do not use or encourage group learning. These traditional methods may be appropriate for technical material, but are inappropriate for alcohol education. The duty of the instructor in group learning is facilitation— encouraging participation with questions, provoking involvement with group exercises, and providing feedback about the possible outcomes that follow various drinking patterns. The peer educator should guide learning, not dictate it.

Participants in alcohol education workshops are part of a larger social group. That group will have built-in norms, well-developed patterns of communication, and probably strong normative beliefs about alcohol use. Against this backdrop, the alcohol educator must conduct a learning experience about highly charged material.

Certain techniques allow a leader to build the group quickly and leave the participants with a sense of accomplishment:

1. If possible, limit the group in size to fifteen to twenty to allow for:
   — more individual communication
   — more chance for feedback to each participant
   — room for some emotional expression of feelings (attitudes) toward consequences of alcohol use

185

— greater group cohesion

2. Use material taken from the participants' everyday experiences as focal points for discussion:
   — slides of drinking scenes
   — home movies
   — a recent incident with alcohol (positive as well as negative)
   — magazine ads for alcohol
   — local political issue in newspaper about alcohol policy and laws
   — a potential alochol problem (litter, rock concert)

3. Conduct short group participation exercises that are entertaining:
   — role play
   — psychodrama
   — new games
   — trust/play exercises
   — wine/cheese tasting
   — breathalyzer demonstration—limit to blood alcohol concentration (BAC) of .10 (0.10 grams alcohol/100 milliliters blood) (caution: can produce competitive atmosphere)

4. Focus on problem-solving techniques to elaborate on a simple theme:
   — brainstorming
   — polling
   — competitive group strategies
   — team building exercises

5. Focus on positive alternatives by:
   — preparing a written list of positive outcomes before workshop
   — avoiding the use of value words (*should, must, ought to*) and instead using verbs that suggest (*can, might, could*)
   — avoiding spelling out the negative consequences of alcohol use that are obvious (sickness, obnoxious behavior, arrests)
   — focusing on the participants' beliefs and attitudes and not upon your evaluation of your beliefs—the participants must form their own evaluation of their own beliefs about the consequences of alcohol use

6. Review key material:
   a. Keep key points simple and relevant. For example:
      — intoxication is more alcohol in blood than metabolized
      — intoxication is detrimental to decisions
      — decisions (two choices or more) are crucial to driving
      — intoxication is detrimental to driving
   b. Keep alternatives simple and relevant:
      — pass car keys to friend who is sober if you feel intoxicated
      — learn to listen to others' judgments on your level of intoxication
   c. Review points should be elicited from participants rather than supplied by the facilitator.

A checklist for the design and delivery of an alcohol education workshop is given below to give an idea of the overall process.

Phase I: Needs Assessment
1. Identify target audience and do a formal or informal needs assessment (questions, surveys).
2. From the survey, you may identify risk situations (time, place, behavior); and inappropriate beliefs, attitudes, and behaviors.
3. Define audience demand—what is acceptable, based on what you have learned in the needs assessment.

Phase II: Design and Delivery
1. Decide on a simple theme.
2. Formulate goals.
3. Formulate instructional objectives (specific observable behavior to be acquired).
4. Describe the conditions for learning/instruction.
5. Design strategies that encourage participation and introduce new beliefs, attitudes, and behaviors.
6. Promote workshops with ads and posters.
7. Arrange scheduling of facilities.
8. Test workshop on small group and evaluate results.
9. Collect feedback from first run and redesign for next section.

Phase III: Evaluation
1. State criteria for successful performance of instructional objectives.
2. Specify performance conditions: written test, role play, behavior practice, personal assessment.
3. Conduct evaluation exercises.
4. Give participants *feedback* on:
   a. individual learning accomplishments;
   b. group participation; and
   c. group learning accomplishment (support functions).

The peer group meeting derives its power from collective and individual experiences with alcohol. Since many of the consequences of alcohol use are unwanted or unanticipated, an alcohol education workshop should strive to strengthen group support for behaviors that result in planned, positive results.

A workshop should always be based upon an analysis of the target audience. A formal survey can provide the instructor with organized data from which a workshop design can be derived. A needs analysis may also be informal: a student group may report that its members complain frequently about others who are intoxicated, about litter after parties, and about neighbors who party late into the evening and make sleep or study impossible.

A needs analysis forces the peer educator to focus upon the requirements and demands of the target audience. A group discussion of beliefs about alcohol use should be specific enough so that participants will find the information pertinent to their own exposure to alcohol. For example, fetal alcohol information is appropriate for married students; information about the effects of alcohol on driving skills may be relevant to commuting students; and concerns about individual drinking patterns might be most relevant to residence hall advisers and counselors. It is wise to remember that it is difficult to fill the needs of the target audience, but relatively easy to satisfy the demands that arise from those needs. (People may need to use more public transportation, but until there is a demand for the service, busses and commuter trains will continue to lose money.) This translation of identified needs to actual demands makes it possible to offer more relevant, significant workshops to the audience.

Using information from the needs analysis, it is possible to begin designing the workshop itself. Three initial design steps include: 1) deciding on a theme; 2) formulating goals; and 3) formulating objectives.

STEP 1: DECIDING ON A SIMPLE THEME
Some themes that might be appropriate for workshops include
1. The influence of alcohol advertising on drinking
2. Women and alcohol
3. Alcohol use and pregnancy
4. Alternative party planning
5. Techniques for setting limits on consumption

Themes that are probably inappropriate for a college audience might include:
1. Treatment for alcoholism
2. Psychological dependence on alcohol.
3. History of prevention in the United States
4. Public policy about alcohol abuse
5. Family therapy for the alcohol abuser

STEP 2: DERIVE GOALS
A goal narrows the type of information that is to be processed, and objectives detail the specific content and process the learner will use to accomplish the desired behavior. Examples of workshop goals include the following:
1. Participants will examine the beliefs behind alcohol advertising directed toward their group (students, women, youth, blacks).
2. Participants will analyze situations (in their own lives) in which there is strong social pressure to consume more than two drinks per hour.

STEP 3: FORMULATE OBJECTIVES
Objectives are derived from goals. Instructional objectives specify in behavioral terms what is to be learned. For example, in the workshop "The Influence of Advertising on Expectations" (see Goal Example 1 above) the goal is to have participants consider the beliefs that advertisers transmit to their groups. The following cognitive objectives might be derived from that goal.
1. The participants will be able to list five distinct themes that advertisers use to associate the product with a positive outcome.
2. The participants will illustrate the principle that alcohol intoxication can serve as a discriminative stimulus for a number of behaviors.
3. The participants will be able to identify at least six specific target groups who would be receptive to positive themes in alcohol advertising.

4. The participants will be able to describe how advertisers generate belief credibility through selective placement of their ads.

Sharing the theme and the objectives with the group sets up an implied contract between the participants and the instructor, and places the learner and the peer educator on a more equal footing. This technique creates a more congenial atmosphere for learning and establishes a modicum of trust between partipant and leader.

Affective objectives are more difficult to evaluate, but are more important for problem-reduction. Typical affective objectives might include the student deciding to:

1. consume no more than two beers Thursday night after work at the airport club
2. consume small amounts of nonsalty food while having some wine at the Wednesday afternoon faculty cocktail party
3. pass the car keys to a friend Saturday night after others suggest that he or she might be too intoxicated to drive
4. drink only two glasses of wine with dinner and refrain from drinking three hours before bedtime.

Objectives that focus on what the participant is not to do or to be are unlikely to be successful. For example, the participant will not *want* to:

1. drink excessively
2. fight while drinking
3. drink beyond his or her limit
4. discuss family problems while drinking
5. go to sleep drunk
6. get drunk at every party

The objectives you have developed reflect sets of beliefs and attitudes that can be used in exercises in your instruction. For example, if the target behavior is to consume only two beers after school Thursday night, then the following *positive beliefs* are likely to be relevant to the workshop::

1. If I drink two beers or fewer beers, my appearance is likely to remain nice. remain nice.
2. People who drink two or less beers are more alert than people who drink six or more beers.
3. Drinking two beers allows me to relax and not become loud or sloppy.
4. Drinking six or more beers increases my chance of getting a DUI (arrest for driving under the influence).
5. Drinking two or fewer beers will allow me to feel part of the crowd.

These belief statements, if credible and relevant to the drinker, are very likely to result in a positive attitude toward drinking two beers and a negative attitude toward drinking six. However, a group discussion of the following topics would *not* be expected to alter consumption patterns on Thursday night (or any night for that matter).

1. Heavy drinkers are more likely to have liver disease.
2. Taxes collected on alcoholic beverages are often used to build highways.
3. Alcohol abusers are also likely to abuse other substances.
4. Government programs often generate policies targeted to per capita consumption.
5. Heavy alcohol use and smoking increases the chances of heart disease.
6. Alcoholics have family problems.

These topics have little to do with an individual's perception of the consequences of his or her consumption as a member of a group.

AN EXAMPLE.

Consider the relationship between driving and drinking. How much have you heard about the problem? How much of that information has affected your behavior? If you were going to make a group presentation about driving under the influence, of all the facts you know what information do you think would be meaningful to your audience?

Through some form of audience assessment, you might isolate two items that would be important for that particular group: (1) the number of drinks a person consumes affects his or her ability to operate a motor vehicle; and (2) if one gets convicted for drunken driving one loses one's license. You could present specific facts about these items; for example, the number of drinks, the effect on driving skills, the criteria and penalties for drunken driving. This information is carefully chosen and limited in scope.

The items above are clearly related to the consequences of alcohol use (in the alcohol use cycle). You might begin with a discussion of intoxication—blood alcohol content (BAC) as a function of the number of drinks, weight of the drinker, and rate of consumption—and move on to specific information about the BAC level that makes one legally drunk in your state. You would also want to design experiences or presentations that could:

1. Increase your peers' awareness of the *situations* (with attendant *pressures*) in which they are likely to drink and drive;
2. Illustrate how different drinking styles (*behavior*), with different beverages, could push the blood alcohol level beyond the legal limit (behavioral and biological *consequences*);
3. Examine *beliefs* and *attitudes* that lead to drinking and driving;
4. Introduce *beliefs* and *attitudes* that would be likely to prevent one from driving while intoxicated; and
5. Review the legal *consequences* of conviction for Driving Under the Influence (DUI), including the variations for one, two, three, or more convictions.

The five items above are the learning objectives for a peer meeting on this subject and include six of the seven parts of the alcohol use cycle: drinking behavior, consequences, beliefs and attitudes, situations, and social pressure. Only the *decision* component is not directly addressed.

Under the first objective (1), you might discuss the implications of holding parties in locations beyond walking distance from the homes of the guests, social events where no alternatives to alcohol are served, and giving parties (and serving alcohol) without provisions for alternative sleeping arrangements or transportation for inebriated guests. For the second objective, a discussion or demonstration might focus on how gulping straight liquor, competitive drinking, or serving drinks without food may lead to a BAC that would impair driving.

"Risky" beliefs and attitudes under goal (3) would include: 'I'll never get caught," "I can always hold my liquor," "I know when I am not in control," or even "I can drive perfectly well because I am used to drinking and driving." An individual holding these beliefs could easily consume five or six drinks per hour and then attempt to drive home. New beliefs and attitudes (4) might include: "A driver is *legally* impaired if he or she consumes more than four drinks per hour, and many people are impaired with as few as three per hour," and "If I drink more than two beers, two glasses of wine, or two straight drinks in an hour, I will try to avoid driving."

References

Finn, P. 1981a. "Teaching Students to Be Lifelong Peer Educators. *Health Education 5* (September/October): 13–16.

———. 1981b. "Institutionalizing Peer Education in the Health Education Classroom." *The Journal of School Health* 2 (February): 91–95.

Gonzalez, G.M. 1978. "What Do You Mean Prevention? *Journal of Alcohol and Drug Education* 3 no. 3 (Spring): 14–23.

———. 1980. "The Effect of a Model Alcohol Education Module on College Students' Attitudes, Knowledge and Behavior Related to Alcohol Use. *Journal of Alcohol and Drug Education vol.25 (3)* Spring 1980: 1–11.

Gonzalez, G.M., and J.M. Kouba, 1979. "Comprehensive Alchool Education: A New Approach to an Old Problem." *NASPS Journal* 16 no. 4 (Spring): 17–14.

Kelly, N.M. 1978. "Health Education through Entertainment; a Multimedia Campaign." *Journal of the American College Health Association* 26: 248–252.

Kraft, D.P. 1979. "Strategies of Reducing Drinking Problems among Youth: College Programs." In *Youth Alcohol and Social Policy* edited by H.T. Blane and M.E. Chafetz, pp. 311–353. New York: Plenum Press.

Mellor, E.T. 1976. "University of Massachusetts Training Program for Peer Alcohol Educators," In *The Whole College Catalog about Drinking*, U.S. Department of Health, Education and Welfare, pp. 89–90. Washington, D.C.: U.S. Government Printing Office (ADM-76-361).

U.S. Department of Health, Education and Welfare. 1976. *The Whole College Catalog about Drinking*, Washington, D.C.: U.S. Government Printing Office (ADM-76-361).

Part II

THE ALCOHOL USE CYCLE
Self-Instructional Modules for Peer Educators

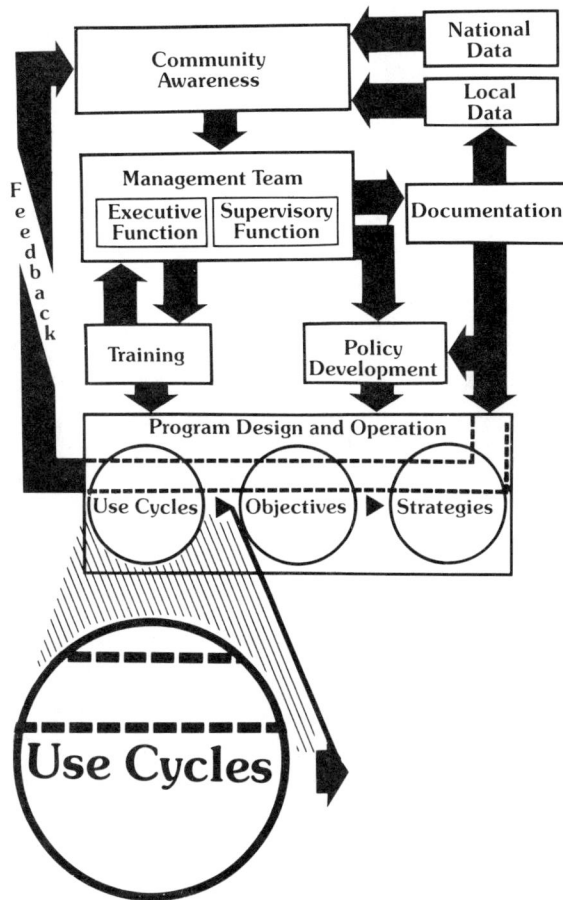

Community Awareness

National Data

Local Data

Feedback

Management Team

Executive Function

Supervisory Function

Documentation

Training

Policy Development

Program Design and Operation

Use Cycles

Objectives

Strategies

Use Cycles

Chapter 13

INTRODUCTION TO MODULES FOR SELF-INSTRUCTION

The last portion of this book is written as a self-instructional manual. It can be used as a training tool for peer educators, as a source of alcohol-specific information for program activities, and as a basis for designing group experiences. Each chapter begins with a list of objectives and ends with an evaluation of your mastery of the objectives. Tests are provided for self-evaluation. We suggest that the best procedure is to study the objectives carefully, refer to them as you read the chapter, and review them before you take the self-test. If you answer any question incorrectly, you should repeat the relevant portions of the chapter. The chapters are sequential, each builds on material from previous chapters, so it is important to master one chapter before moving on to the next.

Before reading any further, you should review the first part of Chapter 7, which is an explanation of the Alcohol Use Cycle. When you have finished reviewing that material, you will be prepared to read the two case studies presented below. In the first one, the parts of the cycle are identified beside the text. In the second, spaces are provided for you to identify the parts of the cycle yourself.

Case Study 1

Clark Reinhold cut a sharp profile for a prelaw student. He was a member of Alpha Kappa, held a 3.8 average in his combined major of political science and business, was apparently in excellent physical condition, and showed many leadership characteristics that suggested he would have little trouble in law practice.

His arrest for driving while intoxicated occurred late Saturday night after the season's first winning football game. **Consequences**

When Clark first saw the flashing blue light of the city patrol car, he assumed that he should pull over to let the officer pass. He was honestly amazed when the police car pulled up behind him and the officer approached him and asked for his license. Clark had just finished the last of the keg and was escorting his date, Julie, to her home. He felt a little tipsy, but when the **Situations** officer told him to step out of the vehicle, he suddenly realized that he was **Biological** drunker than he thought. Clark failed the motor performance tests, and was **Consequences** arrested after he blew a .18 on the breathalyzer at the station. He was to **Legal** appear in the district court in forty-five days and was charged with DWI **Consequences** (Driving While Intoxicated).

Clark had been a light drinker as a freshman when he lived in a north campus dorm. He occasionally would have a beer or two at the floor parties, **Behavior** but seldom got drunk. In fact, when he witnessed his friends obviously **Situations** intoxicated, he felt a little embarrassed and uncomfortable. He thought **Attitudes** drinking was more or less a waste of time. **Belief**

During his sophomore year Clark pledged for Alpha Kappa because his older brother suggested that this was "the group" to give you important contacts in both the business and law fields. During the first year Clark was surprised by the fact that there were often two or three parties a week at the **Situations** House. The fraternity members' grades did not seem to suffer. He joined in occasionally, and found he could handle his liquor quite well. He also found **Belief**

197

Belief
Situation
Consequences
Consequences

Belief

Situations
Beliefs
Attitudes

Consequences

Decisions
Consequences
Situations

Belief

he could talk more freely after two or three drinks. During his junior year, Clark was drinking three or four nights a week. He always managed to rise for class and seldom experienced serious problems while drinking. Occasionally he was bothered by a hangover but this did not seem atypical.

In his senior year Clark continued to drink with the same pattern he exhibited during his junior year. He also found that he was able to meet more people when he attended a variety of campus parties. His older brother began to introduce him to friends in the business world, and would often invite Clark to cocktail parties where mixed drinks were served. Clark found he could handle the drinking in this setting and enjoyed the ability to relax and carry out a glib conversation after a few doubles. However, he was starting to think more and more about his drinking.

At first, Clark thought that his arrest for DWI was a "chance happening." Then, the interviewing court officer asked him about previous arrests, and Clark clearly stated that he had none. When he was asked whether he would be willing to attend classes on alcohol education, he said it might not be a bad idea.

Since Clark began his senior year, he found weekend drinking with the "boys" less appealing. The hangover interfered with his ability to study for Monday exams, especially his course in financial management. He also discovered he enjoyed Julie's companionship more when he remained sober. As Clark began to become more aware of sophomore and junior drinking he toyed with the idea that alcohol education for entering freshmen might be justified.

Case Study 2

Instructions: Identify the parts of the cycle in this case study.

David and Peggy Morrow arrived at the State University campus in late summer to begin their first year of graduate training. David was accepted into the doctoral program in sociology, and Peggy had achieved candidacy for the MBA program a year earlier. After their baccalaureate graduation, David had taken a year off to work for a Chicago advertising agency. Although he had an economics background and was attracted to the business world, he found that the work lacked creativity. He explored a number of graduate training options, and Peggy suggested that he look into the social science departments to widen his interests. Since she had been accepted for the MBA program during the previous spring she audited two courses before she committed herself full time.

1. _____

2. _____
3. _____

4. _____

During their undergraduate years, Peggy and David could both be considered light drinkers. They drank wine infrequently, on special dinner occasions, and David had only been drunk twice during his college career. However, recently, David was discovering new varieties of wine, and drinking was becoming more or less an accepted pattern with the evening meal. He claimed that wine let him relax before the long evenings of study.

During dinner, the conversations were more animated, if not heated, and David claimed the wine added a new dimension to their evening together. David would often continue to drink after dinner while studying, and in the mornings Peggy would find the half-gallon bottle of wine that they opened for dinner—empty. Peggy also noticed that David's sleep was more restless. It was becoming more difficult to rouse David for morning classes. Often he would miss class, but would register the claim that graduate training did not require strict attendance. He was training to be a scientist, not a business mechanic.

5. _____
6. _____

7. _____
8. _____
9. _____
10. _____

During the weekends, David and Peggy found more parties to attend than they had in the past. Peggy was also anxious because they had shifted their recreational activities toward the evening instead of during the day.

11. _____
12. _____
13. _____

They had both given up running when they moved into their new apartment and Peggy gained more than fifteen pounds during the first semester.

When Peggy suggested that they cut down on their wine consumption David reacted by saying that most social science professionals drank moderately, without consequences, and the faculty parties they attended were excellent examples. David also argued that the only important checkpoints were the first year exams and the dissertation. He was confident that his class participation and studying were progressing adequately, and the drinking was unlikely to interfere with his graduate training.

14. _____

15. _____

When David was asked about alcohol education through a telephone survey he chuckled. He reacted and said the notion was absurd and felt that most people were able to control their drinking without formal training.

16. _____

The correct responses were:

1. Behavior
2. Situations
3. Beliefs and behavior
4. Beliefs
5. Behavioral consequences
6. Attitudes
7. Situations
8. Behavior

9. Biological consequences
10. Beliefs
11. Situations
12. Situations
13. Consequences
14. Attitudes
15. Beliefs
16. Beliefs

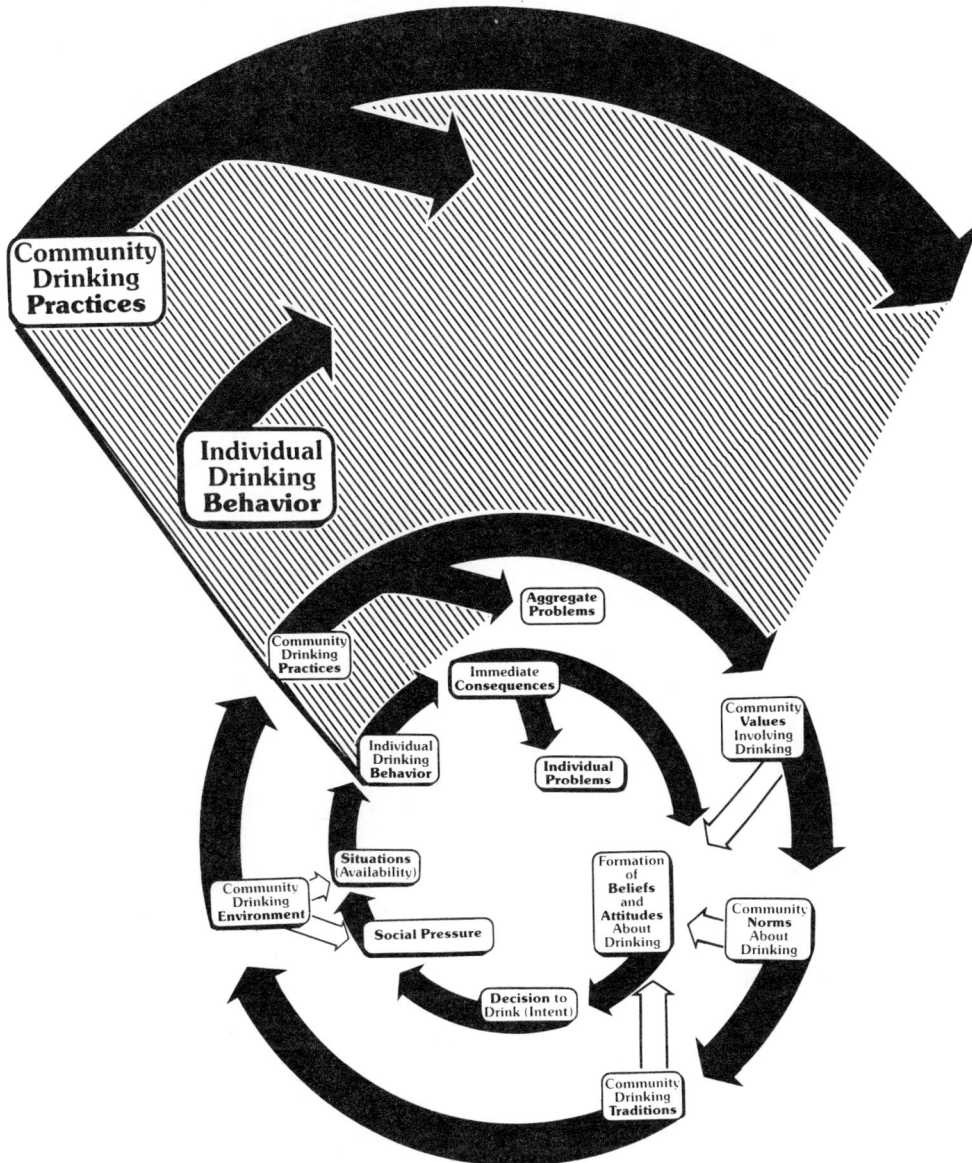

Chapter 14

MODULE 1
Drinking Behavior

When we drink, we usually think of the act as a discrete, single behavior rather than part of a continuous series of behaviors. This unit provides a perspective on drinking behavior that helps to describe it more adequately. Any observable human behavior can be measured along a number of dimensions. Drinking can be analyzed with respect to the type of alcohol consumed, the frequency of consumption, and the contexts in which it occurs. If these measurements are made precisely and reliably, an accurate record of drinking behavior will emerge. Drinking behavior can be calculated by reference to the *acute* (initial) *dose,* by *acute exposure* (alcohol consumed on one occasion), and by *chronic exposure* (repeated occasions of alcohol exposure).

The amount of pure ("absolute") alcohol consumed at one time is called the *acute dose.* The acute dose is usually expressed in terms of the weight of alcohol consumed relative to the drinker's body weight. Each milliliter of absolute alcohol weighs .8 gram, and a 60 kilogram (132 lb) person who consumed 20 grams of alcohol at one time would receive an *acute dose* of .33 gm/kg of absolute alcohol (20 gm ÷ 60 kg = .33 gm/kg). There are approximately twelve grams of alcohol in a twelve-ounce can of beer (or about one gram per ounce), so a 60 kg person drinking two beers would receive an acute dose of .4 gm/kg (24 gm ÷ 60 kg = .4 gm/kg).

Because the liver is able to eliminate alcohol only at a fixed rate—approximately .125 grams per hour—the acute dose is stored in the bloodstream where it is carried to the brain and causes intoxication. Chapter 15 contains a detailed explanation of the biological processes involved in the storage, absorption, and elimination of alcohol, but for the present it is sufficient to say that alcohol stored in the bloodstream can be measured with some degree of accuracy. After drinking two beers in one hour the 60 kg person's blood alcohol concentration (BAC) would be approximately .06 grams per 100 milliliters of blood (see Table 15–2, page 218).

However, a person is unlikely to drink only two beers at the beginning of a party and then stop. It is more reasonable to assume that he/she will continue to drink throughout the evening. Because the liver will eliminate slightly less than one beer per hour, the 60 kg drinker would need only *one* additional beer per hour to maintain a BAC of .06 gm/100 ml. Since .10 gm/100 ml is the legal standard for drunkenness in most states, the implications of this "maintenance dose" are obvious. Drinking more than one additional beer per hour could push the BAC over the limit.

If the 60 kg person drank no more than five beers in four hours, he/she would consume 60 grams of alcohol, and his/her *acute exposure* for the evening would be 1 gm/kg (one gram of alcohol per kilogram of body weight). Acute exposure, then, is a measurement of drinking on a single occasion.

Spirits such as bourbon or scotch contain more alcohol than beer or wine. There are 15 grams of alcohol in a shot (1.5 oz) of distilled spirits, but only 10 to 12 grams in a glass (4 oz) of table wine. This means that a person could drink less wine than beer and less bourbon than wine to reach the same blood alcohol level. Since blood alcohol content is also affected by the amount of body tissue into which the alcohol is absorbed, a person weighing only 100 pounds could drink much less than a 250 pound person and yet achieve the same BAC—they would both have the same *acute exposure.* The amount of intoxication felt by the drinker on a given occasion is affected by the rate of consumption, the type of drink consumed, the drinker's body weight, and the amount of time that he/she continues to drink.

When acute (short-term) exposure to alcohol is repeated in different situations or contexts, it is called *chronic exposure.* Chronic exposure is important because it produces unique effects on the drinker that differ from the effects of acute exposure. Intoxication is an immediate result of acute exposure, but various kinds of biological damage may result from repeated, long-term exposure to alcohol.

Chronic exposure is calculated by multiplying acute exposure times the repetitive frequency of consumption. For example, an initial *acute dose* of alcohol might consist of:

3 beers consumed by a *150 pound person* in *one hour*

in which case the drinker would have an initial blood alcohol level of .08 gm/100 ml. To maintain that BAC level for three additional hours, the drinker would only need to consume two beers each hour, so that at the end of four hours he/she would have had nine beers. The *acute exposure* would total 108 grams of alcohol or about 1.6 gm/kg:

9 beers times *12 grams* of alcohol equals *108 grams;*
108 grams divided by *68 kilograms* (150 lb) equals *1.6 gm/kg.*

If the drinker repeated the performance two times in a given month, he/she would accumulate a *chronic exposure* of 216 grams of alcohol per month, or 3.2 gm/kg per month (216 gm ÷ 68 kg = 3.2 gm/kg).

Chronic exposure, then, is repeated application of acute exposure, and one could calculate a person's chronic exposure for a year, several years, or even a lifetime. Long-term high level exposure to alcohol produces the kinds of biological deterioration often seen in heavy drinkers and alcoholics: damage to the liver, heart, pancreas, muscle tissue, and central nervous system. Recent studies suggest that consuming more than five drinks a day (60 to 80 grams of alcohol) increases the chance of cardiovascular disease and cirrhosis of the liver.

Exercise
Mark through the *incorrect* statements in the list below.
a. Chronic exposure is repeated occasions of exposure to alcohol.
b. Acute exposure is repeated occasions of exposure to alcohol.
c. An acute dose is the amount of alcohol consumed initially.
d. Acute exposure can be expressed in grams of alcohol per kilogram of body weight.
e. Chronic exposure can be expressed in grams of alcohol per kilogram of body weight.

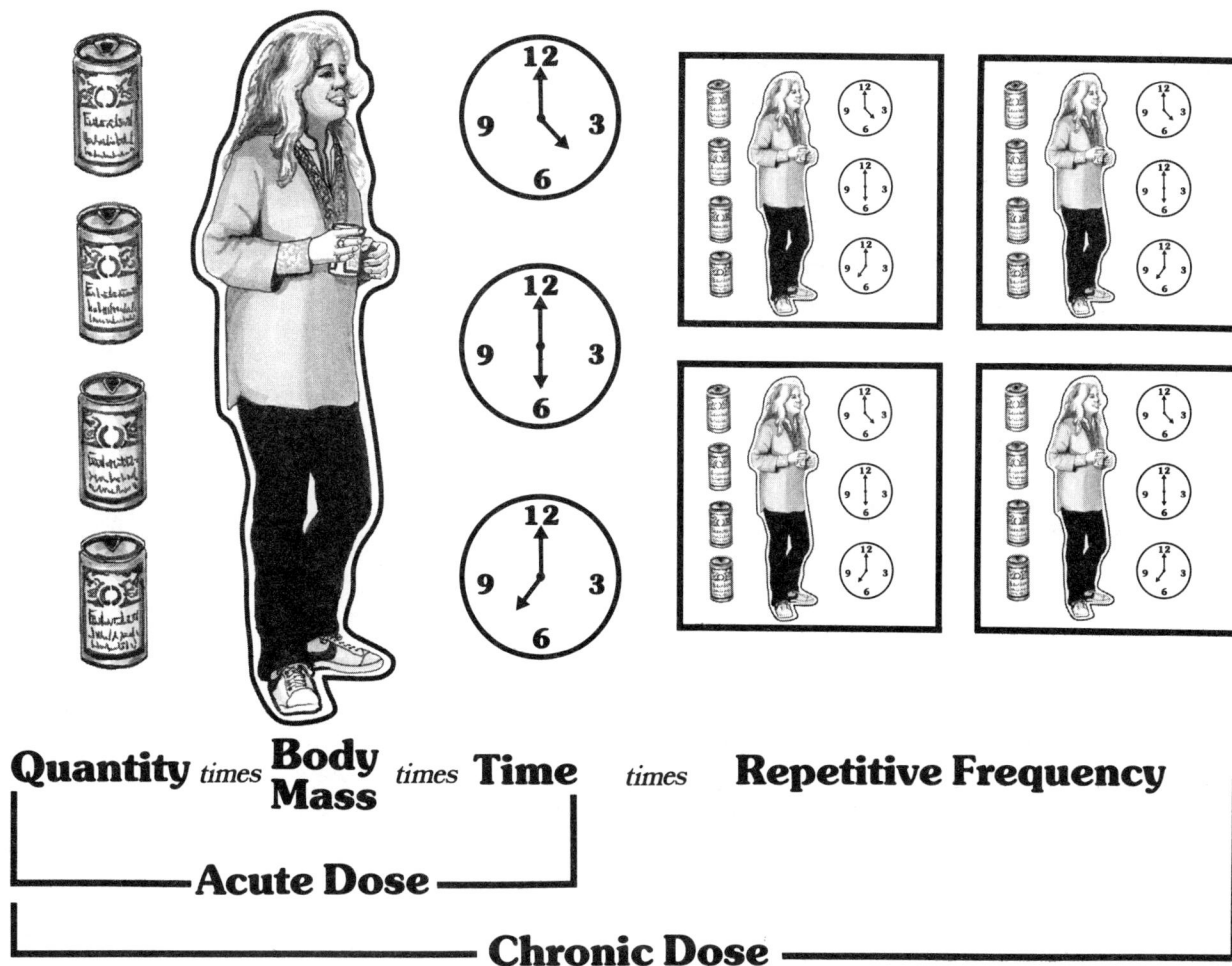

Figure 14–1. Acute dose and chronic dose.

   f. Acute exposure is the amount of alcohol consumed on one occasion.
   g. The effects of chronic exposure and acute exposure are identical.

    Answer: Incorrect statements are items b and g.

The Consequences of Alcohol Use

Although it may seem self-evident, it is important to emphasize that drinking alcohol produces different consequences than drinking milk, coffee, tea, cola, or other nonalcoholic beverages. Drinking alcohol produces intoxication: a unique biological and behavioral event that has the potential to influence and become part of other biological and behavioral events, especially when intoxication is repeated.

The degree to which we become aware of the impact of a behavior on the environment is determined by: 1) how well we are able to define and specify that behavior as distinct from other behaviors; and 2) our sensitivity in measuring the effects (consequences) upon all areas of the environment. This sensitivity, or lack of it, determines whether a consequence will be anticipated or unanticipated. Anticipated consequences are usually derived from personal past experiences or from observation of other people.

The most immediate and anticipated consequences of drinking alcohol are biological. Some biologically anticipated and unanticipated consequences are as follows:

Anticipated Biological Consequences	Unanticipated Biological Consequences
Intoxication	Nausea
Euphoria	Vomiting
Pleasant taste	Hangover
Calories	Injuries

It is important to note that unanticipated consequences of alcohol use are less likely to occur than anticipated consequences, and they are more likely to be negative than positive. Anticipated consequences tend to be immediate, whereas unanticipated consequences are more likely to be delayed. For example, a hangover is less likely to occur than intoxication; is more negative than intoxication; and comes the day after drinking (whereas intoxication is immediate). In alcohol education, we attempt to show that the consequences of moderate drinking are likely to be immediate and positive, whereas the consequences of over-consumption are delayed and negative.

The next module (Chapter 15) examines biological effects in greater detail, and Module 3 (Chapter 16) delves into the behavioral effects generated by chronic doses. In this module we simply wish to emphasize that there are complex effects that go beyond the immediate drinking situation. Unfortunately, as people drink in more situations, both anticipated and unanticipated consequences increase. For example:

Anticipated Behavioral Consequences	Unanticipated Behavioral Consequences

Individual:

1. Stress relief	1. Must have alcohol to relax
2. Forget worries	2. Irritability next morning
3. Feel better about self	3. Sleep loss

Interpersonal:

1. Communicate with boss	1. Family problems
2. Feel in control	2. Criticism by friends
3. Talk more fluently	3. Fight with best friend

Social/Legal:

1. Celebrate	1. Driving under the influence
2. Meet new people at party	(DUI) offense
3. Cut loose once in a while	2. Missed class
	3. Late for work

People usually perceive only the immediate, positive consequences of drinking. These consequences are within the drinker's control. One goal of alcohol education is to raise group awareness of the chronic effects of drinking.

Exercise.   *Place* true *or* false *in the space provided beside each statement below:*

a. _____   Unanticipated consequences of drinking are more likely to be negative than positive.

b. _____   Anticipated consequences are likely to be delayed.

c. _____   Intoxication is an unanticipated consequence.

d. _____   A hangover is an unanticipated consequence.

e. _____   Unanticipated consequences are less likely to occur than anticipated consequences.

f. _____   Nausea is an unanticipated consequence.

g. _____   Sleep loss is an anticipated consequence.

Answers: (a) true; (b) false; (c) false; (d) true; (e) true; (f) true; and (g) false.

Thought Question

How might the information in this chapter be applied to community goals and objectives to reduce problem levels?

Additional Readings

Cahalan, D., I.H. Cisin; and H.M. Crossley. 1969. *American Drinking Practices—A National Study of Drinking Behavior and Attitudes.* New Haven, Conn.: College and University Press.

Ewing, J.A. 1981. *Drinking to Your Health.* Reston, Va.: Reston Publishing Co., Inc.

Keller, M., and M. McCormick. 1968. *A Dictionary of Words about Alcohol.* Richmond, Va.: The William Byrd Press, Inc.

Mayer, J.E., and W.J. Filstead. 1980. *Adolescence and Alcohol.* Cambridge, Mass.: Ballinger Publishing Co.

McCarthy, R.G., editor. 1959. *Drinking and Intoxication: Selected Readings in Social Attitudes and Controls.* New Haven, Conn.: College and University Press.

Miller, W.R., and R.F. Munoz. 1976. *How to Control Your Drinking.* Englewood Cliffs, N.J.: Prentice-Hall, Inc.

Module 1 Final Test

1. Define acute exposure to alcohol.

2. Define chronic exposure to alcohol.

3. Place a "U" beside the unanticipated consequences, and an "A" beside the anticipated consequences of drinking.

   a. _____ family problems
   b. _____ euphoria
   c. _____ relief of stress
   d. _____ loss of sleep
   e. _____ DUI offense
   f. _____ hangover
   g. _____ intoxication
   h. _____ forget worries
   i. _____ late for work
   j. _____ feel less hungry
   k. _____ talk more fluently

ANSWERS TO MODULE 1 FINAL TEST

1. Acute exposure to alcohol is a measurement of drinking on a *single occasion*, and is associated with positive, *anticipated* consequences of drinking.

   quantity $/$ body weight $/$ unit time

2. Chronic exposure to alcohol is a measurement of *repeated occasions* of exposure to alcohol, and is associated with negative, *unanticipated* consequences of drinking.

   acute dose $/$ repetitive frequency

3. a. U   d. U   g. A   j. A
   b. A   e. U   h. A   k. A
   c. A   f. U   i. U

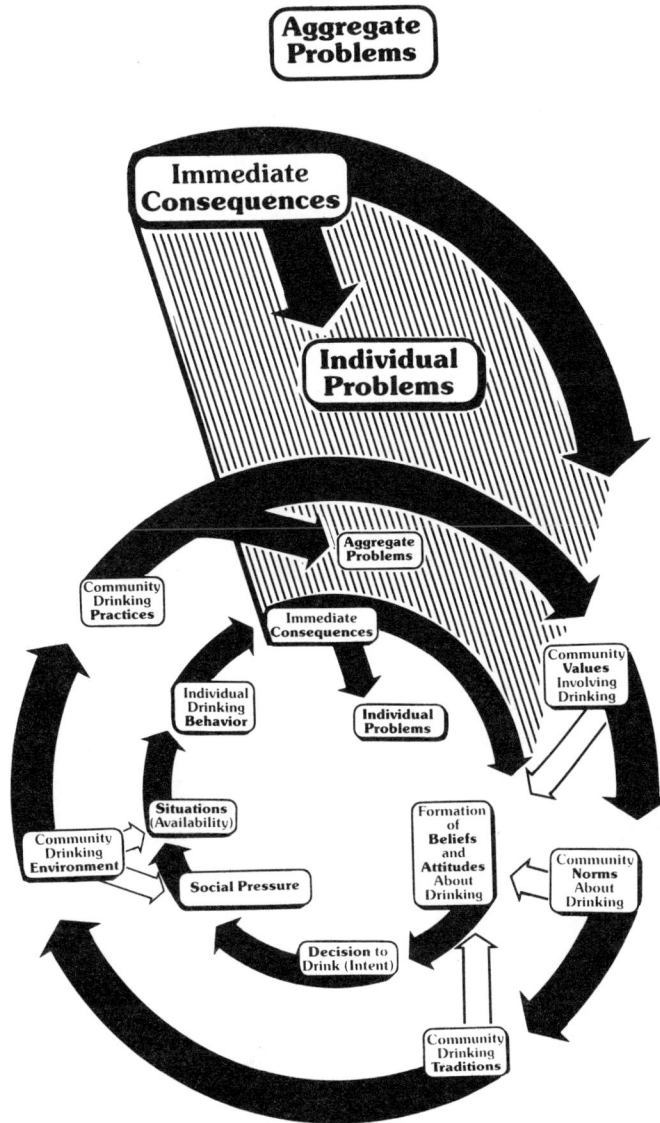

Chapter 15

MODULE 2

Biological Consequences of Drinking

The act of drinking (drinking behavior) has immediate biological consequences. Most people are unaware of the complex chemical and physical interactions that occur in our bodies when we drink. This lack of knowledge has given rise to a number of myths about hangover preventatives, hangover treatments, and the use of various concoctions to sober up an intoxicated person. This module dispels those myths by presenting the biological facts about alcohol's action within the human body.

An acute dose of alcohol, usually taken orally, produces *intoxication,* which is the impact of alcohol upon the brain or central nervous system. Figure 15–1 shows how intoxication follows drinking. The steps are:

1. Intake
2. Storage and Absorption
3. Distribution
4. Detection
5. Oxidation
6. Elimination

Not only does the *dosage* of alcohol determine the degree of intoxication, but so does the *route* of administration. Drinking, of course, is the most common method for consumption, but alcohol could be directly injected into the bloodstream (as it is in some laboratory experiments). The intravenous lethal dose is about one-half the oral lethal dose, since the alcohol bypasses the digestive system. Alcohol can also be introduced into the bloodstream by inhaling the vapors. Studies have shown that laboratory animals can become physiologically addicted as a result of inhaling alcohol.

211

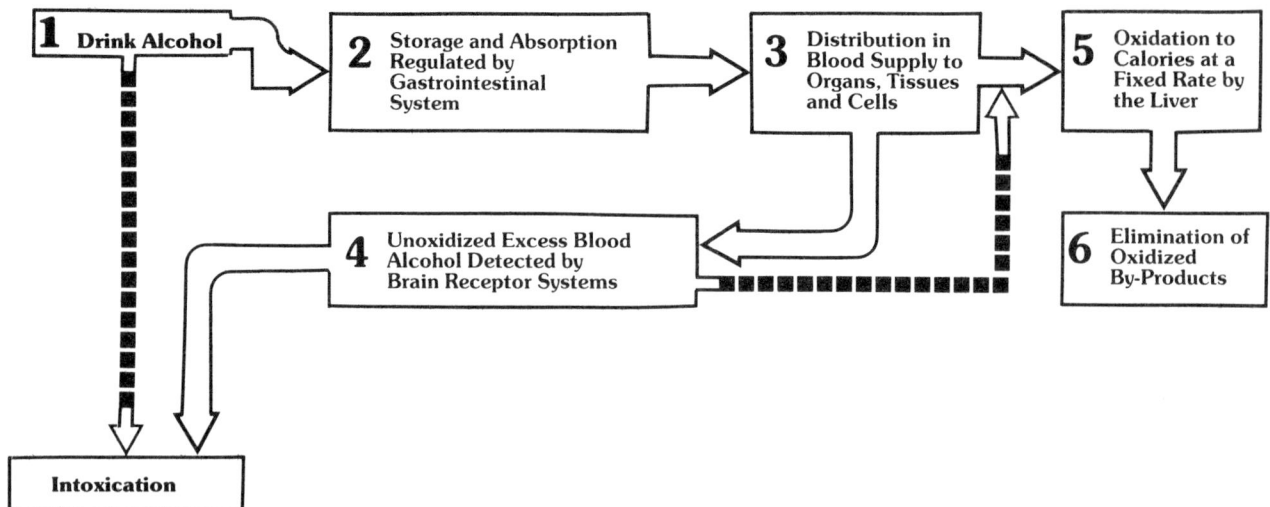

Figure 15–1.   Alcohol metabolism.

Storage and Absorption

Alcohol enters the digestive tract from the mouth, goes through the esophagus and into the stomach. If the drinker has not eaten recently, approximately 25 to 30 percent of the ingested alcohol will be directly absorbed into the bloodstream from the stomach. Alcohol differs from other foods in that it does not require digestion and is partly absorbed directly from the stomach. The remaining alcohol is emptied into the upper small intestine (the duodenum) and readily absorbed there. The duodenum is the main absorption site for alcohol and all foodstuffs. The critical factor determining the rate of absorption into the bloodstream is *the emptying time of the stomach,* which can be influenced by several factors:

1. The presence of food slows emptying, especially fatty foods, milk products, or a heavy meal. Absorption time is stretched out so that the blood alcohol level does not increase as rapidly and does not become as high.
2. Fasting, or any other condition causing rapid emptying of the stomach will increase the rate and subsequent concentration of alcohol in the blood.
3. The volume, character, and dilution of the alcoholic beverage affects absorption. Concentrations of alcohol of up to 50 percent (100 proof) will increase the rate. Higher concentrations irritate the stomach lining.
4. The period of time over which the beverage is consumed alters absorption: slower drinking means slower absorption.
5. Adrenergic drugs delay emptying.
6. Lower body temperature delays emptying.
7. Cholinergic drugs, alkaline salts, and carbonated beverages will *increase* gastric emptying (hence, "mixers" *speed up intoxication*).

8. Emotional and physical state (fear, stress, anger, and fatigue) may speed up the body's rate of absorption of alcohol.

Exercises. 1. *Which of the following is the critical factor that determines absorption of alcohol into the bloodstream? Circle one.*

    a. presence of food in the stomach
    b. volume, character, and dilution of alcoholic beverage
    c. emptying time of the stomach
    d. body temperature
    e. period of time over which beverage is consumed

Answer: The critical factor that determines absorption of alcohol into the bloodstream is the emptying time of the stomach (c).

2. *Which of the following influences the emptying time of the stomach? Circle as many as apply.*

    a. type of food present in the stomach
    b. period of time over which beverage is consumed
    c. physical activity of the drinker
    d. concentration of alcohol in beverage consumed
    e. type of alcohol consumed (i.e., gin, bourbon, rye, etc.)
    f. presence of food in the stomach
    g. body temperature
    h. size of the stomach
    i. fasting
    j. weight of drinker
    k. presence of carbonated beverage in mixed drinks
    l. emotional state of drinker

Answer: Factors influencing emptying time of the stomach include: period of over which beverage is consumed (b); concentration of alcohol in beverage consumed (d); presence of food in the stomach (f); body temperature (g); fasting (i); presence of carbonated beverage in mixed drinks (k); and the emotional state of the drinker (l).

Distribution

Alcohol diffuses easily across all biological membranes except the skin. Apparently there are no barriers to prevent alcohol from reaching all fluid compartments, therefore it distributes uniformly throughout the body. Alcohol concentration in body tissues is directly proportional to the tissue's fluid content; the greater the supply of fluid in tissues the greater the entrance of alcohol will be. Alcohol reaches maximum concentration in the lungs, heart, kidneys, and the brain more rapidly than the skeletal muscle, since these organs have more fluid than muscle. Alcohol concentrations in tissues with a lower fluid supply, such as in fat and skeletal muscle, increase at a slower rate. Since the central nervous system is so highly supplied with blood, the concentration in brain tissue quickly reaches the same concentration as in the bloodstream.

Oxidation (Metabolism) and Elimination

More than 95 percent of the metabolism of alcohol takes place in the liver. The remaining alcohol is eliminated unchanged in urine, saliva, tears and sweat. The first step in metabolism is the breakdown of alcohol into acetaldehyde by an enzyme in the liver. The rate of this reaction is not related to the blood concentration. In other words, *no matter how drunk a person becomes, he or she metabolizes alcohol at the same rate* and one cannot sober them up with black coffee or anything else. Alcohol is processed at a maximum rate from the first dose that reaches the liver, and the limited supply of the liver enzyme is the limiting factor in the clearance of alcohol from the bloodstream.

The maximum metabolic rate for most moderate drinkers is roughly 8 grams of absolute alcohol per hour in an individual who weighs 150 pounds (70 kilograms). This is slightly less than one ounce of straight whiskey or a 12 ounce beer or 4 ounces of wine per hour. Although the rate is fairly constant for young, moderate drinkers, there are individual variations caused by influences such as chronic alcohol consumption and poor nutrition. The second step in metabolism is the oxidation of acetaldehyde to a substance not toxic to the body. Further oxidation yields carbon dioxide and water.

Alcohol is considered to be a food, since complete oxidation produces 7 kilocalories of energy per gram. Three hundred milliliters (10 ounces) of 86-proof liquor represents about 700 calories, which is one half to one third of the normal daily caloric need of the average adult. However, alcohol does not contain sufficient amounts of protein, vitamins, and minerals to be an adequate source of nutrition.

Detection: Unoxidized
Excess Alcohol = Intoxication

The intoxicating effects of alcohol result from the action of the unoxidized excess alcohol on the brain. Different levels of blood alcohol concentration produce various and progressive effects on the brain. If the amount in the blood is known, the effects on the drinker's behavior can be predicted. Blood alcohol concentration depends on several things, including the amount and method of consumption, rate of consumption, rate of absorption into the bloodstream, volume of blood into which the alcohol is diluted, and the rate of metabolism.

Blood alcohol concentration is stated in terms of the weight of the quantity of alcohol contained in a given volume of blood. The amount is commonly recorded as milligrams (or grams) of alcohol per 100 milliliters of blood. For example, one is considered legally drunk in most states if one has a blood alcohol concentration of 0.10 gram of alcohol per 100 milliliters of blood. For the sake of clarity, concentrations should not be expressed as just "percent alcohol" (e.g., .1 percent) but should be specified as percent weight by volume (0.10 gm/100 ml).

Exercises.   1. *Which of the following best defines intoxication? Circle one.*

a. Intoxication is the effect of alcohol on the drinker's behavior.
b. Intoxication is defined by number of drinks, rate of drinking, volume of blood into which alcohol is diluted, and rate of metabolism.
c. Intoxication is defined by the various and progressive effects of drinking on the brain.
d. Intoxication is the effect of unoxidized excess alcohol on the brain.

Answer: Intoxication is the effect of unoxidized excess alcohol on the brain (d).

2. *Match the activity or biological process in Column 1 with the appropriate step in alcohol metabolism in Column 2.*

_____ a. 25 to 30 percent of ingested alcohol directly absorbed from stomach	1. Intake
_____ b. alcohol concentration is lower in fat and muscle	2. Storage and absorption
_____ c. discharge in urine, saliva, and tears	3. Distribution
_____ d. effect of unoxidized excess alcohol on brain	4. Detection
_____ e. intravenous injection	5. Oxidation
_____ f. breakdown of alcohol into acetaldehyde	6. Elimination
_____ g. psychological effects of alcohol	
_____ h. emptying time of stomach is limiting factor	
_____ i. food value of alcohol	
_____ j. is affected by other foods, drugs, body temperature, emotional state, etc.	
_____ k. oral ingestion	
_____ l. alcohol is carried by blood to all body compartments	
_____ m. intoxication	
_____ n. subcutaneous injection	
_____ o. the action of a liver enzyme	
_____ p. duodenum is main site	
_____ q. tissue's fluid content determines concentration of alcohol	
_____ r. changing acetaldehyde into carbon dioxide and water	

Answers: (a) 2; (b) 3; (c) 6; (d) 4; (e) 1; (f) 5; (g) 4; (h) 2; (i) 5; (j) 2; (k) 1; (l) 3; (m) 4; (n) 1; (o) 5; (p) 2; (q) 3; and (r) 5.

Physiological Effects of Alcohol on the Brain

The action of alcohol on brain tissue is not fully understood, however, scientific studies have yielded several theories. Alcohol appears to disrupt the basic regulation and maintenance processes of brain cells. Activity of neurons is affected. The nerve impulse transmission from neuron to neuron is diminished. Moderate intoxication does not result in decreased cerebral metabolic rates, and does not affect production of energy. Although alcohol is a depressant, low concentrations of alcohol can act as a stimulant by increasing excitability of peripheral nerves, nerve muscle junctions, muscle fibers, and neurons in the central nervous system. Increasing concentrations change the excitability of the central nervous system into depression. The spontaneous and excitable electrical activity of the reticular system within the brainstem is depressed progressively. The state and progression of depression is relative to the amount of alcohol in the blood. Intoxication is usually evident at 0.10 gm/100 ml. Progression may depress the reticular activating system or the entire central nervous system, which leads to coma and death if concentrations reach .40 to .50 gm/100 ml. Death occurs when there is paralysis of the medulla oblongata, the area of the brain responsible for respiration and heart rate (see Table 15–1).

Table 15–1. Alcohol's Effects Are Fairly Predictable from the Amount in the Bloodstream

.02 gm/100 ml of blood—Light and moderate drinkers begin to feel some effects. Reached usually after one drink.

.04—Most people begin to feel relaxed.

.06—Judgment is somewhat impaired, people are less able to make rational decisions about their capabilities, and inhibitions are lowered.

.08—Definite impairment of muscle coordination and driving skills, responses to stimuli are slowing, judgment impaired, inhibitions continue to be lowered, and legally drunk in some states.

.10—Clear deterioration of reaction time and control, legally drunk in most states.

.12—Vomiting, unless level is reached slowly.

.15—Balance and movement are impaired. About 1/2 pint of whiskey circulating in blood.

.20—Decreased pain and sensation, marked decrease in response to stimuli.

.30—Many lose consciousness.

.40—Most lose consciousness, depressed reflexes, anesthesia

.45—Subnormal temperature, impaired circulation and respiration.

.50—Death

Exercise.   *Match the effect in the first column with the blood alcohol concentration in the second column.*

_____ a. legally drunk in most states

_____ b. subnormal temperature

_____ c. decreased pain sensation; marked decrease in response to stimuli

_____ d. most people begin to feel relaxed, jovial

_____ e. clear deterioration of reaction time

f. balance and movement are impaired; about one half pint of whiskey circulating in blood

_____ g. many lose consciousness

_____ h. impaired circulation and respiration

_____ i. vomiting, unless level is reached slowly

_____ j. depressed reflexes, anesthesia

_____ k. death

1. .04
2. .10
3. .12
4. .15
5. .20
6. .30
7. .40
8. .45
9. .50

Answers: (a) 2; (b) 8; (c) 5; (d) 1; (e) 2; (f) 4; (g) 6; (h) 8; (i) 3; (j) 7; (k) 9.

How to Measure Unoxidized Excess Alcohol

Examining a blood sample is not the only way to measure blood alcohol concentration. Laws of diffusion and vapor pressure apply also to the distribution of alcohol between blood and air in the alveoli (air sacs) in the lungs. Therefore, a measure of alcohol from a breath sample can give a reasonably accurate estimate of alcohol concentration in the blood. To illustrate, if one sniffs from an open container of alcohol, one can smell the vapors that hover over the surface. The ratio between the concentration in solution and concentration as vapor is determined by solution temperature and pressure. The container is analogous to the blood circulating through the capillaries of the lungs that contain alcohol. If alcohol is in the blood, a portion of it will escape in vapor form into the alveoli of the lungs.

Many studies have shown that the ratio between blood alcohol concentration and breath alcohol concentration in the alveolar sacs is 2,100:1. A reasonably accurate measurement can be obtained using a breathalyzer, but the person must expire a long deep breath sample to deliver a valid sample.

Exercise.   *The breathalyzer can give a reasonably accurate estimate of alcohol concentration in the blood because (circle one choice).*

a. Studies have shown that the ratio between blood alcohol concentration and breath alcohol concentration is 2,100:1.

b. Unoxidized excess alcohol collects in sacs within lungs in proportion to volume consumed.
c. Laws of diffusion and vapor pressure apply to distribution of alcohol between blood and air in the alveoli in the lungs, and breathalyzers measure this distribution.
d. Alcohol diffuses easily over all biological membranes except the skin.

Answer: The breathalyzer's accuracy can be attributed to distribution of alcohol to blood and air in alveoli of the lungs (c).

Amount of Intoxication = Blood Alcohol Concentration

There are three main factors to consider when reading blood alcohol concentration (BAC) tables. (Refer to Table 15–2.) These considerations include: what constitutes a drink, the weight of the person under observation, and the amount of time spent drinking. (Acute dose = quantity/body weight/time.) A "drink" is the amount of beverage that contains ½ ounce of pure alcohol. This amount is contained in one bottle of beer (12 oz; 360 ml), one glass of wine (4 oz; 120 ml), one small glass of fortified win (2½ oz; 75 ml), and 1 ounce of distilled liquor (30 ml). When determining blood

Table 15–2.   Approximate Blood Alcohol Level in Grams Per 100 ML After One Hour of Drinking.

NUMBER OF DRINKS (12 oz. beer, 4 oz. wine or 1 oz. 85 proof liquor)	BODYWEIGHT IN POUNDS					
	100	120	140	160	180	200
1	0.04	0.04	0.03	0.03	0.02	0.02
2	0.09	0.07	0.06	0.05	0.05	0.04
3	0.13	0.11	0.09	0.08	0.07	0.06
4	0.16	0.14	0.12	0.11	0.10	0.09
5	0.22	0.18	0.16	0.14	0.12	0.11
6	0.26	0.22	0.19	0.16	0.14	0.13
7	0.30	0.25	0.22	0.19	0.17	0.15
8	0.35	0.29	0.25	0.22	0.20	0.17
9	0.39	0.33	0.28	0.25	0.22	0.19

Note: subtract .01 grams/100 ml for each forty minutes of drinking.
Source: The Center for Alcohol Studies
School of Medicine
University of North Carolina
Chapel Hill, North Carolina.

alcohol concentration, body weight and structure must be considered. After drinking the same amount, a person who weighs 160 pounds will have a lower blood alcohol concentration than someone who weighs 110 pounds. The alcohol distributes itself over a greater volume of water in the larger person. However, if we consider body *structure,* the obese person may have a higher blood alcohol concentration than the muscular person of the same weight after drinking the same amount. This difference occurs because fat lowers the number of water compartments available as distribution sites for alcohol. Finally, the number of drinks consumed over the *span of time* must be considered. Of course, the slower the consumption the slower the absorption into the bloodstream.

To compute BAC using Table 15–2, locate the weight of the drinker across the top of the chart, then locate the number of drinks consumed in the column at the left of the table. The intersection of the two columns (weight and number of drinks) is blood alcohol content in grams per 100 milliliters of blood, the most commonly used notation. A person weighing 160 pounds who consumes six drinks in an hour will have a BAC of .16 g/100ml. (and be legally drunk in most states). If this individual takes five hours to consume the same amount of liquor, BAC will only be .08 g/100ml. (subtracting .01 g/100 ml. for every 40 minutes). The computation is: 300 minutes ÷ 40 minutes = 7.5; 7.5 x .01 g/100ml. = .08; .16 − .08 = .08.

Exercises.   1. *Which of the following influence blood alcohol concentration? Circle as many as apply.*

    a. the height of the drinker
    b. the weight of the drinker
    c. the body structure of the drinker
    d. the type of beverage consumed
    e. the amount of water in each drink
    f. the number of drinks consumed
    g. the amount of time spent drinking
    h. the rate at which each drink is consumed
    i. the biological tolerance to alcohol of the drinker

Answers: Blood alcohol concentration is influenced by body weight (b); body structure (c); number of drinks consumed (f); and the amount of time spent drinking (g).

2. Use Table 15–2 to determine the following blood alcohol concentrations.

  a. 2 drinks / 140 lbs / 2 hrs   BAC = _____ g/100ml
  b. 4 drinks / 120 lbs / 3 hrs   BAC = _____ g/100ml
  c. 2 drinks / 120 lbs / 1 hr   BAC = _____ g/100ml
  d. 5 drinks / 120 lbs / 2 hrs   BAC = _____ g/100ml
  e. 8 drinks / 180 lbs / 3 hrs   BAC = _____ g/100ml

Answers: a. .03 g/100ml; b. .09 g/100ml; c. .05 g/100ml; d. .15 g/100ml; e. .15 g/100ml.

Tolerance

Another consequence of alcohol use is *tolerance,* which is the biological and behavioral adaptation to the use of alcohol. Both acute and chronic doses of alcohol result in tolerance. Tolerance develops in all elements of the alcohol use cycle. The drinker adapts not only to a new biological requirement for the drug, but also adapts to new beliefs about the consequences of alcohol use, new attitudes toward those beliefs, and new patterns of drinking behavior. As tolerance builds, the individual develops a greater number of salient beliefs about what he or she expects from alcohol; and the cognitive, behavioral, and biological consequences of alcohol use become more prominent.

Tolerance, simply stated, means that the drinker will need larger doses of alcohol over time to achieve intoxication. The beginning drinker may require only one or two beers to feel the effects of alcohol. If he or she embarks on a drinking career, in a short period (depending on psychological and physical factors unique to the individual), he or she will require three or more beers to feel those same effects.

If a high dose is taken before tolerance is established, unconsciousness or death may result. This is as true for a monkey who overdoses on alcohol through a catheter in its vein as it is for a fraternity brother who chug-a-lugs a fifth of bourbon during freshman orientation. In both cases the subjects have not had time to build up tolerance.

There are two types of alcohol tolerance. The first is *acute tolerance,* which refers to the rather short-term tolerance that a person can develop over a single evening of drinking. Acute tolerance is adaptation to an acute dose. The second kind of tolerance is *chronic tolerance:* it represents the experienced drinker's ability to consume greater amounts of alcohol without behavioral impairment. Both kinds of tolerance represent *adaptive responses* to intoxication.

Acute tolerance represents short-term adaptation to the stimulation provided by alcohol. The drinker shows noticeable impairment while consuming alcohol (when the blood alcohol level is rising). When he or she stops drinking, the blood alcohol levels gradually begin to drop, the impairment is not noticed, even though the actual blood alcohol level may be the same during both the rising and falling portion of the blood alcohol curve. The biological and behavioral adaptation to the initial doses makes the rising intoxication more observable. In other words, "going up" has a more severe effect than "coming down."

THE PROCESS OF TOLERANCE

Chronic tolerance occurs after repeated exposures to alcohol. Chronic tolerance is an adaptation to a chronic dose of alcohol. There are four elements that are associated with chronic tolerance: 1) chronic adaptation; 2) compensation; 3) an increased dose requirement; and 4) a voluntary increase in the dose consumer. (See Figure 15–2)

Chronic Adaptation.   When the senses are stimulated, the sense organs adapt by coming into equilibrium with the stimulation in the environment. Adapting to alcohol occurs in the same way. Chronic adaptation occurs when alcohol is consumed

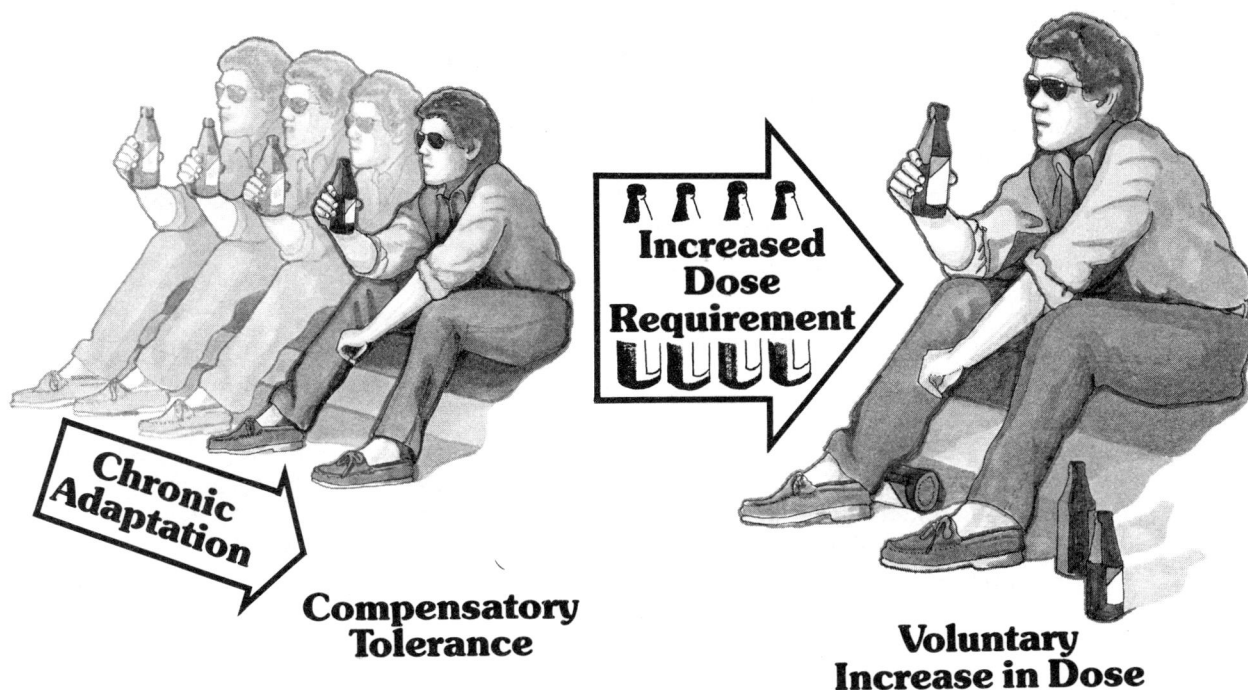

Figure 15–2. The process of tolerance.

repeatedly (every day or several times a day), and a lessening of the drug effect occurs even though the dose is constant. Simple adaptation is illustrated in Figure 15–3. The time between the doses as well as the absolute size of the dose are critical to the development of adaptive tolerance. Adaptive tolerance, also called absolute tolerance, is biological and is determined by the rate of exposure to alcohol.

Compensatory Tolerance. This type of tolerance represents behavioral adaptation to the effects of the drug. The detrimental effects of an acute dose become more difficult to observe upon repeated exposure. Most of the animal and human experiments that explore compensatory tolerance examine early observable (and

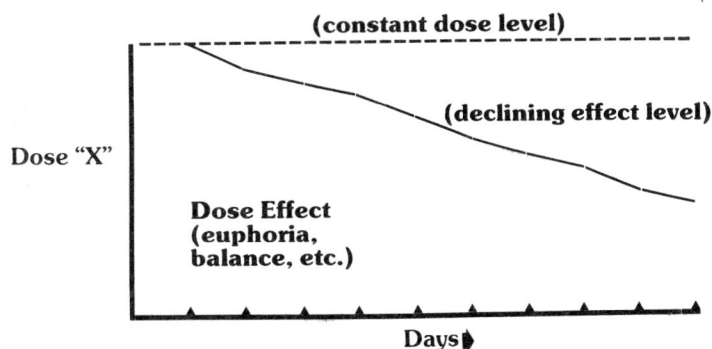

Figure 15–3. Biological tolerance.

undesirable) effects: loss of balance, slurred speech, increased time in an uncomfortable position, falling down, and so on. The subjects in the experiments practice to overcome these unpleasant effects and to compensate for them. The compensation is gradual, occurs over time, and appears to be learned. For these reasons, compensatory tolerance is also called *acquired tolerance, learned tolerance, developed tolerance,* or even *functional tolerance.* It complements simple biological tolerance.

An Increased Dose Requirement Occurs after Repeated Exposures.   The original effect of the drug may result in impaired performance or euphoria, among other possibilities. If the drinker wishes to repeat this effect, then he or she requires a greater dose.

A Voluntary Increase in the Dose Consumed.   This is the final behavioral expression of the increased dose requirement. Because of tolerance, the drinker needs more alcohol to sustain the original pleasures of the drug.

The full implications of developing tolerance to alcohol will become apparent in the unit on behavioral consequences. However, three implications are apparent:

1. Over time (days, weeks, months) the same quantity of alcohol has a lessened biological and behavioral effect;
2. Some people are still able to perform certain physical skills after they *practice* them while intoxicated; but
3. Decision making skills *do not* improve with "intoxicated" practice.

In summary, tolerance to alcohol is an adaptive process that develops gradually. Acute tolerance is short-term adaptation to the effects of one dose of alcohol, whereas chronic tolerance is long-term adaptation to repeated doses of alcohol. Chronic tolerance is characterized by adaptation, compensation, an increased dose requirement, and finally a voluntary increase in the dose of alcohol consumed.

Exercises.   1. *Each of the following is a function of biological tolerance to alcohol. Mark statements that denote acute tolerance with an "A"; those that denote chronic tolerance with a "C."*

_____   a. increased dose requirement
_____   b. "going up" is more severe than "coming down"
_____   c. ability to consume greater amounts of alcohol without behavioral impairment
_____   d. high dose level does not result in passing out or death
_____   e. behavioral effects of rising intoxication are more noticeable than decreasing intoxication
_____   f. occurs after repeated exposure to alcohol
_____   g. short-term adaptation to stimulation provided by alcohol

Answers: (a) c; (b) a; (c) c; (d) c; (e) a; (f) c; and (g) a.

2. *Match each effect in Column 1 with the appropriate descriptor of chronic tolerance in Column 2.*

_____ a. at constant dose level, loss of balance, slurred speech, and so forth, decreases

_____ b. original drug effect is obtained with greater dose

_____ c. a lessening of drug effect occurs even though dose is constant

_____ d. the drinker increases the quantity of alcohol he or she consumes

_____ e. also called learned, developed, or functional tolerance

_____ f. absolute tolerance determined by *rate* of exposure to alcohol

_____ g. the organism strives to overcome unpleasant effects of alcohol

_____ h. the drinker uses more alcohol to achieve a good feeling

1. Chronic adaptation
2. Compensatory tolerance
3. Increased dose requirement
4. Voluntary increase in dose consumed

Answers: (a) 2; (b) 3; (c) 1; (d) 4; (e) 2; (f) 2; (g) 1; (h) 3.

Thought Questions

1. What specific information in this chapter would be useful in a community alcohol education program?
2. Can you think of group activities in which this material could be applied?

Additional Readings

Begleiter, H. 1980. *Biological Effects of Alcohol.* New York: Plenum Press.

Kissin, B., and H. Begleiter. 1971. *The Biology of Alcoholism, Volume 1: Biochemistry.* New York: Plenum Press.

_____. 1972. *The Biology of Alcoholism, Volume 2: Physiology and Behavior.* New York: Plenum Press.

Wallgren, H., and H. Barry. 1970. *Actions of Alcohol, Volume 1: Biochemical, Physiological and Psychological Aspects.* Amsterdam: Elsevier Publishing Co.

Module 2 Final Test

1. The critical factor that determines absorption of alcohol into the bloodstream is _____.
2. List six factors that influence the emptying time of the stomach.

3. Define intoxication.

4. List four factors that influence blood alcohol concentration.

5. Explain briefly how the breathalyzer can give a reasonably accurate estimate of blood alcohol concentration.

6. Describe the effects of nonoxidized excess alcohol on the drinker at each of the following concentrations:

   a. 0.04 gm / 100mls

   b. 0.10 gm / 100 mls

   c. .12 gm / 100 mls

   d. .15 gm / 100 mls

   e. .20 gm / 100 mls

   f. .30 gm / 100 mls

   g. 45 gm / 100 mls

7. Use Table 15–2 to determine the following blood alcohol concentrations:

   a. 6 drinks / 200 lbs / 1 hr   BAC = _____ g/100ml

   b. 4 drinks / 200 lbs / 3 hrs   BAC = _____ g/100ml

   c. 1 drink / 180 lbs / 1 hr   BAC = _____ g/100ml

   d. 6 drinks / 140 lbs / 2 hrs   BAC = _____ g/100ml

8. Define acute tolerance and chronic tolerance, and explain the implications of the difference between them.

9. Explain briefly the four elements that fully describe chronic tolerance.

10. Fill out the following chart (Figure 15–4) with the steps in alcohol metabolism.

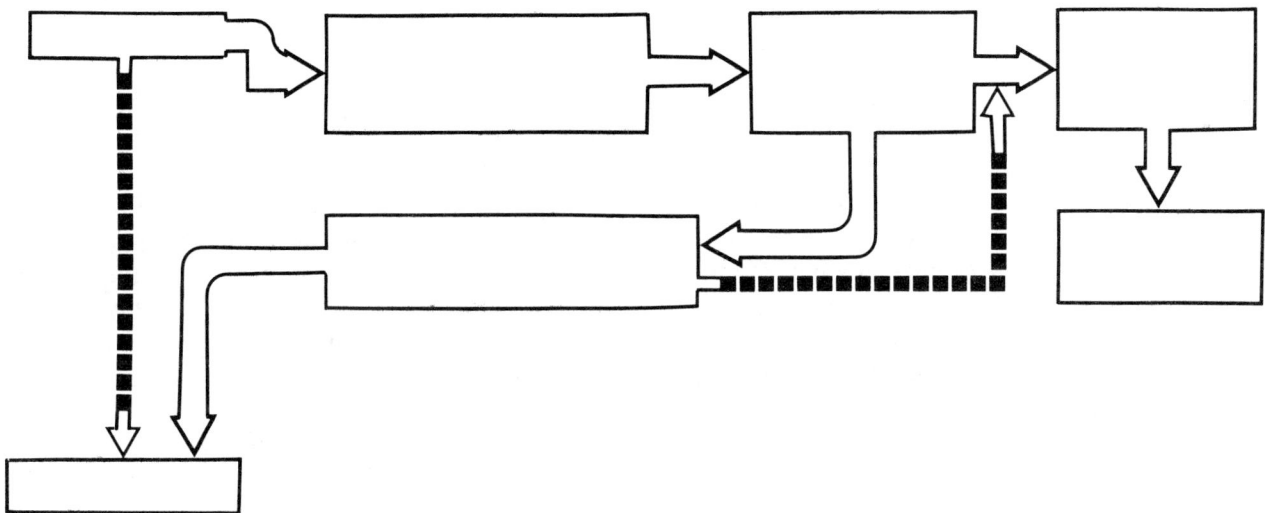

Figure 15–4. Alcohol metabolism.

ANSWERS TO MODULE 2 FINAL TEST

1. ...the emptying time of the stomach
2. a. presence of food in stomach
   b. fasting
   c. volume, character, and dilution of alcoholic beverage
   d. period of time over which beverage is consumed
   e. adrenergic drugs
   f. lower body temperature
   g. cholinergic drugs, alkaline salts, carbonated beverages
   h. emotional and physical state of drinker

3. Intoxication is the effect of nonoxidized excess alcohol upon the brain.
4. a. weight of drinker
   b. body structure of drinker
   c. number of drinks consumed
   d. span of time over which drinks are consumed
5. Laws of diffusion and vapor pressure apply to the distribution of alcohol between blood and air in the lungs (following a ratio of 2,100 to 1), and the breathalyzer measures this distribution.
6. a. 0.04 — most people feel relaxed, jovial
   b. 0.10 — clear deterioration of reaction time and control; legally drunk in most states
   c. 0.12 — vomiting, unless level is reached slowy
   d. 0.15 — balance and movement are impaired; about one half pint of whiskey in blood
   e. .20 — decreased pain and sensation; marked decrease in response to stimuli
   f. .30 — many lose consciousness
   g. .45 — subnormal temperature; impaired circulation and respiration; death
7. a. .13 g/100 ml
   b. .04 g/100 ml
   c. .02 g/100 ml
   d. .17 g/100 ml
8. *Acute* tolerance is the short-term adaptation to the stimulation provided by alcohol. The behavioral effects of rising intoxication are more noticeable than the effects of decreasing intoxication; that is, "going up is more severe than coming down." *Chronic* tolerance is the adaptation to repeated (chronic) exposure to alcohol. The individual acquires the ability to consume greater amounts of alcohol without behavioral impairment, and an increased dose requirement.
9. a. Chronic adaptation: a lessening of drug effect when the dose is constant.
   b. Compensatory tolerance: behavioral adaptation or ability to overcome undesirable effects of the drug.
   c. Increased dose requirement: only increased dose results in preferred drug effect.
   d. Voluntary increase in dose consumed: in order to experience the preferred effect, drinker *must* consume more alcohol.
10. See Figure 15–1.

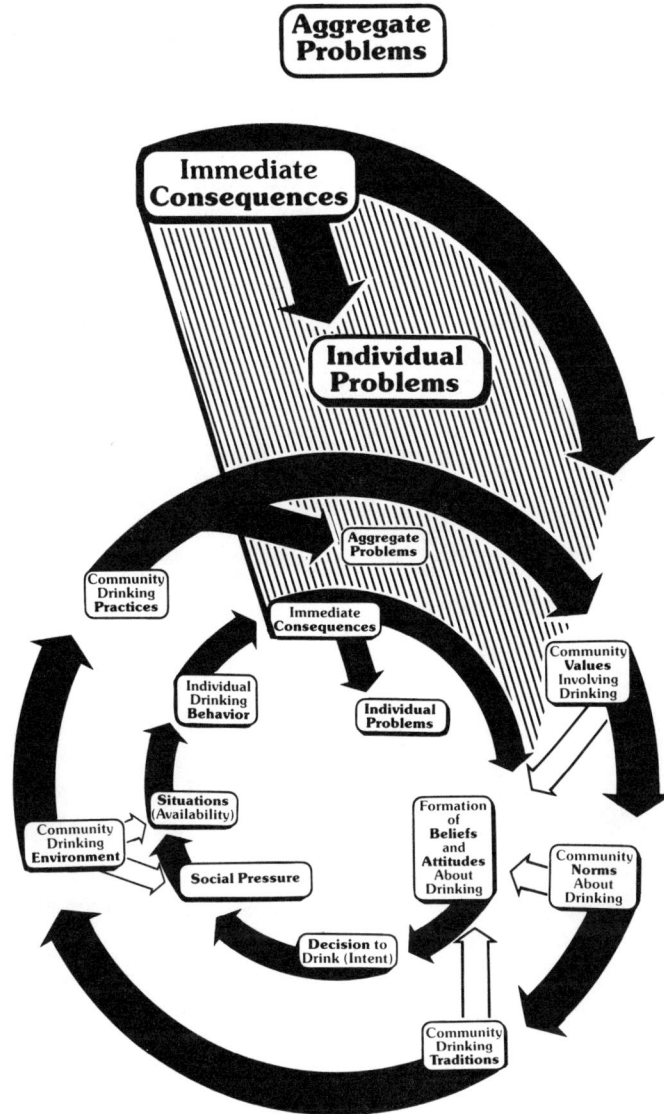

Chapter 16

MODULE 3

Behavioral Consequences of Drinking

Moving from the biological to the behavioral effects of alcohol requires the addition of another element to the drinking equation: *repetition.* However, from Module 1 (Chapter 14), you should already be familiar with the concept of "chronic dose" (repetitive application of an acute dose).

Intoxication is excess alcohol in the bloodstream, distributed to all tissues and organs of the body. Intoxication, therefore, is the perception by the brain of chemical "information." Intoxication as a stimulus is defined subjectively when it is *discriminable* from other sensations. Just as a red light is discriminable from other lights, or a sound is a sensation that is noticeably different from silence, alcohol intoxication is a stimulus that is perceived when it is different from (or contrasts with) the background. The amount of difference that a drug stimulus produces is regulated by the dose. As a stimulus, biological intoxication produces both unlearned and learned effects. When intoxication occurs in a specific setting, it can take on new properties or values beyond the biological effects (euphoria, drowsiness, etc.). In a specific setting, the stimulus assumes a value through *learning:* it occurs repeatedly in relation to some specific behavior. Points to remember about alcohol as a stimulus are:

1. An acute dose provides a *discriminable sensory stimulus* to the central nervous system.
2. The size of the stimulus is regulated by the dose of the alcohol consumed.
3. The stimulus can be repeated (chronic exposure).
4. The stimulus can occur before, during, or after specific behaviors and therefore performs various learning functions.
5. The stimulus *intoxication* can occur in a variety of "learning environments": parties, bars, sporting events, and so forth.

Many behavioral investigators have observed that alcohol or chemical information is similar to other stimuli in our environment. Alcohol stimulus information is also unique from other stimuli because:

1. The quantity and duration of the stimulus received is regulated by the *dose,* and not by environmental limits.
2. It is readily available in a wide variety of settings.
3. Intoxication can be more powerful than other stimuli because it acts on the whole central nervous system.
4. The alcohol stimulus is subject to the biological requirements of tolerance. After repeated exposure to the alcohol stimulus, the size of the dose must be increased to achieve the same behavioral effect.

229

Alcohol Intoxication "Follows" Event or Feeling ━━━━━━

Situation 1

| SOME BEHAVIOR | Result ▷ | Consequence (Meet Attractive Person) |

| DRINKING | Result ▷ | Consequences of Intoxication (Getting High, Stress Relief, Relaxation) |

Pairing of Consequences Leads to Situation 2

Alcohol Intoxication Precedes Event or Feeling ━━━━━━

Situation 2

| DRINKING | Result ▷ | Consequences of Intoxication (Getting High, Stress Relief, Relaxation) | Signal ▷ | Consequence (Meet Attractive Person) |

Alcohol Lets You ... Feel Sexy, Rich ...

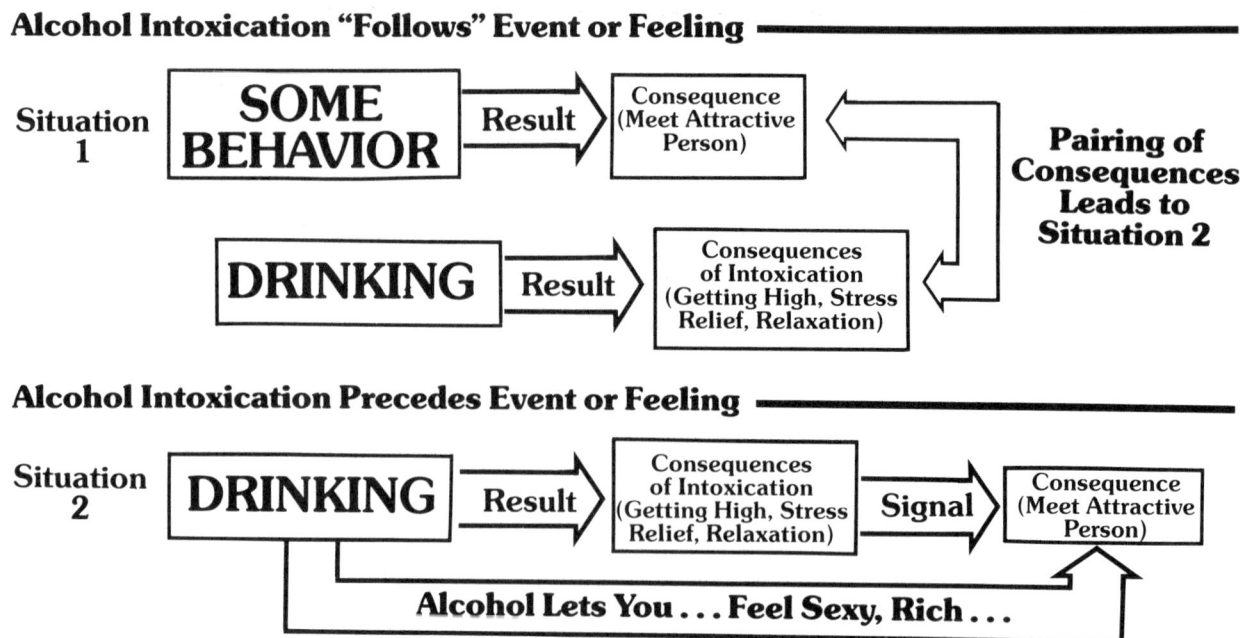

Figure 16–1.   Stimulus properties of alcohol.

 5. The alcohol stimulus is more reliable in regulating behavior than other social or behavioral stimuli.

 These stimulus properties of alcohol can condition the individual to respond in predictable ways, just as a laboratory animal can be taught to perform certain actions through "operant" techniques. A stimulus that repeatedly follows a specific event is called a *reinforcing stimulus*. A stimulus that consistently and repeatedly precedes an event is called a *discriminative stimulus*. It predicts upcoming events for the learner. Alcohol can serve as both a reinforcing and discriminative stimulus. Figure 16–1 shows that in Situation I, intoxication that *follows* an event can provide euphoria, stress relief, relaxation, and sedation. In Situation II, alcohol intoxication *precedes* an event, becoming a sensory event or *cue* that regularly precedes some behavior. It is therefore a *signal* for the other, widely varied, behaviors to occur.

Discriminative Properties of Alcohol

 This section examines the discriminative, or cue properties of alcohol that serve as *social stimuli*. Alcohol and intoxication have the potential to serve as consistent cues for many behaviors. The girl in Figure 16–2 has learned to associate intoxication with making friends, relaxing, and expressing her feelings. To further illustrate the point that many decisions are preceded by some identifiable and distinct signal, assume we have placed a hungry rat in a cage. The rat knows how to press a lever to get food, but there are two levers. Sometimes Lever 1 delivers food and sometimes Lever 2. Above each lever a light has been installed, and each lever will deliver food only when its corresponding light is on.

Which lever should the rat push to get food? If no consistent cues precede the food delivery, the rat will alternate between the two levers. However, if he discovers that the light flashes always come before food delivery on one lever and not on the other, he learns discrimination. The cue (the light flash) that predicts the outcome of the animal's behavior is called a discriminative stimulus. Note that the rat is learning two things: (1) when the cue (light) is present pushing the correct lever will deliver food; and (2) behavior in the presence of the light has *predictable* consequences. The latter point may be more important in the long run because the animal learns about its own potential, which can be applied in a number of different situations. Many animal experiments have shown that the effect of alcohol can serve as a discriminative stimulus under special circumstances. The feelings induced by the drug in experiments are very distinct, consistent, and temporally associated with desirable behaviors.

Figure 16–2. Alcohol as a discriminative stimulus.

Animal experiments indicate that the natural discriminative stimulus in many learning situations may be conveniently replaced by the effect of a drug. In other words, a hungry rat can decide which lever to press if the light is replaced by a drug injection. In a simple learning situation the chemical cue provided by the drug acts effectively as a signal that precedes behavior. The studies have also shown quite consistently that animals learn as well, if not better, under drug stimuli and seem to retain the learning longer. Responses acquired in association with a drug stimulus are also harder to extinguish (unlearn) and are less likely to be influenced by competing stimuli. In short, drug learning is rather quick and complete.

Advertising agencies consistently use the principle that alcohol intoxication serves as a discriminative stimulus for behavior. The "status" ads, for example, imply that individuals will feel rich, suave, and sophisticated if they drink the product. "Macho" ads imply that drinking will result in feelings of sexiness and athletic prowess.

In the next module we will examine how simple stimulus information provided by alcohol intoxication becomes the basis for our beliefs about our own actions when: 1) Alcohol assumes a *variety* of functions for the drinker; and 2) The drinker comes to *expect* the alcohol to serve similar functions in upcoming situations.

Alcohol intoxication acquires this future dimension through learning, and therefore becomes a part of the person's belief system. Beliefs are our expectations about the probable consequences of our behavior. What we come to expect from our behavior is important to us for understanding how to negotiate our environment. Our expectations about behavior also form the nucleus of how we feel about ourselves (our ego, identity, and self-concept).

Exercise.   *In the following list, label each statement with "R" for reinforcing stimulus or "D" for discriminative stimulus.*

_____ a. Alcohol lets me feel sexy
_____ b. Alcohol relaxes me when I'm tense
_____ c. Alcohol makes me sleepy.
_____ d. Alcohol makes me feel powerful.
_____ e. Alcohol lets me be adventurous.
_____ f. Alcohol satisfies hunger.
_____ g. Alcohol picks me up when I'm depressed.
_____ h. Alcohol makes me feel more adult.
_____ i. Alcohol lets me become one of the crowd.

Answers: (a) D; (b) R; (c) R; (d) D; (e) D; (f) R; (g) R; (h) D; and (i) D.

Thought Question

Can you think of occasions in your own life when alcohol served as a discriminative stimulus for some behavior? (Such as meeting people, relaxing, having a good time, and so forth.)

Additional Readings

Harris, R.T.; W.M. McIsaac; and C.H. Schuster. editors. 1970. *Drug Dependence. Part III: Behavioral Aspects of Drug Dependence.* Austin: University of Texas Press.

Ho, B.T.; D.W. Richards III; and D.L. Chute. 1978. *Drug Discrimination and State Dependent Learning.* New York: Academic Press.

Lal, H. editor. 1977. *Discriminative Stimulus Properties of Drugs.* New York: Plenum Press.

Seiden, L.S., and L.A. Dykstra. 1977. *Psychopharmacology: A Biochemical and Behavioral Approach.* New York: Van Nostrand Reinhold Co.

Module 3 Final Test

1. Define "reinforcing stimulus" and describe when alcohol fills that role.

2. Define "discriminative stimulus" and describe when alcohol fills that role.

ANSWERS TO MODULE 3 FINAL TEST

1. A reinforcing stimulus is one that *follows* a behavior. Alcohol consumed *after* a behavior (stressful situation, hard work, exciting situation) leads to euphoria, stress relief, relaxation, and sedation.

2. A discriminative stimulus is one that *precedes* behavior, becoming a *cue* or *signal* for that behavior. Alcohol consumed to create a mood or achieve an effect ("alcohol lets me feel sexy") is a discriminative stimulus.

Chapter 17

MODULE 4
Beliefs and Attitudes

By the end of this module, you should be able to:

1. Define a belief;
2. List four ways in which beliefs are formed;
3. Define the three dimensions along which beliefs may be measured;
4. Define attitude;
5. Define positive and negative beliefs; and
6. Explain how positive beliefs are employed in positive alcohol education.

A belief is a perceived relationship between an object and its attributes (Fishbein and Ajzen 1975). The statement "I believe that jaybirds are blue" expresses a relationship that one individual holds about the attributes (color) of a certain class of objects (jaybirds). A belief is also a perceived relationship between an event (as opposed to an object) and its attributes. For example, "basketball games are exciting" and "the stock market is in an upswing" are beliefs. A belief may or may not be objectively true; it is an individual's perception of objects and events in his or her environment.

People are "objects" and behavior is an "event." Some belief statements about people and their behavior might be:

> "I believe that Jack Jones is very competitive."
> "It is highly likely that Mary is pregnant."
> "I believe that I am outgoing."

Our most important beliefs express relationships between behavior and its consequences. We may hold beliefs about the behavior of others: "If Jack continues to practice, he is likely to make the basketball team," or "Most people who drink and drive will eventually have an accident." We also hold beliefs about the relationship between our own behavior and its consequences.

A belief statement about our own behavior expresses an *expectancy* or a *prediction* of what will happen if we perform certain acts. Therefore, when we anticipate the consequences of our own behavior, we are acting upon our beliefs.

Exercise. *A belief is* (*choose* two):

a. something formed in early childhood
b. a perceived relationship between an object and its attributes
c. attributes that are personal to each individual
d. a perceived relationship between cause and effect
e. a perceived relationship between a behavior and its outcomes
f. a perceived relationship between an attitude and a behavior
g. the result of early training modified by experience

Answers: A belief is a perceived relationship between an object and its attributes or a behavior and its outcome (b and e).

Belief Formation

Beliefs are formed in four ways:

1. Through the direct experience of behavior.
   "If I touch an open flame I am likely to get burned; because I received a burn last week."
   "Drinking three beers at the party Friday night enabled me to have fun."
   "Drinking three beers at the game Saturday enabled me to have fun."
   "Drinking three beers is always a sure way to have fun."
2. Through the observation of the behavior of other individuals or groups (role modeling).
   "I notice that college graduates get better jobs."
   "Bill and Mary seemed to fight a lot before their separation."
3. By acceptance of *others'* stated beliefs.
   "I read in the newspaper that 54th Street has a high rate of robberies, therefore I believe 54th Street is a place that I am likely to get robbed."
4. By inference from established beliefs in one's community.
   "Sports cars are expensive."
   "Drinkers end up on skid row."
   "It's all right to get blasted every Saturday night with your buddies."

As illustrated in Table 17–1 these four methods of belief formation can be used as a basis for alcohol education.

Table 17–1. Belief Formation and Alcohol Education

Method of Belief Formation	*Implication for Alcohol Education*
1. Direct experience of behavior and its consequences.	1. Practicing moderate styles of drinking.
2. Observation of other's behaviors and consequences of those behaviors.	2. Observing peer role models who practice moderate patterns of alcohol consumption.
3. Acceptance of other's statements about the behavior.	3. Introducing new information about drinking, especially information derived from a source the students would find credible.
4. Inference from established community beliefs.	4. Help the community develop a consensus about new beliefs associated with alcohol to displace old beliefs that fostered problems.

Because beliefs are sometimes formed on the basis of our past experience, a *complete* belief statement might read: "In my first year of college, I found that my science test grades improved when I studied; therefore, studying is likely to increase my grades in science," but would be expressed as "I believe that studying is likely to increase my grade point average."

When we relate our past experiences to what we expect in the future, we use beliefs as a bridge. Remember, the individual's perception of the outcome that will follow a specific behavior is a belief. For example: "I *expect* that if I study my grades will improve," or "I *anticipate* that if I am friendly, others will respond to me in a similar fashion," or "I *predict* that Bill and I will have a good time Friday night if we go to an adventure movie."

Exercise. *List the four ways beliefs are formed, and give an alcohol-related example for each one.*

Answers; possible examples:

a. individual experience—my own drinking behavior
b. observation of others' behavior—watching others drink at parties
c. others' views of consequences of use—listening to accounts of how well others hold their liquor
d. inference from established beliefs—reading a university's alcohol policy statement.

Beliefs may be measured along three dimensions: (1) credibility; (2) salience; and (3) valuation. Belief credibility refers to how much an individual accepts each particular belief as true or false. The credibility of a belief is most accurately represented by a probability statement, which reflects the extent to which the person *links* a specific consequence or a specific attribute to a specific object. For example, how likely is it that:

Jaybirds are blue.

Very Likely   1   2   3   4   5   6   7   Very Unlikely

Jaybirds are chrome.

Very Likely   1   2   3   4   5   6   7   Very Unlikely

Jaybirds are evil.

Very Likely		1	2	3	4	5	6	7	Very Unlikely

Similarly we can use a probability statement to tie together a behavior and its consequence:

Disciplined study leads to better grades.

Very Likely		1	2	3	4	5	6	7	Very Unlikely

Drinking three beers enables most people to relax.

Very Likely		1	2	3	4	5	6	7	Very Unlikely

Smoking three cigarettes a day will induce cancer.

Very Likely		1	2	3	4	5	6	7	Very Unlikely

Running improves health.

Very Likely		1	2	3	4	5	6	7	Very Unlikely

Belief credibility therefore refers to the extent to which a person holds a particular belief. One goal of an alcohol education program is to improve the credibility of certain beliefs about alcohol. This can be accomplished in a number of ways. We can provide new information, more accurate information, more clearly defined relationships or more authoritative beliefs. To illustrate:

New belief information: Excessive alcohol consumption (six drinks per day) by a pregnant mother is likely to damage the unborn fetus (generally unknown to the public prior to 1961).

More accurate information: Alcohol can only be metabolized by the liver at a fixed rate and therefore a heavily intoxicated individual *cannot* be sobered up by a cold shower, hot coffee, or any other common remedy.

More clearly defined relationships: If one smokes and drinks, the chances of throat and lung cancer increase tenfold over nonsmokers and nondrinkers.

More authoritative beliefs: Nine out of ten doctors recommend Brand X aspirin to relieve headaches from excessive drinking and smoking.

Exercise.   *Belief credibility refers to:*

a. the relative importance of the belief to the individual
b. the judgment by the individual of a specific belief

c. the attitude the individual holds toward the belief

d. to what degree an individual accepts a belief as true or false

Answer: Belief credibility refers to what degree an individual accepts a belief as true or false (d).

Belief *salience* refers to the relative importance of the belief statement to the individual. Salience, or importance, means that some beliefs can be a part of a person's memory or cognitive processes, but may or may not be important to the individual. Often belief salience is determined by the particular situation or context to which the person is exposed. For example, the following beliefs are highly credible to most people, but are unlikely to be important (salient): "many cars are light blue;" and "beer contains less alcohol than wine."

We can measure belief salience by asking an individual how important a particular belief is, especially if we specify the particular situation in which the belief is applicable. Belief salience is important in establishing the link between specific behavior patterns and long-term undesirable outcomes. People seldom deny that a given belief is true or not true, they simply deny that it applies to them. Hence, they may argue that "it won't happen to me," or "it is not important in my life now." One goal of an alcohol education program is to increase the salience of beliefs that people *already hold*. This may involve introduction of new, related beliefs; repositioning old beliefs ("cigarettes cause cancer"); or changing the relationship of the belief to old salient beliefs ("but it will not happen to me").

New Beliefs:
1. Your mother and father smoked cigarettes and got cancer.
2. Your children are likely to smoke cigarettes and get cancer.

Salience:
1. My children are very important.
2. I will evaluate my smoking.

Exercise. *Belief salience refers to:*

a. the extent to which a person holds a particular belief

b. the attitude the individual holds toward the belief

c. the relative importance of the belief statement to the individual

d. the judgment by the individual of a specific belief.

Answer: Belief salience refers to the relative importance of the belief statement to the individual (c).

Valuation of a belief is the attitude a person holds about that belief. For example, an individual might hold the following belief: "If I consume six beers I am likely to become drunk" (highly credible). *Further,* "It is important for me to know that six beers will make me drunk" (highly salient). *Yet,* "I feel good about the fact that six beers will make me drunk" (a *positive* attitude toward drinking six beers).

The person might also hold the belief with equal credibility and salience and yet have a *negative* attitude toward consumption: *Yet;* "I feel bad about the fact that if I consume six beers, I will probably get drunk" (a *negative* attitude toward drinking six beers). Therefore, one goal of an alcohol educator can be to change attitudes toward some beliefs.

Exercise.   *Belief valuation refers to:*

a. how much an individual accepts a belief as true or false
b. the attitude of the individual toward a specific belief
c. the relative importance of the belief statement to the individual
d. the attitude the community holds toward a specific belief.

Answer: Belief valuation refers to the attitude of the individual toward a specific belief (b).

To summarize:

Belief Statement:	If I drink two beers on Saturday night I will have a good time.
Credibility Dimension:	It is (likely/unlikely) that if I drink two beers on Saturday night I will have a good time.
Salience Dimension:	It is (important/not important) to me to have two beers so that I will have a good time.
Valuation Dimension:	It is (good/bad) to have two beers on Saturday night to have a good time.

The alcohol educator is not interested in the credibility, salience, or valuation of "two beers" or "having a good time on Saturday night," but rather the credibility, salience, and valuation of the *perceived relationship* between two beers and having a good time. It is the relationship that is the crucial focus for alcohol education. This relationship expresses what people expect from repeated alcohol use, and typically it becomes the source of problems with alcohol.

Obviously we can have many "belief systems" about alcohol: its use by teenagers, use that leads to alcoholism, our own alcohol use, alcohol use by the elderly, and so forth. For the alcohol educator, the most important beliefs are the specific set that the individual accepts and applies to his or her own consumption. The beliefs are influenced by the social group to which the individual belongs, so the educator must identify the values, norms, and traditions held by the social group in order to try and promote new values, norms, and traditions about drinking.

If a person drinks alcohol and feels intoxicated, two things happen almost immediately. First, the individual experiences unique biological effects that are stronger (more salient) than other information provided through the natural environment. Second, the individual comes to *expect* the experience again. The predictable and invariant biological effect from an acute dose of alcohol becomes a part of the person's memory. But the individual's *belief* about alcohol intoxication is not invariant; it changes with each drinking situation. As we form beliefs about the feeling of intoxication, we compare these beliefs with our existing belief system about alcohol. Because existing belief systems typically relate to long-term consequences observed in the behavior of others ("if you drink, you will end up on skid row"), the drinker is unlikely to have any beliefs that relate his or her immediate experience with any long-term consequences. While the feeling from alcohol is immediately salient, the beliefs about *others'* alcohol use are not salient.

To review, we learn about alcohol through:

1. our own experiences that follow an acute dose
2. observation of others who consume an acute dose
3. others' expressed views about the consequences of their consumption
4. inference from established (community) beliefs.

As the consequences of alcohol consumption expand to include a greater number of people and situations, our beliefs become more variable. The *biological* consequences of drug action are invariant: within narrow limits a specific acute dose leads to a specific blood alcohol level. The biological impact is predictable. However, the *social* consequences of drug use are variant and flexible, and these *learned* consequences of alcohol use become the basis for beliefs about alcohol.

Although we may devise a number of different strategies for alcohol education (discussion, role modeling, counter-advertising, throwing nonalcohol parties, etc.), our basic aims are few. First, we should strive to introduce *credible* and *salient* beliefs about the varied psychological, social, and environmentally defined consequences of alcohol use. Second, we should attempt to encourage *positive* beliefs. A positive belief links a specific behavior with an outcome that the individual prefers (values, or holds a positive attitude toward).

A belief can be about any number of consequences that follow a specific behavior. For example:

I drink two beers and
    1. I am likely to relax.
    2. I am likely to be more talkative.
    3. I am likely to feel as a part of the group.
    4. I am likely to feel pleasantly tired.
    5. I am likely to meet new people.

A positive belief represents what the individual looks forward to the next time the behavior is performed. For example:

When I drink two beers
    1. I expect to relax.
    2. I expect to be more talkative.
    3. I expect to be part of the group.
    4. I expect to feel pleasantly tired.
    5. I expect to meet new people.

A belief that represents a relationship between a recurring behavior and its reinforced outcome is a positive belief. A belief that represents a relationship between a recurring behavior and its punished outcome is a negative belief. Positive beliefs tend to lead to additional beliefs—the learner's expectations are reinforced.

Positive alcohol education therefore introduces specific beliefs that lead to positively reinforced consequences. Beliefs, behaviors, and consequences are defined as specifically as possible. The positive notion draws its strength from the fact that the belief (and associated behavior) that the educator wishes the group to accept results in positive outcomes. For example:

"Drinking two beers leads to relaxation."
"Drinking two beers in one evening allows the drinker to avoid a possible driving under the influence (DUI) arrest."

The implications of a positive approach to alcohol and drug education are manifold. Emphasis is placed on positive behavior rather than on beliefs about negative consequences of alcohol *abuse* (a negative designation in and of itself). Many consequences of alcohol use are undesirable, but using terms such as "abuse" or "disease" do not elicit positive responses. Seldom does the drinker classify his or her own actions as undesirable or inappropriate, especially in a social milieu that promotes drinking and rewards it.

Most traditional alcohol programs are derived directly from the educator's beliefs about the consequences of alcohol use, and usually revolve around lectures that urge the user to avoid becoming alcoholic. This strategy is exemplified by the alcoholism counselor who is concerned with cirrhosis of the liver, memory loss, financial problems, family alienation, and poor health seen in his or her patients. The alcohol counselor's lectures reflect the beliefs that drinking in general leads to liver damage, brain damage, social isolation, and personal despair. Prolonged, excessive consumption is not distinguished from acute, moderate consumption.

These negative messages, which may be an accurate reflection of the counselor's beliefs, are not related to the behavior of the *youth drinker*. A person who is not alcoholic will not find these messages relevant to his or her own experiences with alcohol.

Exercises.   1. *Fill in the blanks.*

   a. A belief that represents a relationship between a recurring behavior and its reinforced outcome is a _____ belief.
   b. A belief that represents a relationship between a recurring behavior and its punished outcome is a _____ belief.

Answers: a) positive; b) negative.

2. *Suggest a possible positive alternative to the following belief about alcohol:*

"If I drink a six-pack tonight at the party, I'll have a good time."
One possible alternative:
"If I drink two beers tonight at the party I will have a reasonably good time and avoid a possible DUI."

Thought Question

Can you list at least four things you expect to happen when you drink alcohol? (Four beliefs about alcohol.)

Module 4 Final Test

1. Define belief.

2. List four ways in which beliefs are formed.

3. List and define the three dimensions along which beliefs may be measured.

4. Define positive and negative beliefs.

5. Explain how positive beliefs are employed in positive alcohol education.

ANSWERS TO MODULE 4 FINAL TEST
1. A belief is a perceived relationship between an object and its attributes.
2. Beliefs are formed through 1) direct experience, 2) observation of others' behaviors, 3) acceptance of others' statements about the behavior, and 4) inference from established community beliefs.
3. Beliefs may be measured by their 1) credibility—the degree to which a person accepts a belief as true or false, 2) salience—the relative importance of the belief statement to the individual, and 3) valuation—the positive or negative attitude a person holds toward a belief.
4. A positive belief represents a relationship between a recurring behavior and its reinforced (positive) outcome; a negative belief represents a relationship between a recurring behavior and its punished (negative) outcome.

Reference

Fishbein, M., and I. Ajzen. 1975. *Belief, Attitudes, Intention and Behavior: An Introduction to Theory and Research.* Reading, Mass.: Addison-Wesley.

Additional Readings

Bauman, K.E., and E.S. Bryan. 1980. "Subjective Expected Utility and Children's Drinking." *Journal of Studies on Alcohol* 41: 152–158.

Finn, P. 1975. "The Role of Attitudes in Public School Alcohol Education." *Journal of Drug and Alcohol Education* 20: 23–30.

Hochheimer, J.L. 1981. "Reducing Alcohol Abuse: A Critical Review of Educational Strategies." in M.H. Moore, and D.R. Gerstein, eds., *Alcohol and Public Policy: Beyond the Shadow of Prohibition.* pps. 286–335. Washington, D.C.: National Academy Press.

Huebner, R.B.; R.E Slaughter, R.D. Goldman; and G.R. Caddy. 1976. "Attitudes Toward Alcohol as Predictors of Self-estimated Alcohol Consumption in College Students." *The International Journal of the Addictions* 11: 377–388.

Kilty, K.M. 1978. "Attitudinal and Normative Variables as Predictors of Drinking Behavior." *Journal of Studies on Alcohol* 39: 1178–1194.

Kinder, B.N. 1975. "Attitudes Toward Alcohol and Drug Abuse. II. Experimental Data, Mass Media Research, and Methodological Considerations." *International Journal of the Addictions* 10: 1035–1054.

Macoby, N.; J.W. Farquhar; P.D. Wood; and J. Alexander. 1977. "Reducing the Risk of Cardiovascular Disease: Effects of a Community Based Campaign on Knowledge and Behavior." *Journal of Community Health* 3: 100–114.

McAlister, A.; P. Puska; K. Koskela; U. Pallonen; and N. Macoby. 1980. "Mass Communication and Community Organization for Public Health Education." *American Psychologist* 35: 375–379.

McCarty, D.; S. Morrison; and K.C. Mills. 1982. *Attitudes, Beliefs and Alcohol Use: An Analysis of Relationships.* In press, Journal of Studies on Alcohol.

Rokeach, M. 1967. "Attitude Change and Behavior Change." *Public Opinion Quarterly* 30: 529–550.

Schlegel, R.P.; C.A. Crawford; and M.D. Sanborn. 1977. "Correspondence and Mediational Properties of the Fishbein Model: An Application to Adolescent Alcohol Use." *Journal of Experimental Social Psychology* 13: 421–430.

Schlegel, R.P., and J.E. Norris. 1980. "Effects of Attitude Change on Behavior for Highly Involving Issues: the Case of Marijuana Smoking." *Addictive Behaviors* 5: 113–124.

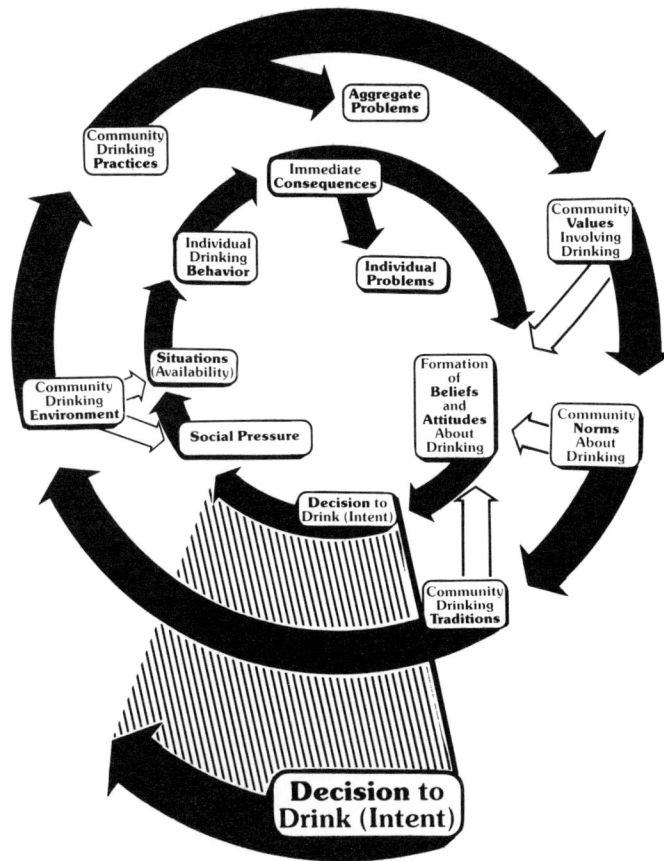

Aggregate
Problems

Community
Drinking
Practices

Immediate
Consequences

Community
Values
Involving
Drinking

Individual
Drinking
Behavior

Individual
Problems

Situations
(Availability)

Formation
of
Beliefs
and
Attitudes
About
Drinking

Community
Norms
About
Drinking

Community
Drinking
Environment

Social Pressure

Decision to
Drink (Intent)

Community
Drinking
Traditions

Decision to
Drink (Intent)

Chapter 18

MODULE 5

Decisions About Drinking

By the end of this unit, you should be able to:

1. Define the decision-making process;
2. Name the three key elements in the decision-making process;
3. Define a personal decision;
4. Explain the five factors that influence personal decisions;
5. List the five conditions that must be met when trying to alter an individual's decision-making process; and
6. Define learned helplessness and explain how excessive alcohol use can create such a condition.

The ability to make responsible decisions regarding the use of alcohol relates directly to the individual's general decision-making competence. This competence develops within both the personal and social arenas for learning; learning about self and learning about others. The decision-making process involves three key elements: the person, the process, and the object of the decision.

Decision-making is a learned behavior that is influenced by repetitive practice, new information from the environment, and exploration by the individual attempting to gather new information. Most learning also includes some room for error. That error is neither good nor bad in itself, but allows the growing individual to adopt new patterns of behavior that may be more productive. In short, decisionmaking is a *continual and recycling process* modified by feedback from the environment. The young man in Figure 18–1 remembers his arrest for driving under the influence. This form of "environmental feedback" influences his decision not to drive, since he has chosen to drink.

Although many decisions seem to occur unconsciously, some are quite conscious and require endless hours of struggle. Some insignificant decisions may occupy an inordinate amount of time, while major decisions may be reached in a few minutes. Different types of decisions are associated with different consequences for behavior.

It is important to understand that decisions about our own behavior do not always result in clear-cut consequences or specific outcomes. We must often act upon incomplete information. We react to feelings and attitudes that may not be expressed explicitly. Often, we are forced to act in situations that demand a decision before we are ready. Sometimes old beliefs interfere with newly formed decisions.

Decisions about drinking are unique because they deal with repetitive patterns of behavior rather than simple isolated events. Alcohol use is a prolonged and repetitive pattern of behavior, regulated by the immediate, biological effects of intoxication as well as the positive and negative consequences of the behavior.

Exercises. 1. *The three elements in the decision-making process are* (*circle* one):

a. the person, the environment, and the belief system
b. the situation, the person, and the consequences

251

Figure 18–1. New decisions based on feedback.

  c. the person, the object of the decision, and the situation
  d. the behavior, the decision, and the consequences
  e. the person, the object of the decision, and the process
  f. the person, the probability of the decision, and the consequences

Answer: Three key elements in the decisionmaking process are the person, the object of the decision, and the process (e).

 2. *The decision-making process (circle all that apply)...*

  a. is a learned behavior influenced by repetitive practice.
  b. is a continual and recycling process modified by feedback.
  c. is a totally unconscious process in which we weigh probabilities.
  d. always results in clear-cut consequences and specific, measurable outcomes.
  e. reacts only to feelings and attitudes explicitly expressed.
  f. may require hours of struggle.

g. includes some room for error.

h. has no evaluative component to measure success or failure of the decision.

Answer: The decisionmaking process is a learned behavior influenced by repetitive practice; is a continual and recycling process modified by feedback; may require hours of struggle; and includes some room for error (a, b, f, g).

Decisions

A personal decision is an *intent to act* based upon our beliefs about a particular situation. Our beliefs represent *information,* and our attitudes represent our *valuation* of that information. Therefore a decision is a summary statement about what we expect to happen, based upon information from our past and information available in the immediate environment.

As a potential action a decision becomes a means for reducing inconsistent information. The decision to purchase a Ford instead of a Toyota, or the decision to attend college instead of joining the military both reduce the amount of information presented to the individual in the long run.

A personal decision is a decision about our own behavior. The primary function of a personal decision is to maintain consistent information to the individual and to reduce the amount of conflict or stress that results from different sources of input.

A personal decision is influenced by:

1. Information stored in our cognitive memory. This information comprises our belief and attitude system. Beliefs are formed in various ways and represent an individual's personal history. Personal history also influences the salience or importance of certain beliefs.

2. The amount and type of information available at any specific time and place. This is called *situational information.*

3. The amount and type of information held by the individual's reference group regarding behavior and its consequences in a particular situation. These are called *normative beliefs.*

4. The particular *object* of the decision. Different objects carry different value weights, varying degrees of importance, and interest an individual to different degrees.

5. The success or failure that the individual has experienced with decision-making in the past. This is often called the person's self-concept, general decision-making competence, or self-image, and reflects the individual's beliefs about the decision-making process itself.

Exercise. *A personal decision is (circle all that apply)*:

a. a potential action
b. a means for reducing inconsistent information
c. a decision about one's own behavior
d. based only on personal information from one's past
e. a reflection of our attitudes toward something

f. influenced by success or failure in past decision-making
g. an intent to act based upon one's beliefs
h. influenced by information stored in one's cognitive memory
i. not likely to reduce conflict or stress from inconsistent information
j. influenced by situational information
k. based partially on normative influences
l. unrelated to the individual's self-concept

Answers: a, b, c, e, f, g, h, j, k.

A goal of alcohol education is to encourage decisions that result in the smallest number of unanticipated consequences. The alcohol educator can also encourage decisions that improve the individual's decision-making competence and his or her self-concept. To achieve these goals, several conditions must be met:

1. People must be offered behavioral alternatives having distinct, identifiable *consequences*.
2. The outcome of the appropriate behavior must be specified, identified, and acceptable to the group to which he/she belongs.
3. The place, time, and target of the behavior and its consequences must be clear to the individual making the decision.
4. The decision must be reinforceable. The appropriate response must have an outcome that is clearly preferred by the decisionmaker.
5. The decision must be specific to the situation, involving only a restricted set of beliefs about particular objects and a limited number of attitudes toward the beliefs.

For example, let us examine a situation in which the beliefs, attitudes, and situational cues seem to present inconsistent cues to the individual. Our subject is a college statistics student who has won round-trip tickets to Reno, Nevada for a weekend. The student is methodical, and on the plane ride he clearly articulates his salient beliefs about gambling to his girlfriend.

Belief Statement 1: The laws of probability strongly suggest that the betting and payoff ratios offered in organized casinos favor the House in the long run.

Belief Statement 2: Casinos are businesses that must show a profit in the long run.

Belief Statement 3: It is very likely that if I participate in organized gambling I will lose money in the long run.

The student's attitude toward the last belief statement might be: "My participation in organized gambling is more 'bad' than 'good.'" Therefore, he attempts a presituational decision: "I do not intend to gamble (at least beyond $5.00 fun money)." However, he may also hold another set of beliefs about having fun that might sway the presituational decision:

1. There are few other options for entertainment in a gambling town.

2. The appropriate behavior, engaging in gambling, is clearly designated by the casino through example, modeling, and training films in the hotel.
3. The positive consequences of gambling (winning) are given public attention: bells ring, the participants receive social approval, and so forth.
4. The negative consequences of gambling (losing) are not given public attention, thus long-term losses are not visible, and short-term gains receive social support.
5. Other rewards are arranged by the casino for participation in gambling. The participant receives free drinks, smiles, entertainment, and so forth.
6. There is extremely high normative pressure to gamble; others are gambling and enjoying their stay in Reno.

The student may begin to question his previous beliefs. True, the laws of probability still hold, but now it is more important to enjoy the weekend and not be "cheated" out of the fun. Beliefs about having fun have therefore become more salient than beliefs about winning or losing.

Another popular belief in gambling resorts is "I'll put aside x amount of money to lose and have a good time." If our potential gambler places $5.00 on the craps table and wins $35.00 at 7:1 odds, he may question his previous belief about the laws of probability. If he loses, the losses may reinforce his previous beliefs about gambling. He may seek out a fairer game. Similar pressures are often at work in a drinker's environment, and work either to reinforce or to change the individual's beliefs about consumption.

Exercise. *Complete the following statements involving the conditions that must be met when trying to improve an individual's decisionmaking competence.*

a. The individual must be offered behavioral alternatives having _____, _____ consequences.
b. The outcome of the appropriate behavior must be specified, identified, and acceptable to the _____.
c. The _____, _____, and _____ of the behavior must be clear to the individual making the decision.
d. The decision must have an outcome clearly _____ by the individual (and is therefore reinforceable).
e. The decision must be _____ to the situation, involve only a restricted set of _____ and a limited number of _____.

Answers: a. distinct, identifiable
b. group
c. place, time, target
d. preferred
e. specific, beliefs, attitudes

Thought Question

Can you think of an occasion on which your decision not to drink was changed by feedback from the environment?

Additional Readings

Becker, M.H., editor. 1974. "The Health Belief Model and Personal Health Behavior." *Health Education Monographs* 2: 324–500.

Birnbaum, I.M., and E.S. Parker, editors. 1977. *Alcohol and Human Memory*. Hillsdale, New Jersey: Lawrence Erlbaum Associates.

Heilbrun, A.B.; A.R. Tarbox; and J.K. Madison. 1979. "Cognitive Structure and Behavioral Regulation in Alcoholics." *Journal of Studies on Alcohol* 40: 387–400.

Jones, M.K., and B.M. Jones. 1980. "The Relationship of Age and Drinking Habits to the Effects of Alcohol on Memory in Women." *Journal of Studies on Alcohol* 41: 179–186.

Moskowitz, H., and M. Burns. 1971. "Effect of Alcohol on the Psychological Refractory Period." *Quarterly Journal of Studies on Alcohol* 32: 782–790.

Moskowitz, H., and D. Depry. 1968. "Differential Effect of Alcohol on Auditory Vigilance and Divided-Attention Tasks." *Quarterly Journal of Studies on Alcohol.* 29: 54–63.

Parker, E.S., and E.P. Noble. 1977. "Alcohol Consumption and Cognitive Functioning in Social Drinkers." *Journal of Studies on Alcohol* 38: 1224–1232.

Parker, E.S., and E.P. Noble. 1980. "Alcohol and the Aging Process in Social Drinkers." *Journal of Studies on Alcohol* 41: 170–178.

Parsons, O.A. 1980. "Cognitive Dysfunction in Alcoholics and Social Drinkers." *Journal of Studies on Alcohol* 41: 105–118.

Tarter, R. 1975. "Psychological Deficit in Chronic Alcoholics: A Review." *International Journal of the Addictions* 10: 327–368.

Tharp, V.K.; O.H. Rundell; B.K Lester; and H.L. Williams. 1974. "Alcohol and Information Processing." *Psychopharmacologia* 40: 33–52.

Module 5 Final Test

1. Define the decisionmaking process and name its three key elements.

2. Define a *personal decision* and list the five factors that influence personal decisions.

3. List the five conditions that must be met when trying to alter an individual's decision-making process.

ANSWERS TO MODULE 5 FINAL TEST

1. The decisionmaking process is a learned behavior influenced by repetitive practice, new information, and exploration by the individual. It is a continual and recycling process. Its three key elements are: the person, the process, and the object of the decision.

2. A personal decision is an intent to act, based upon our beliefs about a particular situation, and it is influenced by 1) our belief and attitude system, 2) situational information, 3) normative beliefs, 4) the object of the decision, and 5) our decision-making competence.

3. To alter the decision-making process, 1) individuals must be offered alternatives with identifiable consequences, 2) the outcome must be specified, identified, and acceptable, 3) the place, time, and target of the behavior must be clear, 4) the decision must be reinforceable, and 5) the decision must be specific to the situation.

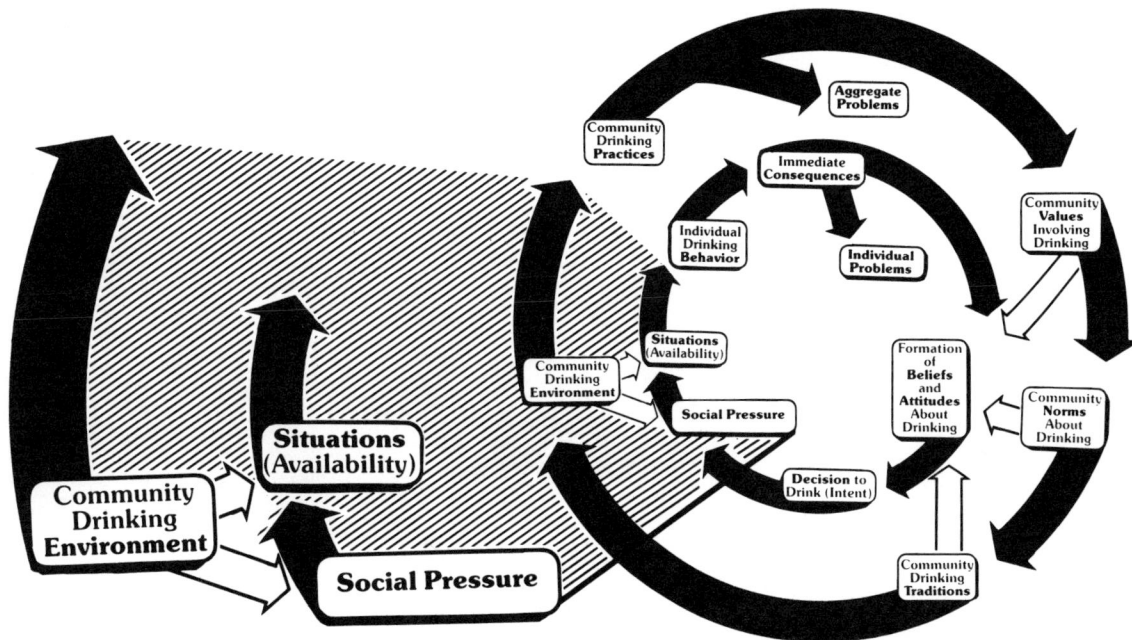

Chapter 19

MODULE 6
Situations

Alcohol is available in a variety of beverages, to a wide variety of individuals, in an even wider variety of settings (a street carnival, a local bar, the Saturday evening party, or at home, just to list a few). Each drinking situation consists of several elements: 1) a place; 2) a time; 3) specific behaviors (and consequences) likely to occur; 4) shared goals/group expectations (normative beliefs); and 5) participants.

In order to perform a situational analysis on drinking behavior, it is necessary to describe the key elements as specifically as possible. Place, time, and participants are fairly easy to specify, while behaviors, consequences, and normative beliefs may be more difficult. For example, there are 16,807 possible drinking situations among the options listed below.

Place

1. a bar
2. a party in an apartment
3. a football game
4. *a restaurant*
5. home alone
6. the cocktail party
7. the drive-in

Time

1. *after classes—Friday*
2. Saturday night
3. before bed nightly
4. while dancing
5. while watching TV
6. Saturday afternoon while working on car
7. during a beach weekend

Specific Drinking Behaviors

1. *two beers*
2. six beers
3. one glass of wine
4. three mixed drinks
5. one pint of scotch
6. a keg of beer
7. a glass of Seven-Up

Participants

1. *close friends*
2. new friends of opposite sex
3. business acquaintances
4. spouse, date
5. employer
6. strangers
7. brothers, sisters

261

Shared Goals (Normative Beliefs)

1. have fun together
2. share growth experiences—conversations
3. *relax together*
4. meet one another
5. cut loose
6. celebrate
7. be a part of the group

The italicized options above are repeated below as an example to illustrate how specific beliefs or expectations about alcohol develop within a specific situation:

Specific Behavior: drink two 12 ounce beers
Participants: close friends
Time: 5:15 Friday evening
Place: Johnny's Restaurant/Bar
Shared goals (Normative Beliefs): two beers after class allows a group to relax and be more sociable

Anticipated Consequences:
1. relaxation with friends
2. feel more sociable and good about self
3. feel less hungry
4. find out about dating opportunities

Unanticipated Consequences:
1. Disagree with roommate
2. Spend a bit more than expected for two beers
3. Feel very hungry after drinking
4. Miss campus bus and wait an extra forty-five minutes

On a more practical level, it is often useful to think in less general terms about our alcohol use and focus on a specific recurring situation in which drinking occurs. Situational analysis enables us to do this and to suggest alternative behaviors to the drinker based on new decisions.

Decisions reflect a subjective probability that a person will perform some specific behavior. The decision is based upon the individual's expectations about what will happen in a particular setting. A decision is commonly referred to as choice between alternative courses of action or behaviors that result in varied consequences. All our beliefs are our memories of different consequences; our beliefs supply the primary information from which we make decisions. Each specific situation in which we drink is also likely to create new expectations or beliefs. If people become aware of the beliefs associated with specific drinking situations, it frees them to develop alternative beliefs and expectations and thereby break old cycles. Groups can be helped to develop this awareness and to create new norms through alcohol education strategies.

The following analysis model can help in the examination of a drinking situation:

1. Define the key elements of the situation.
   a. place
   b. time
   c. behavior most likely to occur
   d. consequences most likely to occur
   e. participants
   f. group expectations about what will occur
2. Describe the situational antecedents (what has occurred *prior* to the situation) that influence what occurs.
3. Describe the alcohol-specific beliefs (expectations) about what will occur in the *next* similar situation.
4. List alternative beliefs that could replace the alcohol-specific beliefs. (In order for new beliefs to be accepted by the group, they must provide many of the same benefits as the alcohol-related beliefs.)
5. Examine the group norms relating to the two belief sets to discover which ones conflict with the new beliefs and which ones support them.
6. Develop a group consensus about which new beliefs will be adopted as a group norm for drinking behavior.

Exercise.   *In the following case study, in the space provided, identify each of the key determinants of a "situation" and personal beliefs, attitudes, and decisions, including those that are situation specific.*

Brad had been working on his garden most of the day, and like most Saturdays, the day had been pleasant. The soft cool spring breeze had been blowing, and the troubles that had plagued him all week— getting a job; the newly arrived daughter; and moving to a new city without a garden, seemed to ebb as he worked the soil. As he thought about the evening party at the Claxtons, Brad grew noticeably more nervous. His tension built as Jackie began to prepare for the evening.

a. _____
b. _____

Brad knew that there would be about thirty of his old friends from graduate school there, not to mention several of his professors. They would be curious about his new job, his future plans, and would generally want "heavy" conversation. Brad wanted time to think and plan rather than announce his future. He knew there would be a lot of pressure to drink, and he felt that at this time in his life, drinking was not the best remedy for his problems.

c. _____
d. _____
e. _____

Lately, Brad and Jackie had experienced some mutual tension, and once Brad had a few drinks, he tends to flirt with the other women at the party. Drinking lets Brad relax, and lets him not only forget about his worries, but enables him to engage in smooth conversation. When intoxicated, he is not as reluctant to discuss the future.

f. _____

g. _____

h. _____

The Claxtons usually throw rather lavish parties. In a small town, there is little else to do. There is mostly hard liquor, and beer is discouraged, at least implicitly. Brad had noticed that at the last party the older teenage set was encouraged to drink beer; the younger ones,

i. _____

j. _____

k. _____   coke. Beer was definitely the teenage drink, while the adults worked on
l. _____   mixed drinks. As the Claxtons' party grew to a close, most of the adults
m. _____   were well ripped, and several ended up in the swimming pool.

                      Brad suggested to Jackie that they call the Claxtons to say they
                      were ill, but Jackie replied that the notion was silly. He sincerely wished
n. _____   he had some way to insure that he would not get drunk and feel
                      horrible on Sunday. But, Brad thought, perhaps a good drunk was just
o. _____   what he needed.

Answers:

a. place
b. time
c. key participants
d. group expectations (normative beliefs)
e. group expectations
f. personal beliefs
g. personal beliefs
h. personal beliefs
i. normative beliefs
j. behavior
k. normative beliefs
l. group expectations
m. unanticipated consequences
n. anticipated consequences
o. personal beliefs

For the case study given above, what alternatives are acceptable to Brad in the
situation?

Answers: It is evident that Brad's beliefs and attitudes about
alcohol use have begun to change because he does not want to go
to the Claxtons' party. However, Brad needs support, particularly
from his wife, Jackie. Brad needs to know that he can be with
adults and feel OK about not drinking alcohol. The following
would provide Brad with support:

New Group Norms:
Adults who drink beer or cola are OK.
Adults don't need to get drunk to have a good time or to engage in "heavy"
    conversation.

New Decisions for Brad:
I will drink *only* cola at the party.
I will drink a maximum of two drinks at the party.

New Behavior for Brad:
Slow sipping of one or two drinks at the party.
Brad might read a current magazine before going to the party and divert
    discussion from personal life to magazine topics.

New Personal Beliefs:
I am a competent person and therefore I can discuss my life plans with others
    confidently without alcohol.
Adults don't have to answer questions just because they are asked.
I can leave a party before the party is over.

Other solutions are possible.

Additional Readings

Babor, T.F.: J.H. Mendleson; I. Greenberg; and J. Keuhnle. 1978. "Experimental Analysis of the 'Happy Hour'; Effects of Purchase Price on Alcohol Consumption." *Psychopharmacology* 58: 35–41.

Dericco, D.A., and W.K. Garlington. 1977. "The Effect of Modeling and Disclosure of Experimenter's Intent on Drinking Rate of College Students." *Addictive Behaviors* 2: 135–139.

Kessler, M., and C. Gomberg. 1974. "Observations of Barroom Drinking: Methodology and Preliminary Results." *Quarterly Journal of Studies on Alcohol* 35: 1392–1396.

Mass Observation. 1970. *The Pub and the People.* Second Edition. London: Seven Dials Press.

Moore, M.H., and D.R. Gerstein, editors. 1981. *Alcohol and Public Policy: Beyond the Shadow of Prohibition.* Washington, D.C. National Academy Press.

Partanen, J. 1975. "On the Role of Situational Factors in Alcohol Research: Drinking in Restaurants vs. Drinking at Home." *The Drinking and Drug Practices Surveyor* 10: 14–16.

Schaefer, H.H.; M.B. Sobell; and K.C. Mills. 1971. "Baseline Drinking Behaviors in Alcoholics and Social Drinkers: Kinds of Drinks and Sip Magnitude." *Behavior Research and Therapy* 9: 23–27.

Thomas, A.E. 1978. "Class and Sociability Among Urban Workers: A Study of the Bar as a Social Club." *Medical Anthropology* 2: 9–30.

Module 6 Final Test

1. List the five key determinants of a situation.

2. Describe situational analysis.

3. Explain how beliefs and behavior can contribute to chronic patterns of alcohol consumption.

266   *A Handbook for Alcohol Education*

4. In the following case study, identify the key determinants of a situation; personal beliefs, attitudes, and decisions including those that are situation specific; and those factors that occurred prior to the situation that influence it (situational antecedents). Write in the column to the left of the text.

Monday was horrible and Tuesday was already hectic. The studio wanted changes in the new fall format and the scheduling department had yet to submit their alternate plans. Joan had not had a chance to get a second cup of coffee that morning. She had a splitting headache, her phone was ringing every time she settled down to the typewriter to complete her memo to the program personnel, and her secretary complained that she needed the first part of the afternoon off to walk down to the county courthouse to pick up legal documents for the firm.

When Joan and her four program executives walked through the front door of the Riverside Room at the Sheraton for lunch, the cool air, the dark atmosphere, and the soothing music all delivered one message—relax. Joan was starved, but before ordering from the menu, she ordered a double martini—hold the vermouth—from the bar.

Ten minutes later, Joan regained the vitality that won her the executive job. She kidded about the "nuts" that must run the scheduling department, and even started to brag that her department was really "on top" of the fall program strategy. The others joined her in the kidding, and for at least one hour, Joan felt that the workday was worth the effort.

After twenty minutes and another martini, Joan decided to skip the food, and just let her system relax. She daydreamed about the vacation coming up in two weeks in the Bahamas with her boyfriend Ted. In fact, the rest of the group became more relaxed and quiet as the lunch wore on and they rambled back to the office at 2:00 to resume the battle. Joan downed a valium in the restroom after lunch, and was ready for more.

5. For the case study given above, suggest acceptable alternatives for Joan in her situation.

ANSWERS TO MODULE 6 FINAL TEST

1. The five determinants of a situation are: a place, a time, specific behaviors, normative beliefs, and participants.
2. Situational analysis is a description of the five key elements of a situation for purposes of determining the possibilities for change.
3. Beliefs supply the primary information from which we make decisions about behavior, and each drinking situation is likely to create new beliefs. Therefore every time a drinking situation is repeated, it reinforces beliefs about drinking and its consequences. This process increases the likelihood that the situation will be repeated.
4. Paragraph 1 describes elements of presituational stress.
   Paragraph 2: "Cool air, dark atmosphere, soothing music" all are attributes of *place*.
   Paragraph 3: "Joan regained vitality" indicates personal *belief* that intoxication leads to vitality.
   Paragraph 4: "After another martini, Joan decided to skip lunch and just relax" reflects *beliefs* that drink leads to relaxation, drink is associated with pleasant daydreams, and finally, drink is an antidote to stress.
5. Alternatives:

   Presituational 1. Don't wait until lunch to relax, take a midmorning break.
                      2. Find another job with less stress.
   Situational 1. Have a snack before drinking the martini.
                      2. Lunch with nonwork colleagues or friends.
                      3. Take a long walk after lunch instead of sitting in the lounge.
                      4. Try lunching without the martini—ice water might achieve the same effect.

Alcohol educators can help people develop alternative beliefs that are acceptable to the group, provide many of the same benefits as the alcohol-related beliefs, and do not require a challenge to the old beliefs.

Reader's Responses

Your comments on this book would be of great value for future revisions and as an aid in designing community alcohol programs. Please take a few moments to answer the questions below and mail the form to:

Kenneth C. Mills
Center for Alcohol Studies
Wing B Medical School Building 207H
University of North Carolina
Chapel Hill, North Carolina 27514

1. What parts of the book have been the most useful for you?

2. What parts of the book have been the least useful?

3. How could the book be improved?

Index

About the Authors

Kenneth C. Mills received his Ph.D. in psychology from Claremont Graduate School in 1971. He has been active in alcohol research since his predoctoral work and is the author of numerous publications about the behavioral effects of alcohol on animals and people. From 1978 to 1982, Dr. Mills directed a primary prevention program contracted by the National Institute on Alcohol Abuse and Alcoholism. The program sought to establish alcohol education programs in a university setting. His current papers include a review of "Guidelines for Alcohol Abuse Prevention on the College Campus" in the *Journal of Higher Education.* His recent lab studies report on a newly developed, computer simulation to test the cognitive performance of the drinking driver. Currently, Dr. Mills is a research psychologist and associate professor of psychology at the Center for Alcohol Studies, School of Medicine, University of North Carolina at Chapel Hill.

Ed Neal is a consultant to faculty in higher education, specializing in teaching improvement techniques. He has ten years of college teaching experience and has been associated with training programs for military, academic, and medical personnel. He is currently director of the Faculty Development Division of the Media and Instructional Support Center, the University of North Carolina at Chapel Hill.

Iola Peed-Neal is assistant director of the Instructional Development Division of the Media and Instructional Support Center, the University of North Carolina at Chapel Hill. As a consultant to faculty in higher education, she is involved in curriculum and instructional development with a focus on learning, including content selection, strategy and message design, and evaluation of instructional activities. She is also a consultant in the design and production of media.